Arthur Wilde Little

Reasons for being a churchman

addressed to English speaking Christians of every name

Arthur Wilde Little

Reasons for being a churchman

addressed to English speaking Christians of every name

ISBN/EAN: 9783337373986

Printed in Europe, USA, Canada, Australia, Japan

Cover: Foto ©Lupo / pixelio.de

More available books at **www.hansebooks.com**

REASONS

FOR

BEING A CHURCHMAN.

ADDRESSED TO ENGLISH SPEAKING CHRIST-
IANS OF EVERY NAME.

BY
THE REV. ARTHUR WILDE LITTLE, M. A.,
RECTOR OF SAINT PAUL'S CHURCH,
Portland, Maine.

MILWAUKEE, WIS.:
THE YOUNG CHURCHMAN CO., PUBLISHERS.
1885.

COPYRIGHTED, 1885,
BY ARTHUR WILDE LITTLE.

PRINTED BY
KING, LAWTON & FOWLE,
MILWAUKEE.

TO
THE COMMUNICANTS OF THE CHURCH
IN
SAINT PAUL'S PARISH, PORTLAND, MAINE,
THIS VOLUME
IS
AFFECTIONATELY DEDICATED
BY THEIR
PASTOR AND FRIEND, THE AUTHOR.

PREFACE.

THESE Reasons for being a Churchman are addressed to *English*-speaking Christians, because the ANGLICAN CHURCH is that part of the CATHOLIC CHURCH which has lawful jurisdiction over that part of the earth which is occupied by the English-speaking race. Our Church can lay no just claim to the obedience of Orientals, Italians, Frenchmen, Mexicans, and the like. They owe allegiance to the Dioceses and Provinces of the Church Catholic in their respective countries. Of their peculiar difficulties, of their need of reformation, and of their proper courses of action, it is no part of this book to treat.

The object in view is twofold:—

First, to *strengthen* those who are already in actual conformity with the Anglo-Catholic Church. It was a profound observation of our great Archbishop, St. Anselm:

"*Neglegentia mihi videtur si, postquam confirmati sumus in Fide, non studemus quod credimus intelligere.*"[1]

This "negligence" among Churchmen is lamentable and appalling — a chief cause of indifferentism and apostacy. The Primate of All England recently declared: "There is perhaps not even now one Churchman in ten who is as well instructed

---

1. It seems to me the part of negligence if, after we have been confirmed in the Faith, we do not try to *understand* what we believe.

in the reasons why he is a Churchman, as Dissenters or Roman Catholics are instructed in the arguments whereby their position is defended. *This should surely be remedied.*" If the two million nominal adherents of the Church in the United States did but fairly appreciate the history, the claims, and the blessings of *American Catholicism*, the individual faith and piety and the general influence of our Church, would be increased an hundredfold.

The second object in view is to call the attention of our nonconforming brethren — Roman and Protestant alike — to the historic continuity, the divine authority, the lawful jurisdiction, the true Catholicity, and the practical advantages of the venerable Church of *their* ancestors and *ours*, the Mother-Church of the English-speaking race. Those who have of late conformed to the Church (and they are a numerous company) agree in saying that the reason they did not "come home" sooner, was because they were ignorant of their "Father's House." Surely the claims of the Reformed Catholic Church of our race — *reformed* indeed, but *Catholic* still — are worth considering.

The argument is stated frankly and from the Catholic standpoint. It first took shape in a course of Sunday evening lectures in the Parish Church of St. Paul, Portland, Maine. It next appeared as a series of thirty-six articles in a leading Church weekly.[2] It is now, at the request of many readers — Bishops, Priests, and laymen — sent forth in book form, with the prayer that it may contribute something to the glory of Incarnate God and the upbuilding of His Kingdom of Grace.

A. W. L.

PORTLAND, MAINE, St. Matthew's Day, 1885.

---

[2] "The Living Church," Dec. 13th, 1884, to Aug. 22d, 1885.

CONTENTS.

CHAPTER I.
THE QUESTION STATED.
The Three Divisions of English-speaking Christians — Churchmen — Recusants — (The essence of the Reformation — The Italian Schism in England and Ireland) — Dissenters — (Their origin and position) — Plan of Argument — Authority — Expediency — Future Prospects,   1-6

CHAPTER II.
DID GOD FOUND A CHURCH WHICH STILL EXISTS?
The *raison d'etre* of Man-made Churches — Church in Eden — Covenant of Redemption — Patriarchal Dispensation — Mosaic — Jewish Church a type and promise of the Catholic Church — "The Kingdom of God" at hand,   7-14

CHAPTER III.
DID CHRIST FOUND A CATHOLIC CHURCH WHICH STILL EXISTS?
Christianity not an "Idea," but an Organism — Christ's Parables — His Promises — He founds His Kingdom on Earth — Appoints a permanent self-perpetuating Ministry — Apostolic Succession in a single clause,   15-21

CHAPTER IV.
THE PENTECOSTAL CHURCH.
Christ's Commands carried out by the Apostles — The Descent of the Holy Ghost — Picture of the Apostolic Church — No Romanism — No Protestantism — Both Inconceivable in the Early Church,   22-31

CONTENTS.

CHAPTER V.

MARKS OF THE HOLY CATHOLIC CHURCH.

PAGE.

Baptism — The Doctrine of the Apostles — The Fellowship of the Apostles — The Breaking of the Bread — The Prayers, - 32–35

CHAPTER VI.

THE ANGLICAN CHURCH AND HOLY BAPTISM.

Continuity of the Anglican Church — What is Baptism? — Regeneration not Conversion — Teaching of the Bible — Of the Fathers — Infant Baptism — Uninterrupted theory and practice of the Anglican Church — Importance of the Sacrament of the New Birth, - - - - - - - - 36–44

CHAPTER VII.

THE ANGLICAN CHURCH AND "THE APOSTLES' DOCTRINE."

Episcopacy not everything — Anglican Church not Roman, and not Protestant — The Primitive Faith — Holy Scripture — The Apostolic Creed — Eastern form, Western form — Nicæa and Constantinople — The Athanasian Creed — The XXXIX. Articles not a Creed — The Anglican Church always Orthodox — "Infallible" Bishops of Rome sometimes *heretical* — Greek, Anglican, and Roman Churches have the same Creed — Roman Additions — Relation of Dissenters to the Apostolic Faith, - - 45–57

CHAPTER VIII.

THE APOSTLES' FELLOWSHIP: WHAT SAITH THE SCRIPTURE?

Apostolic Episcopacy necessary to the unity, continuity and authority of the Church — The Apostolic Office permanent — *The Three Orders* — The Perennial Ivy — St. Matthias the 13th Apostle — St. James the 14th — Evidence that He was Bishop of Jerusalem — Twenty-three Men called Apostles in the N. T. — Timothy Bp. of Ephesus — Titus Bp. of Crete — Eighteen others, 58–66

CHAPTER IX.

PRIMITIVE EPISCOPACY AND ITS OFFICIAL TITLES.

Three Orders — Apparent Confusion of Names — No Confusion of Orders — Priests sometimes called "Bishops" in the sense of *Pastors* or Overseers — *A postoli sunt Episcopi* — Evidence that the Apostles who Succeeded the Twelve gradually Appropriated the title of Bishop — The title of Apostle lingered in some places — The *Didache*, - - - - - - 67–71

CHAPTER X.

PRIMITIVE EPISCOPACY AND THE TESTIMONY OF THE APOSTOLIC FATHERS.

Episcopacy not defended in the Early Church because not an open question — Apostolic Order Universal — Early Church Presbyterial only, *if* you leave out the *Apostles* — Diaconal, if you leave out both Apostles and Presbyters — Episcopacy not Necessarily *Diocesan* — Earliest Witnesses — St. Clement — St. Polycarp — *St. Ignatius* — His Epistles to the Ephesians, Magnesians, Trallians, Romans, Philadelphians, Smyrnæans, and to Polycarp, - - - - - - - - - 72–84

CHAPTER XI.

THE WITNESS OF THE FATHERS—Continued.

Admissions of Gibbon, Guizot, *Grotius* — Strength of our Position — Churchmen "No Fools" — Unanswered Challenge of Hooker — "Epistle to Diognetus" — Testimony of Dionysius; of *St. Irenæus;* of Polycrates; of St. Clement, of Alex.; of Tertullian; of Origen; of St. Cyprian, etc. — "Study the Fathers," - 85–97

CHAPTER XII.

IF THE PRIMITIVE CATHOLIC CHURCH WAS NOT EPISCOPAL, WHAT WAS IT?

Experiment of a learned Presbyterian Minister — The Historic Church Episcopal *because it started so* — If not, when and how did it become so? — No instance of a non-Episcopal Church — A Camel larger than the wooden Horse of Troy — While the Apostles lived the Church undeniably Episcopal — The post-Apostolic Episcopate dove-tailed into the Episcopate of the Apostles — No room for a radical change of polity — Could such a change take place in a Protestant denomination? — A "tempest in a tea-pot" — How revolutions occur — Rise of the *Papacy* an example, - - - - - - - 98–104

APPENDIX TO CHAPTER XII.

DESPERATE EXPEDIENTS TO GET RID OF THE BISHOPS OF THE EARLY CHURCH.

The assumption that a Bishop was only a Pastor of one Congregation — How about TITUS ? — One hundred Cities in his Parish — ST. JAMES, the over-worked Pastor!—"Tens of thousands" of parishoners, at least fifty Churches — IGNATIUS in Antioch, 200,000 inhabitants, calls himself the Bishop of *Syria* — ONESIMUS; one Parish in Ephesus simply preposterous — Case of ST. MARK in Alexandria — St. *Cyprian* in Carthage: great multitude of clergy (not "ruling elders" but "Glorious Priests"); Cathedral and Ten Churches — The "Moderator Hypothesis," - - 105–108

CHAPTER XIII.

A FEW FRAGMENTS THAT REMAIN TOUCHING APOSTOLIC SUCCESSION.

Evidence of Canons — Apostolic Succession not a Chain but a NET — Illustrations — Quotations from Dr. Hopkins — From Bishop Neely — Evidence from Early Schismatics, Novatian and Fortunatus — From Pagan Writers — From Would-be-bishops, Colluthus, Aerius, his "*dogma furiosum et stolidum*" — The Six General Councils — Archbp. Potter and Lord Macaulay on the Fact of Apos. Success, - - - - - 109–116

CHAPTER XIV.

THE ANGLICAN CHURCH AND THE "FELLOWSHIP OF THE APOSTLES."

Importance of the Catholic Episcopate — Anglican Church Never Without It — Early Origin of Christianity in Britain — First Bishop of Rome a Britain — Did St. Paul Preach in Britain? — Testimony of Gildas, Fortunatus the Poet; Theodoret, St. Jerome, Eusebius, Origen, Tertullian, Justin Martyr, St. Clement — Church at Glastonbury — St. Alban, our Proto martyr — Constantine — British Bishops at Councils of Arles, Nicæa, Sardica, Rimine — The Anglo-Saxon Conquest, - - - - 117–124

CHAPTER XV.

ANGLO-CATHOLICISM; OR, THE MAKING AND ESTABLISHING OF THE PRESENT NATIONAL CHURCH OF ENGLAND.

The Celtic Churches, Catholic, independent — Queen Bertha and Bishop Luidhard — The Italian Mission — Romish errors then unknown — Gregory and the title of "Universal Bishop" — Augustine ordained in France — Saxons converted mainly by the Celtic Christians — Canterbury — Two schools of thought — Theodore — The unification and establishment of the Anglo-Catholic Church long before the State, - - - 125–131

CHAPTER XVI.

THE ENGLISH CHURCH NEVER THE ROMAN CHURCH.

The *Ecclesia Anglicana* — Lease of Church property for 999 years — Mediæval corruptions — Usurpation of the Bishop of Rome, illustrated by Napoleon, Sinbad, etc. — Roman influence slight before the Norman Conquest — Wilfrid — Cuthbert — Image-worship — Offa — The "Forged Decretals" — Robert and Stigand — William and Lanfranc defy the Bishop of Rome — The Archbishop of Canterbury called "the Pope and Patriarch of another world" — Anti-Roman legislation — King John — *Magna Charta* — Two reforms necessary: to free the State; to free the Church — The *legal* freeing of the Church in the Fourteenth Century — The prestige of Rome broken — "Rival Popes" — "Reforming Councils" — Greek Churchmen — Henry VIII. — The "Gordian Knot" — The Bishop of Rome no more than any other "foreign Bishop" — Queen Mary and the second subjugation of our Church — Accession of Elizabeth, - - 132–144

CHAPTER XVII.

ANGLICAN ORDERS.

True Catholics — Elizabeth and the Papal usurpation — Vacant Bishoprics — Election, confirmation, and consecration of Archbishop Parker — Overwhelming evidence of the fact — The "Nag's Head Fable" — Marc Antonio de Dominis — Irish succession — R. C. admissions — American and Colonial succession, 145–159

APPENDIX TO CHAPTER XVII.

PIUS IV. AND THE ENGLISH REFORMATION.

Hore — Jennings — Cutts — Blunt — Van Antwerp — Butler, - 160–163

CHAPTER XVIII.
ANGLICAN JURISDICTION AND CATHOLICITY.

Declaration of Lambeth Council — Novelty of the Ultramontane Theory of Jurisdiction — Inherent Jurisdiction of Provincial and Autocephalous Churches - Early English Church Complete in Itself — Our Reformers did not Commit the Sin of *Schism* — English Romanists Schismatic — Pius IX. and Westminster — English Church never claimed to be Anything but *Catholic* — Quotations from Dr. Coit, and Dr. Seabury — The "Golden Rule of Faith," - - - - - - - - 164–176

CHAPTER XIX.
THE ATTITUDE OF DISSENT TOWARDS EPISCOPACY.

Difference Between the *Catholic Reformation* in England and the *Protestant Revolutions* on the Continent — Changing Attitude of Protestants toward Episcopacy — (1) They Believed in It, and Regretted their Loss of It; Luther, Melancthon, Beza, Calvin, etc.— 2) They Blindly and Ignorantly Assailed It; Drs. Miller and McCloud — (3) Scholarly Protestant Reaction in Favor of It; Drs. Schaff and Fisher; the Concessions of Mosheim, Gieseler, etc.—*An important consideration*, - - - 177–183

CHAPTER XX.
THE ANGLICAN CHURCH AND CONFIRMATION.

Definition of Confirmation — Practiced by the Apostles — Scriptural evidence — Patristic — Retained in the Greek, Roman, and Anglican Churches — Confirmation not "joining the Church" — Protestants feel the need of it, - - - - - 184–193

CHAPTER XXI.
THE ANGLICAN CHURCH AND " THE BREAKING OF THE BREAD."

One true *Sacrifice;* prefigured in the Jewish Church, commemorated in the Christian Church — *The Altar* — The Eucharist also a *Communion* — What the N. T. says of it — The Fathers — Two parts of the Sacrament — *Transubstantiation* denies the real presence of the Bread and Wine — *Zwinglianism* denies the real presence of Christ's Body and Blood — Growth of Transubstantiation — Forced on the English Church in the thirteenth century — The Catholic Doctrine restored in the sixteenth century — Rise of "Half Communion" — Declared *heresy* by three Bishops of Rome — Received unwillingly in the English Church in fifteenth century — The Chalice restored in the sixteenth — Growth of the Zwinglian impiety — *Never* sanctioned in the Anglo-Catholic Church, - - - - - 194–205

CONTENTS.

CHAPTER XXII.

"THE PRAYERS."

Liturgical Worship a Mark of the Church — Jewish Worship: Temple, Synagogue — The Apostles Trained to Liturgical Worship — Endorsed by Christ — Glimpses of Liturgical Worship in the N. T. — The Liturgy of the Passover — Oral Liturgy of the Apostles — Four Great Types — Parts Common to Each — Worship of the Early Church — Pliny, Justin Martyr — Specimen of the Oldest Extant Liturgy — Remarkable Agreement of Our Liturgy, - 206-220

CHAPTER XXIII.

THE ANGLICAN CHURCH AND "THE PRAYERS."

Our Church *Inherited* Catholic Worship — Liturgy of St. John — British Liturgy — Influence of Augustine — The *Roman* Breviary and Missal *never* Used in England — Latin Services — Creature-worship — Devotional and Liturgical Reform — The Prayer Book of 1549 — Subsequent Revisions — Anglican P. B. dear to outsiders — Luther, Calvin, Knox, etc., Believed in Liturgical Worship — Amazing Devotions of English and American Dissenters — "Sam. Lawson's" Philosophy of Prayer — Dr. Mines — Extemporary Prayer the Work of Jesuits in England — Protestant Reaction in Favor of Liturgical Worship — Thank God for the Prayer Book, - - - - - - 221-229

CHAPTER XXIV.

CLOSE OF THE ARGUMENT FOR THE CHURCH'S AUTHORITY BASED ON HISTORIC CONTINUITY.

Our Church has retained the accessories of Catholic worship — Bodily reverence — Scriptural warrant — Usage of Early Church — Bowing at the SACRED NAME — The Christian Year — Jewish Feasts and Fasts — Origin of the Church's Calendar — Retained in the Anglo-Catholic Church — So with other things: Ordination, Absolution, Church Architecture, Vestments, etc. — Special defense of Vestments — CONTINUITY, the key-note of the Anglo-Catholic position — Summary of the Historic Argument — Charity to non-conformists, - - - - - 230-240

CHAPTER XXV.

THE ARGUMENT FROM EXPEDIENCY.

PAGE.

Authority ought to be sufficient — "*Præscriptio in limine*" — Comparison of the three Systems — The Anglican holds to the Past and adapts itself to the Present — All the Elements of true Catholicity not only authoritative but *practically advantageous* — Protestant Dissenters adopting the Church's Ways — Two noted Tributes to the Church by disinterested Observers — The Power of the Historic Church to evoke enthusiastic Love — "The Bride of Christ" — The *Catholic Idea*, - - - 241-251

CHAPTER XXVI.

THE ARGUMENT FROM FUTURITY.

(I.) Which System has the Brightest Outlook? — Anglican Prospects Last Century — Revival of Church-life — The Wesleys, the "Evangelical Movement," the "Oxford" — Church Growth in England and the United States — Prospects of the Anglo-Saxon Race and the English Language — An unfair Comparison — Anglican Prospects Brighter than Roman — Roman Schism losing Ground in England — Dependent on Immigration in the United States — The United States the Paradise of Protestantism — Elements of Disintegration and Decay — Protestantism about to Pass through a Fearful Ordeal — *Protestant Paralogism* — The Churchman has Nothing to Fear.

(II.) The Anglican Church *Surest to Keep the Faith* — Roman Additions to the Faith Driving Men to Infidelity — "Infallibility," What Next? — Protestantism Losing the Faith (Unitarianism) — Lacks the Conservative Orthodoxy of the Church.

(III.) Which System Offers the Best Basis for the Reunion of Christendom? — Not the *Roman*, Unless it Gives Up the Papacy, etc.— The Anglican Church a Medium of Reunion — So Acknowledged by French Roman Catholics — Catholic and Reformed — Let Romanists Lay Aside Novel Additions, and Protestants Restore Omitted Essentials, and they will find themselves *Catholics* — Nothing Unreasonable is Asked — Summary and Conclusion, 252-266

BISHOP JEREMY TAYLOR'S
PRAYER FOR THE WHOLE CATHOLIC CHURCH.

CHAPTER I.

THE QUESTION STATED.

"Be ready always to give an answer to every man that asketh you a reason of the hope that is in you."—1. St. Peter, iii. 15.

ENGLISH speaking Christians are divided into three great classes—Churchmen, Recusants, and Dissenters. These terms have established themselves in literature; and without implying any opprobrium, stand for important historical facts.

Churchmen are those who adhere to that old Catholic and Apostolic Church which, after sundry deformations, and reformations, but without losing its corporate identity, its historic continuity, or its divine authority, still maintains primitive faith, order, and worship, and exercises lawful jurisdiction throughout the British Empire and the American Republic. Churchmen are variously called Anglicans, Anglo-Catholics, or Episcopalians. They number about 225 Bishops, 30,000 priests,[1] and some 25,000,000 adherents.

Recusant means *Refuser*. The term was originally applied to those members of the English Church who, after the Reformation, *refused* the Church's ministrations; and,

---

1. Including a small number of Deacons.

at the instigation of the Bishop of Rome, formed the first English schism.

The essence of the Reformation in our Mother Church was the assertion of her ancient independence of the Bishop of Rome, together with the correction of certain abuses. The English Bishops, clergy, and laity, as a body, acquiesced in the change which was a mere episode in the chequered history of Anglo-Catholicism. Out of 9,400 clergy only 189 refused to accept the new order of things. The laity, including those who really believed in the Papacy, were quietly settling down in the freed and purified Church of England ;[2] when in the year 1570, the Bishop of Rome, Pius V., lost his temper, and commanded the "faithful" to withdraw from the English Church. A mere handful obeyed his mandate ; and leaving the ancient Catholic Church of their country, formed the Roman Schism or Italian Mission in England. That they were conscientious in so doing we cannot doubt. They have borne up bravely against *civil* persecutions, and manifold difficulties ; but have made almost no impression on the nation at large, and are now relatively losing ground. It was only as late as 1850 that they effected a regular organization in England with diocesan Bishops and a full Roman hierarchy. In Ireland, however, owing mainly to political causes, the Italian Mission was more successful and drew away a large majority of the laity,

---

2. "For diverse years in Queen Elizabeth's reign there was no Recusant known in England; but even they who were most addicted to Roman opinions, yet frequented our Churches and public assemblies, and did join with us in the use of the same prayers and divine offices, without any scruple, till they were prohibited by a papal bull for the interest of the Roman Court."—ARCHBISHOP BRAMHALL. I. 248.

but not many of the clergy, of the venerable Church of St. Patrick's planting.[3]

Such is the position of the Recusants or *Refusers* of Anglo-Catholic reform. They are variously styled Romanists, Roman Catholics or Papists. They have intruded also into the jurisdiction of the American Church, and have many adherents, mainly Irish and Germans.

The third division of English-speaking Christians comprises the Dissenters. As Romanists objected to the English Reformation because they thought it had gone too far, so certain others, who had imbibed the novelties of German Protestants and French Calvinists, objected because, forsooth, they fancied it had not been sweeping enough. At first they were few in number, and for the most part remained in communion with the Church—which even to this day shelters in her bosom many whose real sympathies lie with those who went out from her.

Recusants and Dissenters alike left their Mother Church, but with this distinction: the former in seceding placed themselves under the jurisdiction of a foreign Bishop, the Italian Pontiff; while the latter broke altogether with the Church of the past, cast aside all ecclesiastical authority, organized themselves into new voluntary societies—not at first calling them churches, though they have since come to do so—and ordained their ministers by the authority of the congregation. The action of the Recusants was *schism;* that of the Dissenters, *sectarianism.*

---

3. Of all the Irish Bishops (and there were a great many of them for the size of the country), only *two,* Walsh, Bishop of Meath, and Leverous, Bishop of Kildare, refused to accept the Reformation, and left the "Church of Ireland." The rest remained in the old Church, and the Bishops of the present "Church of Ireland" are their successors.

It is not my purpose to describe the different dissenting communions. The principle of sectism once introduced is fruitful of sub-division—like a fresh-water *Polypus* it multiplies by "fission" in a geometrical ratio. The Presbyterians left us in 1573. The Brownists or Independents, afterward called Congregationalists, began to secede ten years later. They were followed by the Baptists, the Quakers, the Methodists, etc., etc., for their name is legion. There are now nearly 150 dissenting bodies in England, and while the actual number of Dissenters is diminishing, the number of sects into which they are splitting up is constantly on the increase.[4] Even the Methodist body which began but a century ago has already broken up into at least 25 distinct denominations. In the United States the fragmentary and disintegrated character of Christianity is simply appalling.

All these denominations, of course, differ among themselves; but from a Church standpoint they may be classified together as having certain general characteristics, viz: the breaking away from the historic Church, the rejection of the Apostolic Ministry—with a special disbelief both in the Episcopate and the Christian Priesthood—a lowering or distortion or even abolition of the Sacraments, a rejection of Common Prayer and impressive services in place of which are substituted much preaching and the extemporaneous devotions of a leader, the abandonment of the Christian Year which is so precious and profitable to us, and finally a great confusion in doctrine occasioned sometimes by elevating philosophical systems to the place

---

4. See "Cutt's Turning Points in Eng. Ch. Hist.," p. 317.

of dogma, and again, as in the case of the Unitarians, by actual apostacy from the fundamentals of the Christian religion.

The Dissenters are variously styled Nonconformists, Separatists, Sectarians, or, from an Anglo-Catholic standpoint, Protestants, as *protesting* against the old historic Church. They number about one-fourth of the English, the major part of the Scotch among whom Presbyterianism is established by law, a small proportion of the Irish, and a vast majority of American Christians.

To one or other of these three great classes of Christians we all belong, many of us perhaps without being able to justify our position or to give a reason for the hope that is in us. It is my purpose to state as simply, clearly, and accurately as I can, the chief reasons for being Churchmen instead of being Romanists, or Dissenters—and this I do with the prayer for divine guidance, "*with charity for all, with malice toward none.*"

The first question is: Did God found an universal Church which claims the allegiance of mankind? Does that Church anywhere exist in its essential purity, and if so, does the Anglican Church fulfill the requirements? This may be called the *argument from authority*, and is based on an appeal to history.[5]

The second consideration is that of *present expediency*, based on the comparative merits of the three systems so far as their practical methods of worship, teaching and work are concerned.

---

5. "It may be asserted without fear of contradiction that the whole case of the Romanising movement on the one side and of popular Protestantism on the other, rests upon perversions of history."—(English) *Ch. Times.*

The third argument, or *argument from futurity*, will be drawn from a consideration of future prospects. Which system is likeliest to be the basis for restoring the broken unity of Christendom, and likeliest to hold the Faith till the Master comes?

Our theme then is: THE CHURCH, *her authority derived from the past, her present advantages, and her future prospects.*

CHAPTER II.

DID GOD FOUND A CHURCH WHICH STILL EXISTS?

[*"Ab origine mundi incipiens."*]

IT ought not to be necessary to ask this question. But it is. The *raison d'etre* of man-made churches, the only possible justification of dissent, must logically be the assumption either that God did not found a Church, or else that the Church He founded has perished from the earth. Now, if it can be shown that God did found a Church which still exists, surely no one can fail to see his personal duty with reference to it.

Our first parents, even before they fell into sin, were admitted into covenant relation with God, which was the germ of all subsequent ecclesiastical dispensations. "Eden was an enclosure from the outside world, the CHURCH where the Son of God personally met man and told him of his duty of faith and obedience, and of the penalty that would follow unbelief and disobedience. That Church was the root of Christianity, and it was designed to pass through several stages of development before it attained its maturity."[1]

After the fall of man God continued that Church, but

---

1. Dr. C. C. Adams in Am. Ch. Rev., Oct., 1884.

altered its character to suit the changed relation between Him and His now disobedient children. Sin had destroyed the sweet communion of Eden, and in its place God appointed a *Covenant of Redemption*, based on the sacrificial death of the promised Seed of the woman who should bruise the serpent's head, the Lamb of God who, in the knowledge and purpose of the Almighty, was "the Lamb slain from the foundation of the world."[2] All history, ancient or modern, centres in the Incarnation and sacrifice of the Son of God; and so, from the offering of righteous Abel to the latest Eucharistic Oblation upon the Table of the Lord, *Sacrifice* has ever been the chief characteristic of God's Church; while even the heathen who left the worship of the true God, never entirely lost the God-given conviction that without the shedding of blood there is no remission of sin.

Thus the Church of the Patriarchal Dispensation was ushered in, and as we read in Gen. iv., 26, "Then began men to call on the name of the Lord." Before the flood, however, dissent in its worst form, as utter apostasy, prevailed to a greater extent than at any subsequent period. The "Sons of Men" so far outnumbered the "Sons of God," that the Church was narrowed down to one family of but eight souls. After the flood God renewed His Covenant with man in the person of Noah; and again in the case of Abraham, at which time He appointed an additional rite for the initiation of infants and of adult converts into His Church, viz: Circumcision. At the same time he cut off the apostate races, so that the Church was

---

2. Rev., xiii., 8.

continued in the family of Abraham, whose descendants in the line of his grandson, Jacob, became the "chosen people," whose great work in history was the keeping alive the worship of Jehovah in the midst of an idolatrous world, in order that there might be one orthodox nation of which, according to the flesh, the Son of God should be born, and which should form the nucleous of a new, higher, world-wide and eternal Dispensation which God was about to introduce.

God's revelation of Himself and the building up of His Kingdom of Grace on the earth have been progressive. We have seen something of the Patriarchal Dispensation in which the priesthood was vested in the eldest son. A great step was made in the development of revealed religion, when God through Moses gave Israel the Decalogue and the Ceremonial Law. From that time to the coming of Christ no Christian can deny that there has existed on the earth an organization fully entitled to be called *the Church of God*. As under the previous Dispensation, so here, sacrifices typifying the one great Sacrifice to come, were the most notable feature of the Church. "Gather my saints together unto me," saith the Lord, "those that have made a covenant with me with sacrifice."[3] God, moreover, gave explicit directions as to the polity and worship of the Jewish Church. "See thou make all things according to the pattern showed thee in the mount."[4] Instead of the Patriarchal Priesthood there was now established a Ministerial Succession *in three orders* in the tribe of Levi—the High Priest, the Priests and the Levites. And when once God had ordained this ministry,

---

3. Ps., l., 5.   4. Heb., viii., 5.

He showed that He meant it to be sacred and exclusive by making a fearful example of those who presumed to usurp its functions. Witness Korah, Dathan, and Abiram[5]; or Saul[6], Uzzah[7], and Uzziah[8]; and when, after the secession and schism of the ten Northern tribes, Jeroboam intruded into the Priestly Office men who were not of the house of Aaron, we read, "this became a sin unto the house of Jeroboam, to cut it off and to destroy it from the face of the earth."[9]

In the matter of public worship in the Jewish Church, we see clearly that God recognizes—what modern Protestants have affected to ignore—the *material* as well as the spiritual side of human nature; for He ordained in the Tabernacle and Temple worship, a grand, stately, ornate, symbolic office of sacrifice and thanksgiving, of prayer and praise—a liturgic service the most ritualistic the world has ever seen, or that in all probability we ever shall see, until with angels and archangels and all the company of Heaven we join in the celestial ritual of the Triumphant Church. Bodily reverence accompanied the devotion of the heart. There was the mitred High Priest resplendent in purple and gold; there were the white-robed Priests and Levites, and the singers with their accompanying instruments; there were the Holy of Holies, the Ark with its overshadowing Cherubim, the altar of incense, the golden Candlesticks, the table of Shew-bread, the great Altar of Sacrifice, and, all about, the prostrate multitudes worshipping the God and Father of all.

The Jewish Church had also its God-given ecclesiastical

---

5. Numbers, xvi. 6. I. Samuel, xiii., 9-13. 7. II. Samuel, vi., 6-7. 8. II. Chronicles, xxvi., 16-21. 9. I. Kings, xiii, 34.

year with its round of Holy Days—the three great Festivals, the Solemn Fast Day of Atonement, the Minor Feasts, and the fifty-two Sabbaths.

Later on, probably in the time of Ezra, there grew up also, under divine approval, if not by direct command, the system of Synagogue worship and instruction, with its eighteen Collects, its versicles and responses, its singing, its reading of Scripture Lessons, and the preaching and expounding of God's word.[10]

Such was the Jewish Church, with its long line of Prophets, Priests and Kings; Martyrs and Confessors; holy men and saintly women; and the little children who were also admitted into the Covenant, who, like Samuel, were "given unto the Lord." "These all died in faith, not having received the promises, but having seen them afar off, and were persuaded of them, and embraced them, and confessed that they were strangers and pilgrims on the earth."[11] And yet, as glorious as was that Church, as exalted in point of privilege as were the saints of old, we read that God had "provided some better things for us, that they without us should not be made perfect."[12] Yes, this Church was not a final Dispensation. It was a type of an ultimate and glorious one to come. "The Law was our Schoolmaster to bring us unto Christ."[13] The root of the olive was there, but new branches were to be grafted into it.[14] The Jewish Church was National. It is true, Gentiles, who abandoned their Paganism, might enter it through the door of circumcision; yet it was not, as then constituted, adapted for universal dominion. But all the

---

10. Geikie's Life of Christ, Chap. xiii. 11. Hebrews, xi., 13. 12. Hebrews xi., 40. 13. Galatians, iii, 24. 14. Romans, xi., 17–24.

while the Prophets used to sing of a Coming Era, when Zion should lengthen her cords and strengthen her stakes.

Bear in mind that the point here to be proved is that God founded a Church which still exists. I have shown that God did have a Church in the days of old, the Jewish Church. It is now my purpose to show that Christ did not change the divine plan by abrogating the Church as a visible organism, but that He continued it, only on a higher plane rendered possible by virtue of the Incarnation. The old Dispensation was but the shadow of good things to come. The first step in proving the existence of the Christian Church is *a priori*, that is to say, we gather from the types and prophecies of the Jewish Church the presumption and promise of the Catholic Church. If God saw that it was best to embody His revelation of old in an organized society with a threefold Priesthood, rites and ceremonies, it is fair to *presume* that He would continue the Church in the Christian Dispensation on the same general principles This presumption, however, becomes a *promise* when we open the treasury of divine prophecy. The prophecies of the Catholic Church in the Old Testament are intimately associated with the predictions of the coming Messiah. To give the tenth part of the prophecies which taught that the Jewish Church should widen into an universal Church, would require more space than is at my command. But this was the meaning of God's words when he said to Abraham : " In thy seed shall *all the nations of the earth* be blessed." [15] Such, too, was the testimony of the dying Patriarch, Jacob, when he said of Christ, " Unto Him shall the gathering of the people be," [16] — the

---

15. Genesis, xxii., 18. 16. Genesis, xlix., 10.

same truth which the Holy Ghost spake through the Sweet Singer of Israel, "Ask of Me, and I will give thee the heathen for thy inheritance and the uttermost parts of the earth for thy possession,"[17] and again: "All kings shall fall down before Him; all nations shall do Him service,"[18] the truth which Isaiah perceived when he cried out: "Lift up thine eyes round about and see; all they gather themselves together, they come to Thee. The forces of the Gentiles shall be converted unto Thee."[19] This truth pervades all holy prophecy, but is, perhaps, most clearly set forth in Daniel's vision of the *stone cut out without hands*, which smote the image and became a mountain, and filled the whole earth.[20] This, Daniel interpreted to mean that in the days of the fourth kingdom (the Roman Empire) "shall the God of Heaven set up a Kingdom which shall never be destroyed; and the kingdom shall not be left to other people, but it shall break in pieces and consume all these kingdoms, and it shall stand forever."[21] And again he says he looked, and "Behold one like unto the *Son of Man* came with the clouds of heaven * * * and there was given unto him dominion and glory, and a kingdom, that all people, nations, and languages should serve him."[22] Yes, from that far off antiquity, as from a lofty mountain top, the holy Prophets, with the eye of Inspiration, saw the narrow covenant of Judaism widening into the Church Catholic throughout the world — saw by faith what we now see with the eye of sense, the universal and everlasting kingdom of our Lord Jesus Christ.

Buoyed up by this hope, the Saints of the old Dispen-

---

17. Psalms, ii., 8. 18. Ps., lxxii; Read the whole Psalm. 19. Is., lx. 20. Dan., ii., 34-5. 21. Dan., ii., 44. 22. Dan., vii., 13-14.

sation clung to their Church, looking for the "Consolation of Israel" and the ingathering of the Gentiles.

Eighteen hundred and eighty-six years ago Christ was born—the WORD was made flesh and dwelt among men; God stooped to earth to redeem, to sanctify and to save mankind. We have seen that God's plan of saving men is not merely as individuals, but in and through an organized society. And so just before our blessed Lord began His ministry, St. John the Baptist, the Morning Star of Christianity, preached, saying, "The *Kingdom of God* is at hand." Notice he did not teach that the *Church idea* of religion was to be done away so that there should no longer be a visible organization. On the contrary he, the Forerunner of Christ, prepared the hearts of the people to receive the religion of Christ, not as an abstract philosophy, but as a *Kingdom*—and that word implies more strongly than any other could do, that the Christian Dispensation was to be an organized authoritative body, "a city that is at unity with itself," a state having God-given laws and divinely commissioned officers. In short, the Kingdom of God which St. John Baptist proclaimed to be at hand, can only mean the Catholic Church. This we shall find was the teaching of the great Head of the Church Himself; and the Apostles at His command, preached Christianity, not as a sentiment, but as a kingdom; not as an abstract faith, but a faith indissolubly blended with an organized and sovereign institution, THE CHURCH OF THE LIVING GOD, THE PILLAR AND GROUND OF THE TRUTH. [23]

---

[23] I. Tim., iii., 15.

CHAPTER III.

DID CHRIST FOUND A CATHOLIC CHURCH WHICH STILL EXISTS?

On this Rock I will build My Church, and the gates of hell shall not prevail against it.—*Words of Christ.*

GUIZOT has said, "Christianity came into the world as an *idea to be developed.*" Christianity did nothing of the kind. The Christian "idea" of which the learned Frenchman speaks can only mean the truth which Christ revealed, which was definite and complete, the "faith which was *once for all* [1] delivered to the Saints." And that was given to develop men, not to be developed by men. (It is not our duty to develop the faith, but, by the grace of God, to develop ourselves in the faith.) According to our Lord's teaching that Faith was embodied in a visible organism, which He calls *His Church*, or *His Kingdom.* Indeed the Faith is so identified with the Church that Christ calls His Gospel *the Gospel of the Kingdom.* The Church is an integral part of the Faith, and a belief in the Church is an article of the Apostolic Creed.

Observe, then, the teaching of our Divine Master. He began His ministry by authoritatively repeating the words of St. John Baptist. For we read (St. Mark, i:14), "Jesus

---

1. St. Jude, 1., 3. See Revised Version.

came into Galilee preaching the Gospel of the Kingdom of God, and saying, 'The time is fulfilled, and the Kingdom of Heaven is at hand."' Later on, after He had appointed the twelve Apostles, He says to the multitude: "No doubt the Kingdom of God is come upon you."[2] Though our Lord occasionally uses *Kingdom* to mean Heaven, and perhaps once or twice to mean His spiritual dominion in our hearts, yet more than nine times out of ten it means simply His Church in the world, the Empire He was founding on the earth, but not of the earth. Out of His thirty-two recorded parables, nineteen are "parables of the Kingdom." More than half of His discourses were what some people now-a-days would call "Churchly." But He spake with authority. Notice a few of the wonderful prophetic parables which bring out the visible character of Christ's Church.

In one He likens the Church to a field of wheat and tares which grow together until the harvest,[3] showing that the Church while on earth will contain good and bad, and that it is wrong to make separations in the Church even for so laudable a purpose as to weed out the unworthy. And this phase of the Church, its unity even at the cost of having some bad men in it, He emphasizes by an additional parable, that of the Net,[4] —"which tells us how the Church, having swept through the ages from one end of the world to the other, will finally land those whom it has caught on the shore of eternity, and *there* the separation shall take place." The parable of the Mustard Seed,[5] shows the Catholic or universal extent of the

---

2. St. Luke, xi., 20. 3. St. Mat., xiii., 25. 4. St. Mat., xiii., 47. 5. St. Mat., xiii., 31.

Church. That of the Vine and its Branches, [6] our Lord's last and crowning parable of His Kingdom, shows that His Church is a *visible organism* which, like a plant, however complex, has a unity dependent on the branches remaining in physical vital connection with the root. Some of our Lord's parables refer to doctrine, some to morals, some to individual religious experiences ; but I challenge any one to show a parable which teaches that His Church is not *one, visible and Catholic*, or which can possibly justify the "developments" of Romanism or the separations of Protestanism. He prays for the unity of all Christians, "that they may be one."[7] He says of the sheep that *hear His voice*, "There shall be ONE FOLD and one Shepherd."[8] He admits that "the wolf" may *catch* the sheep, or *scatter* the sheep ;[9] but not that the wolf or any one else may construct a new fold, much less three or four hundred new folds, for the flock of which He Himself is the Good Shepherd, and for which He has already built the "one fold." The first miraculous draught of fishes[10] implies that the "Net" may break and some of the fishes slip out through the breach ; but not that the Great Net may be made over into little hand nets, or that the fishes who swim back into the lake are still *in the Net*, or surrounded, forsooth, by an "invisible net."

But in addition to the figurative language in which Christ illustrates the unity, the visibility, and the authority of His Kingdom, He gives what a learned priest

---

6. St. John, xv., 5.   7. St. John, xvii., 21.
8. St. John, x., 16. The rendering "one flock" instead of one fold, adapted by the Revisers, scarcely alters the metaphor at all, and certainly does not in the slightest degree affect the argument.
9. St. John, x., 12.   10. St. Luke, v., 6.

has well called "a prophecy of the foundation of the Church, of its endless duration, and of the name by which it should be called." When St. Peter confessed the Divinity of Christ, what said the Son of God? "*On this rock* I WILL BUILD MY CHURCH *and the gates of Hell shall not prevail against it.*"¹¹ Again He says as a matter of discipline in the case of an erring brother: "Tell it to the Church, but if he neglect to hear the Church, let him be unto thee as an heathen man and a publican."¹²

A still clearer view of the origin of the Church will be obtained if we notice the steps which Christ took to found and organize it. One of His first acts was to choose, out of the whole body of His Disciples, twelve men to whom He made known the "mysteries of the Kingdom of God."¹³ He called them Apostles, and sent them forth to preach— what? "*The Kingdom of God.*"¹⁴ On the night in which He was betrayed, at that most solemn moment, immediately after the institution of the Lord's Supper, He told them plainly of the dignity and authority of the office to which He had elevated them in His Church: "I appoint unto you a KINGDOM, as My Father hath appointed unto Me, that ye may eat and drink at My Table in My Kingdom, and sit on thrones, judging the Twelve Tribes of Israel."¹⁵ The Twelve thus raised by Christ Himself to

---

11. St. Matthew, xvi., 18. See the masterly exposition of this passage by Dr. J. H. Hopkins in the *American Church Rev cw*, October, 1884.
12. St. Matthew, xviii., 17. 13. St. Luke, viii., 10. 14. St. Luke, viii., 1, and ix., 2.
15. St. Luke. xxii., 29. Christ appointed also 70 men called "Elders," and sent them to preach the "Kingdom" (St. Luke, x., 1 and 9). It is an open question whether they constituted the nucleus of the Presbyterate to which the Apostles added others by ordination; or whether theirs was a temporary commission. I incline to the former view.

pre-eminence in the Church were of *equal* rank and power. To borrow the words of Dr. Mahan : " In their relations to one another, they were 'brothers,' colleagues, peers. They called no man ' father ' on the earth.[16] According to the type of the Old Theocracy, a ' Kingdom ' was given to them, but the Head was to be invisible till the time of the final 'appearing and kingdom ' of Jesus Christ."

After His resurrection from the dead, when in His Human nature as well as in His Divine, He could say: " All power is given unto Me in Heaven and in Earth,"[17] He said to the Apostles : "As My Father hath sent Me, so send I you." He endued them with a power such as no Priesthood had ever before received, the power of Absolution ; for " He breathed on them and said : ' Receive the Holy Ghost ; whosesoever sins ye remit, they are remitted unto them ; and whosesoever sins ye retain, they are retained."[18] At the same time He issued that far-reaching and tremendous command : " Go ye into ALL THE WORLD, and preach the Gospel to EVERY CREATURE. He that believeth and is baptized shall be saved."[19] And lastly, when He was about to re-ascend into Heaven, He gave them their final and perpetual commission : " Go ye therefore and make disciples (*i. e.* make *Christians*) of ALL nations, baptizing them in the Name of the Father, and of the Son, and of the Holy Ghost ; teaching them to observe all things whatsoever I have commanded you ; and lo, I am with you ALWAY, EVEN UNTO THE END OF THE WORLD. AMEN."[20]

The phrases, " All the world," " Every creature," " All

---

16. St. Matthew, xxiii., 9. 17. St. Matthew, xxviii., 18. 18. St. John, xx., 21-23. 19. St. Mark, xvi., 15-16. 20. St. Matthew, xxviii., 19-20.

nations," show that the Church is *Catholic*. They prove also *incontrovertibly* that the Apostolic Ministry is to be *perpetuated* in the Church, for the *individuals* to whom the command was given, could not go *personally* into ALL the world. And this fact our Lord enforces by His promise to be with the Apostles—*how long?* Till the end of their natural lives? That would have been ten years in the case of St. James, and sixty years in the case of St. John. No, it was longer than that. Mark His words, for there is no evading them : " Lo, I am with you ALWAY, even unto the END of the world." Here, then, we have the whole subject of Apostolic Succession in a single clause. Christ ordains the Apostles, sends them into all the world, and promises to be with them to an age which has not yet come—nay, which still lies beyond the reach of Archangels' ken. And what does this prove? Why, it proves just this : That in ordaining the Apostles He did more than commission twelve men for their natural lives. He *created* the Apostolic Episcopate, a self-perpetuating Hierarchy, like the tree of creation " yielding fruit after his kind, whose seed is in itself, upon the earth."[21] He knew that His Church would need Overseers through all the ages ; and so He established a Ministerial Succession, instinct with a perennial vitality, not to be impaired by the suicide of Judas, nor diminished when blessed James is slain with the sword. What matters it though St. Thomas be flayed alive in India, and gentle Andrew crucified in Greece ? Though the aged Peter " stretch forth his hands," and the beloved Disciple, last of the twelve, breathe out his pure spirit in the Episcopal

---

21. Genesis, i., 11.

Mansion of Ephesus? It matters not. God had promised to be with His Apostles to the end of the world ; and God has been with them, and is with them still. We shall see how that little company of Apostolic Bishops ordained not only the two lower orders of Priests and Deacons, but imparted by the "laying on of hands," all the permanent grace and authority of their own Office to their successors —who form a line of Princes in the Church of God, compared with which the oldest dynasty of Europe is but the child of a day, and which numbers at this hour nearly two thousand Bishops throughout the world.

CHAPTER IV.

THE PENTECOSTAL CHURCH.

"Christ's Church was holiest in her youthful days,
Ere the world on her smiled."
—*Lyra Apostolica*, p. 175.

"*Quis nobis dabit videre Ecclesiam sicut erat in diebus antiquis?*"—ST. BERNARD.

IN assigning reasons for being a Churchman, the first thing to be proved is that Christ founded a Church which still exists. That He did found a Church with a self-perpetuating ministry, with definite faith, and with sacraments and ordinances, has been shown from His own words and His own acts. The question whether His Church still exists ought to be sufficiently answered for any one who believes in Christ, by His promise that against His Church the gates of hell shall not prevail, and that He will be with the ministry of His Church even unto the end of the world. Nevertheless, to make assurance doubly sure, let us look at the Apostolic Church, that we may see in what way the blessed apostles carried out the divine plan, what are the essential marks or characteristics impressed on the Church by Apostolic hands, and whether these essentials have, through all the ages, been preserved in the Catholic Church of the English speaking race.

AUTHORITY.

Christ Himself left no written word; what He commanded can be learned only from what the *Apostles* did. If, at the Battle of Waterloo, Napoleon had been known to summon twelve generals to headquarters to receive instructions from him; and forthwith the twelve generals, in all parts of the battlefield, had begun and carried out a definite plan of *concerted* action, who would doubt that *that* was what the great leader had commanded? Behold then, in the concerted action of the Apostles, and in the uniform faith, order and worship of the early Church, the mandates of the Church's Head!

The first recorded act of the Apostles shows as clearly as anything could show it, that the Apostleship of the Church was not to be confined to the original twelve. For the Apostles and 109 brethren who constituted the membership of the Church in Jerusalem ("the number of the names together was about 120")[1] under divine guidance chose Matthias to "take part of this ministry and *Apostleship* from which Judas by transgression fell,"[2] thus fulfilling the prophesy of David; "His Bishopric let another take."[3]

The Lord had told the Apostles to tarry in Jerusalem until they should be "endued with power from on high." They waited in prayer, which the Church reproduces each year between Ascension and Whitsun-Day, and then when they were all assembled with one accord in one place, God, the Holy Ghost, came down from heaven to quicken, inspire, guide, teach, and comfort them, and to be the Vice-gerent of Christ on earth, until He shall come again. Thus the dead organism of the Church was

---
1. Acts, i., 15. 2. *id.*, 25. 3. *id.*, 20.

quickened into a *New-creation*, just as into the spiritless body of Adam, God breathed the breath of life, and man became a living soul. Then was preached the first Christian sermon, and 3,000 hearts were smitten, and the cry arose: " What shall we do to be saved?" Then that staunch Churchman, St. Peter, replied (in words which show that God's plan for bringing men into the Church Triumphant in Heaven, is by membership in His Church Militant upon Earth): "Repent and be baptized every one of you in the name of Jesus Christ, for the remission of sins, and ye shall receive the gift of the Holy Ghost." Repentance from sin, Baptism into the Faith of the Son of God. How exactly this agrees with the recorded teaching of Christ, Who not only demanded repentance and faith, but ordained Baptism or the New Birth of Water and the Spirit, as the door of His Church, the means by which all nations were to be made disciples, and without which none should enter into His Kingdom. Then " they that gladly received the word were baptized " to the number of 3,000.

Here then we have a picture of the Church—with its twelve Apostolic Bishops and about 3,108 members. They were not a mere voluntary society or debating club, but a divinely organized Church, indwelt by the Spirit of God. Every baptized member had, by virtue of his Baptism, been cleansed from all his sins past, endued with grace, and admitted to certain privileges and duties. The twelve Overseers of this Church had received power from Christ Himself to Baptize, to celebrate a Sacrificial Memorial of Christ's death (of which more anon), to teach with authority whatsoever He had commanded them, to sit upon thrones judging the tribes of Christ's Church, His spiritual Israel, and to keep alive that Apostolic Ministry even unto the end of the world. Such was the Catholic Church in Jerusalem, our Holy Mother, on the tenth day after the Ascension of the Lord.

I gave at the start a picture of the present aspect of Christianity among the English-speaking race. Wherein does it differ from the picture we have just seen? The only important difference is just this: In *that* Church there was no Romanism, and consequently no Protestantism. All was truth and oneness, peace and beauty and joy—in a word, *Catholicity*. And who, O! who would wish to mar that fair picture, to shatter that stately image? Who would presume to sew scarlet patches on the vesture of Christ, or worse still—which even the soldiers of Pilate would not do—to rend that seamless robe? We have, in these days, grown so accustomed, on the one hand, to the usurpations of the Bishop of Rome, and the additions which Trent and the Vatican have made to the primitive Faith; and on the other hand, so accustomed to the lopping off of the articles of that Faith, to the manufacture of new churches (of which there are now nearly 400), and the breaking up of Christianity, that we have become hardened to the scene which Christendom presents to-day, and over which the angels weep. Do you want to see these *innovations* in all their hideousness? Then, imagine them, if you can, breaking out all at once, like the boils of Egypt or the leprosy of Gehazi on the Pentecostal Church.

Nothing, indeed, will so help one to realize the Catholicity of the primitive Church, as to try, by a violent effort of the imagination, to fit the pseudo-Catholicity of Rome or the anti-Catholicity of Protestant Dissent upon the Apostolic Church. The first is like taking the Apollo Belvidere and decking it out with coat and hat and cane; the second is like shattering the image and mounting each fragment on a separate pedestal.

As to the first, fancy St. Peter, who had just missed being expelled from the ministry, when the Lord said to him :[1] "Get thee behind me, Satan!" who had fallen lower than any of his brethren by his threefold denial of Christ; who had been restored to an equal footing with the rest by the special grace of Christ, but not without special warnings; fancy him—with the words of Christ to the *whole twelve* ringing in his ears; *Call no man Father for ye are brethren*, and rebuking them for the slightest rivalry among themselves—fancy him sitting on the Altar Table of that upper room, the infant Cathedral of Jerusalem, putting a crown upon his head, and saying : *I am the Infallible Head of the Church !* the vicar of Christ, a Bishop of Bishops! while John and James, the Elders and the holy brethren rejoice to kiss his foot! But this is no exaggeration; it is precisely what one of the successors of the Apostles, the *pretended* successor of St. Peter, actually as well as metaphorically demands of his brethren today.

Nor is this all. Fancy those early Christians, their hearts aflame with the love of God and the worship of Christ, fancy them taking the gentle, lowly Virgin Mother (who depends for her salvation on the merits of Christ as much as any child of Adam), and putting her in her Son's place,

---

1. St. Matt, xvi. 23.

as an object of worship, as the "Mediatrix" between God and man! Assuredly, like blessed Paul and Barnabas, when the Priest of Jupiter would do them sacrifice, she would have cried out: "Sirs, why do ye these things? * * * Turn from these vanities unto the living God."

Nor is this all. Picture to your minds the first Celebration of the Holy Eucharist, when the newly baptized make their first Communion. They kneel about the Holy Table; perchance St. John, who lay on his Master's bosom, makes the Memorial before God, uttering the awful prayer of Consecration. He breaks the Bread, "the Communion of the Body of Christ," and blesses the "Cup of Blessing, the *Communion of the Blood of Christ;*"[2] he has repeated the words of the Lord, not only "Take, Eat, this is My Body;" but, "Drink *all* ye of this, for this is My Blood;" he remembers the words of Christ at Capernaum :[3] *Except ye drink the Blood of the Son of Man, ye have no life in you*; he himself receives under both kinds, but to the kneeling Apostles and brethren he gives only the Consecrated Bread, he withholds the Chalice, he mutilates the Blessed Sacrament, he disobeys his God, he robs the sheep! Who does not turn away from that picture in horror, as a caricature of the early Church? Nevertheless, these three things, the Supremacy and Infallibility of the pretended successor of St. Peter, the worship of the Blessed Virgin Mary, and the denial of the Cup to all but the ministering Priest, these three things, which are the chief *differentia* of Romanism, are required to-day by that part of the Catholic Church, which claims to be the only true and Catholic part.

---

2. 1, Cor., x., 16. 3. St. John, vi., 53.

Nor will the multi-cloven foot of Protestantism fit the crystal slipper of primitive Catholicity one whit better.

Fancy a certain section of the brethren saying: "It is enough to have the *Elders* over us; down with the order of *Apostles!* Let us break their bands asunder, and cast their cords from us." And so they leave the Church, and make the Presbyterian fold. Fancy another set saying: "We don't want even Elders who claim any divinely given authority; 'Ye take too much upon yourselves, ye sons of Levi, seeing all the congregation is holy.'" And so they leave the Church, appoint their ministers by the authority of the congregation, and erect the "Congregational" or "Independent" folds.

Others object to the worship and the Sacraments which the Apostles, at Christ's command, have established. One faction abolishes Confirmation or the Laying on of Hands (which the Holy Ghost declares to be a part of the foundation of the Gospel of Christ).[4] Another decides that once a month, once a season, once a year or not at all, is often enough for the Holy Eucharist. Another restricts the Sacrament of Holy Baptism to a *small minority* of mankind, and to a singular and arbitrary mode of administration. Another says: "Away with it altogether!" Still others say: "There is no visible Church, or mystical Body of Christ; we can make as good a Church as God Himself." Accordingly small *coteries* of the brethren take each some one doctrine which *all hold* in common, and make a special "church" to emphasize that one point at the expense of other truths equally vital.

---

4. Heb., vi., 1 2.

Again, others assail the rule of Faith, the "Form of Sound Words"[5] which the Apostles together inculcate, the heirloom of the Church, the Apostolic Creed. And here one phase of Protestantism fits the early Church so badly as to be positively ludicrous. One says: "I don't want a Creed imposed by Apostolic authority. Away with it! The Bible and the Bible only is my religion. Give me the New Testament." But lo! St. Matthew rises and says: "My brother, I am the author of the first Gospel, but I shall not begin to write it for twenty years yet. In the meantime my word is as good as my pen." And then, methinks, I hear the beloved John exclaim: "I am the author of the fourth Gospel, but all you who hear my voice will have gone to the spirit-world, or ever I write down the first word." Then St. Peter jumps to his feet and says: "Ye fools and blind! A large part of the New Testament is to be written by one who is now a persecutor and injurious, making havoc of the Church. And even when the Canon of Scripture is closed, it will contain many things hard to be understood [6] which they that are unlearned and unstable will wrest to their own destruction, by their 'private interpretations.'[7] *Sixty years* will elapse before the Bible is finished; *three hundred* before THE CHURCH decides which of the many religious writings are inspired; and fourteen or fifteen centuries ere the inventive genius of man will make it possible to put the open Bible into the hands of all Christians. Meanwhile what is the Church to do? Why, the Lord has directed us [8] to *teach you* to observe *all* things whatsoever He has com-

---

5. II. Tim., i., 13. 6. II. St. Peter, iii., 16. 7. II. St. Peter, i., 20. 8. St. Matthew, xxviii., 20.

manded us. He spent forty days with us after His Resurrection, teaching us the things pertaining to His Church. [9] We *know* what we are about. And if you are willing to accept our writing, will ye not receive our spoken word?"

Thus would St. Peter have shown the folly of the Protestant novelty that *the Church is founded on the New Testament.* The fact is that, as the Jewish Church, which was fully organized under Moses, lived a thousand years before the Old Testament was completed, so the Catholic Church flourished for *two generations*, as the perfectly organized and authoritative Kingdom of God, before the New Testament was finished. Late in the fourth century St. Chrysostom mentions the Acts of the Apostles as a book which probably no one in the vast cathedral congregation of Constantinople had ever read. Yet all the while the Church was *perfectly organized,* and achieved its most glorious triumphs. It had its Rule of Faith, which crystallized into the Creed; it had its worship (the "Divine Liturgy"), the threefold Ministry, the Sacraments, and the oral Gospel which the Apostles preached many years before it was put on paper, and which the Christians knew and loved whether they could read or not. And the Church would still be the Church, even had God chosen to withhold from it the written word; and would continue to be the "Church of the Living God, the Pillar and ground of the truth," even if (as humanly speaking seemed probable at one time) every copy of the Bible had been destroyed. Christianity is not a MS., but a Kingdom; not a book, but a living, believing, worshipping, governing and working Church. Officers of this Church, it is true, were inspired by the

---

9. Acts, i., 3.

Holy Ghost to write a Book, which is thus a most precious revelation from God, and " profitable for doctrine, for reproof, for correction, for instruction in righteousness."[10] But it must be remembered *the Book* was written by Churchmen, for the Church already existing, and must be interpreted according to the Church's Rule of Faith.[11] The Bible divorced from the Church is like a constitution without a nation, a code of laws without a government to give them sanction and authority.

Thus the three distinctive features of modern Romanism, and the illogical, unecclesiastical, uncatholic novelties which are the foundation of Protestant Dissent are incompatible with—nay, inconceivable in—the One Holy Catholic and Apostolic Church as founded by Incarnate God, and builded by those to whom He gave authority and power until the end of time.

---

10. II. Tim., iii., 16.
11. "Without the Creeds, the Holy Scriptures are as a treasure-house of which we have lost the key."

CHAPTER V.

MARKS OF THE HOLY CATHOLIC CHURCH.

"I obey,
Following where'er the Church hath marked the ancient way."
—*Lyra Apostolica*, p. 132.

WE read that the three thousand converts who were *baptized* on the day of Pentecost, "continued steadfastly" in four things: [1] *The Doctrine of the Apostles; The Fellowship of the Apostles; The Breaking of the Bread; and The Prayers*. Churchmen of old, then, in addition to being baptized, had four marks by which they were known, and all Christians who are *Churchmen* bear those same marks to-day.

(*a*) They continued steadfastly in the Doctrine of the Apostles, *i. e.*, the Faith ; the othodox Catholic Faith which the Apostles taught the Church ; or, in brief, the Creed. Any departure from this standard, either by false additions or by diminutions, is *heresy*.

(*b*) They continued steadfastly in the Fellowship of *the Apostles*—not merely of *one* of the Apostles—*i. e.*, they remained in communion with the Church and loyal to the Apostolic Episcopate. This fellowship or communion is broken to-day by those who say: [2] "I am of CEPHAS" [PETER]. They assert (though mistakenly) that St. Peter was an Apostle of Apostles, the Head of the Church, having sole jurisdiction over the whole world ; that he was

---

1. Acts, ii., 42. 2. 1 Cor., i., 12, and iii., 21-22.

Bishop of Rome (which he wás not); and that this [imaginary] authority has come down in unbroken line (though it has not) in the Bishops of Rome. On the strength of a *non-existent* authority which St. Peter did *not* possess, which he did *not* bequeath to the Bishops of Rome, and which the Bishops of Rome have *not* kept in unbroken succession, they have broken fellowship with *four* out of the *five* Patriarchs of Catholic Christendom, with their Bishops, clergy and laity who at the time far outnumbered those who adhered to the Patriarch of Rome ; and have broken fellowship with the autocephalous [3] Churches, like the Churches of Great Britain and Cyprus, and set up altar against altar, notably within the jurisdiction of the Anglican Church since 1570.

This Fellowship with the Apostles is still more violently broken by all Protestant Dissenters who have rebelled against the Apostolic Episcopate and seceded from the historic Church. For individual believers in Christ, who by

---

3. *Note.* "The dioceses are grouped into provinces, with an Archbishop over each. The provinces are grouped, except those in the far West of Europe, *England among them,* and except a few in the East, which are still left autocephalous, into Patriarchates with a Patriarch over each," viz., Rome, Constantinople (which Canon III. of the Second General Council declares to have "*equal privileges*" with Rome), Alexandria, Antioch and Jerusalem.

"The exclusive theory of Rome was resisted from the time it made its first faint appearance in the Catholic Church until to-day. * * * As it grew in strength and insolence during the darkest time of the Middle Ages, the whole Eastern and Greek part of the Catholic Church, at that time by far the largest, most enlightened and numerous part, with the Patriarch of Constantinople at its head, rose and excommunicated the Bishop of Rome and all his adherents. Thus four out of the five great Patriarchates of the world cut off the one Western or Roman Patriarchate. The Roman theory then, left to itself, easily gained additional strength and self-assertion in the West, until in the sixteenth century the Catholic part of the Church in England could endure it no longer. * * * So the Roman part of the Church cut itself off first from the whole Eastern part of the Church, and then from the Anglican."—*Catholicity in its Relationship to Protestantism and Romanism. By Dr. Ewer,* pp. 236 *and* 155.

3

heredity or by erroneous teaching are to-day not in communion with the Church, all Churchmen should entertain feelings of sympathy and brotherly love. But with the systems of Dissent and with their founders, those sons of Nebat who make Israel to sin, there can be no compromise.

It should be remembered also that in the long run, the breaking of the Fellowship of the Apostles is always accompanied by more or less of a departure from the Doctrine of the Apostles, as well as from the two remaining marks of the Church, which must now be considered.

(c) The early Church continued steadfastly in *the Breaking of the Bread, i. e.,* the Holy Eucharist. Those who do not regularly, lawfully and frequently participate in the Holy Communion, do not continue steadfastly in the Breaking of the Bread. This sign of true Catholicity is marred or obliterated by those who mutilate the Blessed Sacrament (like the modern Romanists); by those who make superstitious additions to it; by those who parody it by attempting to consecrate it without the lawful Priesthood, or without the proper *matter* (*i. e.*, bread and wine), or without the proper *form* (*i. e.*, the essential part of the Divine Liturgy); and, of course, by those who abolish it altogether, like the Quakers. And surely this mark is very much dimmed in those parishes of our own Church where Matins takes the place of Holy Communion *forty* Sundays out of the year, and where on the First Day of the week we come together not, like the early Christians, "to break Bread," but to hear sermons.

(d) They continued steadfastly in *the Prayers*, not merely in prayer in general, but in THE PRAYERS. The definite article is there in the Greek, and has been restored in the Revised Version of the New Testament. What *the* Prayers means no one need be ignorant. The Church, like the Jewish Synagogue, has always had a form of worship. The Liturgy of the Church, though elastic and flexible, has in it an element invariable and divine, a norm or skeleton which is demonstrably of Apostolic origin, the common heritage of Catholic Christendom.

Of the three divisions of English-speaking Christians (Churchmen, Romanists and Dissenters) which has continued the most steadfastly in these four things? Which holds the Doctrine of the Apostles without additions and without diminutions? Which holds the Fellowship of the Apostles and the Communion of Saints?—the Catholic Episcopate free from tyrannous usurpation, a reasonable and reformed Priesthood, but without breaking the Apostolic Succession? Which holds the Breaking of the Bread, without mutilating the Sacrament, without superstitious additions, with lawful priestly ministrations, with proper matter and form? Which holds *the* Prayers, the Catholic Liturgy— enriched, it is true, and adapted to present needs — but not overlaid with *creature*-worship, nor dissipated into the extemporaneous devotions of an individual man?

It remains then to show that the Mother Church of English-speaking Christians to-day, like the Church in the days of the Apostles, having admitted to membership by Holy Baptism, holds its members steadfast in the Faith; in the Apostolic Ministry (carrying with it Ordination and Confirmation); in the Blessed Sacrament of Christ's Body and Blood; and in the Prayers, the devotional heritage of the Church.

CHAPTER VI.

THE ANGLICAN CHURCH AND HOLY BAPTISM.

> "All in the unregenerate child
> Is void and formless, dark and wild,
> Till the life-giving holy Dove
> Upon the waters gently move,
> And power impart, soft brooding there,
> Celestial fruit to bear."
> — *Keble, Lyra Innocentium, II.*

IT has been shown that the Apostolic ministry of the early Church admitted to membership by Baptism; and then that the baptized members of the Church continued steadfastly in four things which may be called the marks of true Catholicity. All Christians have at least some measure of these four things, some element or elements of Catholicity; but it is the glory of the Anglican Church that she has retained them *all*.

The Church was early planted in the British Isles, probably by St. Paul himself. This Church, during the British ascendency, during the Saxon ascendency, during the Norman ascendency, and down to the present day, is the *same* Church. She has passed through sundry deformations and reformations, has never been absolutely perfect nor radically imperfect; has never been without the Orthodox Faith, the Apostolic Ministry, the Sacraments, the Liturgy, and good works. She has at times been tyrannized over by a foreign ecclesiastical power, and again robbed and oppressed by the State, but she has never ceased to be the Church. Her escapade with the Bishop of Rome, especially from about A. D. 1200 to the middle of the sixteenth century, was unfortunate in the extreme, and brought her much trouble, but she never lost her personal identity, nor her lawful jurisdiction ; and is to-day the same Church and in the same position that she would be in, had England become totally isolated from all the rest of Christendom, and never so much as heard of the rise of the " Papacy " and the other strange " developments " which have taken place within the Latin Church.

A comparison of the principles of the early Church, as seen in the New Testament and the writings of the Fathers, with those of the Anglican Church to-day, will show that the latter has not departed therefrom in any *essential* point, if indeed in any respect at all farther than local circumstances and the progress of civilization justly demand. *Nor can this be said of any other Communion in Western Christendom.*

As to Holy Baptism, which is the door of entrance from the world into the Church, she holds and has *ever* held what Christ taught, what the Apostles carried out, and what the Universal Church has practiced always and everywhere. There is here no difference between us Churchmen and the rest of Catholic Christendom. It will be well, however, to. consider briefly what this Sacrament really means, this New Birth which made the early believers members of Christ, and of which our Church both in theory and practice makes so much account. *Baptism* and *Regenera-*

tion are synonymous terms. They both in Scriptural phraseology and in Church usage, stand for the initial rite of the Christian religion, viz., *Christening* or the act which makes one a Christian. Almost everything has two or three names, each emphasizing some special characteristic. The Sacrament of the Altar is variously called "the Breaking of the Bread," the Holy Communion, the Lord's Supper, the Holy Eucharist, and the Mass. So likewise the first Sacrament of Christianity is called Baptism with reference to its outward visible sign or form, and Regeneration or the New Birth with reference to its inward spiritual grace. St. Paul couples the two ideas together when he says we are saved "by the Washing of Regeneration,"[1] or as it might be rendered, *the Baptism of the New Birth*. Regeneration then is that death unto sin and new birth unto righteousness which constitutes the inward part or grace of the Sacrament. What could be simpler? We are born or generated into the world by the act of our parents; we are *born again* or *re*-generated into the Church by "Water and the Spirit," receiving at the same time forgiveness of all past sins, original or actual.[2]

There is a shocking abuse of the word *regeneration* which has of late become prevalent among people ignorant of language and of Theology. They make it synonomous with *conversion* (*!*) It has no more to do with conversion than it has with getting married or being buried. Conversion is a change of heart for which we pray, when we say: "Create and make in us new and contrite hearts."[3] Regeneration is that Christening grace for which we pray, when

---

1. Titus, iii., 5. 2. Ch. Catechism. St. John, iii., 5; Acts, iii., 38. 3. Collect for Ash Wed.

we say: "Give Thy Holy Spirit to this Infant that he may be born again," and when we pray that "these persons coming to Thy Holy Baptism may receive remission of their sins by spiritual Regeneration."[4] Conversion is the act of the prodigal in returning to his Father; Regeneration is the act of the Father in receiving him and admitting him to His house. To call conversion Regeneration, as most Dissenters do, is simply an abuse of language and a confusion of ideas. One might just as well call repentance, Confirmation; or Faith, Ordination; or a man, an eagle; or a fish, a bird. We may be converted a hundred times; we can be baptized, christened, regenerated but *once*. And so, as soon as the infant is baptized the priest says, "Seeing now, dearly beloved brethren, that this child is *regenerate* and grafted into the body of Christ's Church, let us give thanks," and then he prays: "We yield Thee hearty thanks, most merciful Father, that it hath pleased Thee to *regenerate* this infant with Thy Holy Spirit, to receive him for Thine own child by adoption, and to incorporate him into Thy holy Church."

It is common in these days to hear some well-meaning Christian say, "O, I believe in Baptism, but I don't regard it a 'saving ordinance.'" It is well to remind such that they differ from the Catholic Church which St. Peter[5] taught to believe, "Baptism doth also now *save* us," and to which St. Paul writes, "According to His mercy He saved us by the Washing of Regeneration."[1] In no less than twelve passages of the New Testament do Christ or His Apostles associate Salvation with Baptism, *e. g.* "Christ loved the Church, and gave Himself for her that He might

---

4. Baptismal Offices. 5. 1 Pet iii., 21.

sanctify and cleanse her by the Washing of Water."[6] A faithful disciple sent by God, says to the penitent and believing Saul of Tarsus, "Arise, be baptized and wash away thy sins."[7] St. Peter says in answer to the question, "What shall we do to be saved?" "Repent and be baptized every one of you for the remission of sins."[8] When Christ commissioned the Apostles to baptize all nations, He adds, "He that believeth AND *is baptized*, shall be saved."[9] And He said to Nicodemus, "Except a man be *born of Water and of the Spirit*, he cannot enter into the kingdom of God." There is no such thing as an unchristened Christian; an unbaptized person is an "alien from the commonwealth of Israel, and a stranger from the covenant of promise." By Baptism, then, a person is cleansed from sin, born again, admitted into the Church, made a member of Christ and inheritor of the Kingdom of Heaven, brought into a state of salvation from which, of course, he may fall, if he be unfaithful.

Such, in brief, is the Church's doctrine of Holy Baptism, as we gather from the New Testament, and from the writings of the Fathers — from Justin Martyr, writing before 148 A. D.; from Irenæus and Tertullian but a little later; from the great and godly Cyprian, Bishop of Carthage A. D. 246; from St. Cyril, Bishop of Jerusalem, A. D. 351, whose admirable lectures on Baptism are still extant; from the unvarying testimony of hosts of others, as well as from the early Baptismal Offices; from the constant use of the Catholic Church; and, what is of special interest to us, from the *uninterrupted* theory and practice of that part of the Catholic Church to which it is our privilege to belong.

---

6. Eph., v., 25-6.   7. Acts, xxii. 16   8 Acts, ii., 38   9. St. Mark, xvi., 16.

These sources of authority also demonstrate beyond all cavil or doubt, that (as Dr. Blunt expresses it) "Baptism has been given to *infants* from the time of its first institution." At the start, of course, there were very few infants to be reached by the Church, but whenever we read in Holy Scripture of the older members of a family being converted, we always read that not only they but the *entire household* were baptized.[10] As the Church grew, and children were born to Christian parents, those parents always brought their little ones to the Church that they might be born into the family of God, believing, as St. Cyprian says that "one cannot have God for his Father, unless he have the Church for his mother." So often were parents or sponsors seen wending their way to church with babes in their arms, that the Pagans started the dreadful slander that Christians met together to slay little children and drink their blood!

There was a controversy in the early Church of North Africa about infant Baptism, but the question was not whether infants should be christened, but whether they should be christened *before they were eight* days old. And the great Bishop of Carthage, above mentioned, with fifty Bishops in council assembled, ruled that no infant was too young for Baptism. The eighth day used to be a favorite time for christening, after the analogy of Jewish Circumcision, that type of Baptism, by which a child of a week was admitted to all the privileges and grace of God's ancient Covenant. Justin Martyr, who was almost contemporanous with St. John, speaks of many aged people who had

---

10. Acts, xvi., 15 and 33, and 1 Cor., i., 16.

been made *disciples of Christ from infancy.* St. Irenæus speaks of "*infants and little children,* and boys and young men" all being alike born anew to God by Holy Baptism. St. Augustine speaks of "infants baptized in Christ," and says: "In infants born and baptized, and thus born again, let Christ be acknowledged." When the Good Shepherd builded the "one fold," He meant it for the lambs as well as for the sheep. We may rest assured that the Catholic Church, after baptizing infants for nearly 1900 years, knows what she is about. That heartless heresy which denies the mercies of the Covenant to the little children whom Jesus blessed,[11] which shuts out of the Kingdom of God those very ones concerning whom the Saviour said, "Of *such* is the Kingdom of God,"[12] was born of ignorance, nourished on prejudice, and has been propagated by a mistaken zeal worthy a better cause. It has also brought it to pass that, even under the shadow of the old English Church, multitudes grow up *unregenerate* — oftentimes subjectively believers, but objectively *heathen.* From the conversion of England to the Church until the seventeen years when Puritanism drove the "Elect Lady" into the wilderness (1645-1662) such a thing as an unbaptized Englishman was practically unknown. And it was only after the restoration of the Church that it became necessary to insert in the Prayer Book an Office for "the Baptism of *Adults,*" to make up for the neglect of Regeneration during that period of sacrilege and self-will.

To sum up, then, as one has said, "All testimony of writers down to the twelfth century approves its use [infant

---

11. St. Mark, x., 16. 12. St. Mark, x., 14.

Baptism], and there is not one saying, quotation, or example, that makes against it."

Consequently the Anglican Church is right in declaring that the "Baptism of young children is in any wise to be retained in the Church, as most agreeable to the institution of Christ;"[13] and in instructing the people "that they defer not the Baptism of their children longer than the first or second Sunday next after their birth, * * * unless upon great and reasonable cause."[14]

It is worthy of note that it is only such sects as have lost, not only the Apostolic Ministry, but the whole "Church Idea," that distort, underrate, or abolish Holy Baptism, or stumble at the doctrine of Regeneration which the Bible and the Church inculcate. The fact is, if one have a low or vague opinion of the Church, he will have a low or vague opinion of that Sacrament which makes us members of the Church. If the Church is anything less than she, on the authority of the Holy Ghost, claims to be, then Baptism is only an empty ordinance, an indifferent rite, a strange ceremony, a meaningless symbol, a powerless instrument. *But what is the Church?*—that "Church which God purchased with His own Blood,"[15] giving Himself for her "that He might sanctify and cleanse her by the *Washing of Water?*" What is the Church into which we are baptized? St. Paul says: "*The Church is* His Body, the fulness of Him that filleth all in all."[16] And the baptized—what of them? They have "all by one Spirit been baptized into *One Body*."[17] They are "in Christ." "As many of you as have been baptized into Christ have put on Christ."[18]

13. Art. XXVII. 14. Private Baptism of Children, P. B. 15. Acts, xx.,28. 16. Ephesians, i., 23. 17. 1 Cor., xii., 12. 18. Gal., iii., 26.

They are the "Body of Christ and members in particular." Their very "bodies" are "members of Christ," [19] and they are "partakers of the *Divine Nature*." [20] The Church, then, is the Mystical Body of Incarnate God. A metaphor? Perhaps so—but God's figures of speech stand ever for *realities*, for realities heavenly and eternal. As a late writer has said : "The Incarnation is a perpetual fact. What is the supernatural law, then, under which Christ's own personal Body continues to expand? It is this: human beings are *baptized into Christ*, according as it is written, 'We are members of His Body, of His Flesh and of His Bones.' [21] Human beings, sprouting like so many separate branches from the poisoned roots of Adam, are plucked thence by the Holy Ghost, and, in Baptism, grafted into the new tree, Christ; our bodies into His; our souls into His; our hopes, our imaginations, our passions, our reason into His ; and so the Tree enlarges; so His Body Visible expands; so the Stone [cut out without hands] grows and becomes a Great Mountain, and fills the whole earth; according as it is written: 'We are the Body of Christ.'"

The act, then, which unites human beings to Incarnate God, through His Body, the Church, is beauteous in its simplicity, intelligible in its meaning, transcendently important in its sublime and far-reaching effects. And this, the Foundation Sacrament of Christ's Religion, the Anglican Church, in common with all parts of Catholic Christendom, not only holds *to-day*, but has *always* retained, used, and prized ; otherwise she could lay no just claim to that true Catholicity which is based on the historic continuity of Apostolic truth.

---

19. 1 Cor., vi., 15. 20. 2d Peter, i., 4. 21. Eph., v., 30.

CHAPTER VII.

THE ANGLICAN CHURCH AND "THE APOSTLES' DOCTRINE."

"It is of the essence of the Church that it teach the Catholic Faith."—*Bishop Forbes.*

"Mark how each Creed stands in that test revealed,
Romish, and Swiss, and Lutheran novelties."
—*Lyra Apostolica,* p. 130.

ZEAL for the vindication of Episcopacy, which is of course one of the essentials of the Christian Church, has led many defenders of the Church to make it the chief argument why we should be Churchmen rather than Dissenters. The possession of a valid Episcopal Succession makes us "Episcopalians," but does not necessarily prove us to be Orthodox Catholic Churchmen, free from "false doctrine, heresy, and schism." The Arians were Episcopalians, but heretics; the Novatians and Donatists were Episcopalians, but schismatics. The historic continuity of the Anglo-Catholic Church depends not alone on the Apostolic Succession, but on the uninterrupted possession of *all* the marks of primitive Catholicity. Had our Church abolished the Sacrament of Baptism, Episcopacy would not save her; had she lost the "Doctrine of the Apostles," "the Breaking of the Bread," or "the Prayers," the mere fact of having "Fellowship with the Apostles" through a Succession of

Bishops, would not make her a true or complete Church, nor afford satisfactory reasons why we should be Churchmen, unless and until, in the Providence of God, the golden crown of Apostolic Order should draw back the lost jewels of Apostolic Faith, Eucharist and Worship. These, however, the English Church never lost. I therefore deprecate the phrase, "the *restored* Catholicity" of the English Church. She was never without it. In *theory* the Anglican Church was never Roman, and never Protestant, though at times like a storm-tossed bark she has felt the whirlpool of Charybdis, and seen the broken crags of Scylla. If we leave out of account certain *practical* departures from that theory, which were forced upon her by the brute might of the Papacy [1] or the grim and selfish tyranny of Kings, [2] we shall find that the general faith, order and worship of the English Church have always been substantially the same. That this is so in the case of Baptism has been shown. If it is so also in the case of the four marks of Catholicity — Apostolic Faith, and Fellowship, the Eucharist, and the Prayers — then the Anglican Church may, more

---

1. *e. g.* The evils, which accompanied the mediæval intrusion of Monastic orders from Italy, which claimed exemption from the jurisdiction of the English Bishops, which, by the way, was a direct violation of Canon IV., of the General Council of Chalcedon, which says: "No monk shall live anywhere, nor establish a monastery or an oratory contrary to the will of the bishop of the city; and that the monks in every city and district shall be subject to the bishop." In Canon VIII. of the same council we read: "Let the clergy of the . . . monasteries . . . in every city remain under the authority of the bishops, according to the tradition of the holy fathers; and let no one arrogantly cast off the rule of his own bishop; and if any shall contravene this canon in any way whatever, and will not be subject to their own bishop, if they be clergy, let them be subjected to canonical penalties, and if they be monks or laymen, let them be excommunicated."

2. *e. g.* The tyranny of Henry VIII., and William of Orange, or the silencing of Convocation, and the usurpations of Parliament and the Privy Council under the Hanoverian Sovereigns.

justly than any other Branch of the Church or than any sect, claim the allegiance of all English-speaking Christians.

Taking these things in their order then, what was the "Faith once delivered to the Saints," the Faith of the Early Church which the Anglican Church has kept? It was a belief in GOD, THE FATHER; in JESUS CHRIST, His only Son, Who became *Incarnate* of a Virgin, in His life and death, His Resurrection, His Ascension into Heaven, and His coming again as Judge; in the HOLY GHOST; *the Holy Catholic Church*, the Forgiveness of Sins, the Resurrection of the Body, and Everlasting Life.

The *narrative* portions of the New Testament show that this, in brief, was the Faith of the Early Church; the *dogmatic* portions authoritatively assert these truths with their necessary implications. This Summary of revealed truth, grand in its simplicity, vast in its comprehensiveness, was taught orally by the Apostles, as "the Form of Sound Words," and was early used, throughout all parts of the Church, as a Profession of Faith for Candidates for Holy Baptism. [3] Christ had commanded all nations to be

---

3. A very ancient form of the Creed, adapted to a baptismal profession, in size and expression midway between the longer, or Eastern form of the Apostolic Creed, which was adopted at Nicæa, or the shorter or Western form, commonly called the "Apostle's Creed," is preserved in the earliest fragment extant of the Baptismal Liturgy, in Book VII., Chapter XLI. of the "Apostolic Constitution," a work compiled by an unknown writer, probably between 250 and 300 A. D., but the materials of which were much more ancient. The person to be baptized says: "I renounce Satan and his works, and his pomps and his worship," etc. * * "And after this renunciation, let him, in his dedication say: 'I associate myself with Christ, and—I BELIEVE in (and am baptized into) one Unbegotten Being, the only true GOD ALMIGHTY, THE FATHER of Christ, the Creator and Maker of all things, from Whom are all things;—and into the LORD JESUS CHRIST, His only begotten Son, the Firstborn of the whole creation, Who, before the ages was by the good pleasure of the Father, begotten, not created; through Whom all things were made, both those in Heaven and those on Earth,

baptized, "in the Name of the Father and of the Son and of the Holy Ghost." Accordingly the Apostles, having stated this Doctrine of the Trinity, with a few of the precious results of the Incarnation in the only natural and logical order,[4] required this belief of those who were admitted to the Church. The tradition that the Creed was composed by the Apostles has been general in the Church for some 1600 years. The Creed, in substantially its present form, is given by St. Irenæus, less than a century after the death of St. John, as something well known in his day. Traces of it are found in Justin Martyr (who died about 150 A. D.), St. Polycarp for more than fifty years the Bishop of Smyrna ("for twenty years the disciple of St John," probably the one addressed as the "Angel of the Church in Smyrna," Rev. ii., 8), St. Clement the third Bishop of Rome (the "fellow laborer" of St. Paul, "whose name is in the Book of Life," Phil. iv., 3), and in St. Ignatius (for thirty years Bishop of Antioch, and a contemporary of all the Apostles). As Dr. Blunt observes, "There is more reason for believing that the Creed was composed

---

visible and invisible; Who in the last days descended from Heaven, and took flesh, and was born of the Holy Virgin Mary, and lived a holy life according to the laws of His God and Father, and was crucified under Pontius Pilate, and died for us; and rose again from the dead, after His Passion, the third day, and ascended into the Heavens, and sitteth at the Right Hand of the Father. And again is to come at the end of the world, with glory, to judge the quick and the dead, of Whose Kingdom there shall be no end. I am baptized also into the HOLY GHOST, that is, the Comforter, Who wrought in all the Saints from the beginning of the world, but was afterwards sent to the Apostles by the Father according to the promise of our Saviour and Lord, Jesus Christ, and after the Apostles, to all who believe in the Holy Catholic Church; into the Resurrection of the Flesh, and into the Remission of Sins, and into the Kingdom of Heaven, and into the life of the world to come."

4. For a clear exposition of the unity and logical order of the articles of the Creed, see Ewer's "Catholicity in its Relation," etc., p. 53.

by the Apostles, under Inspiration of the Holy Ghost, than for believing the contrary." Be that as it may, the "Apostles' Creed" is at least the form into which Apostolic teaching crystallized in the West, as the equivalent Symbol which was witnessed to, ratified, and made universal at Nicæa and Constantinople, is the bright gem cut and bequeathed by Apostolic hands in the East. Properly speaking the "Apostles' Creed" and the Nicene Creed are equally the *Apostles'* Creed, the only difference being that the form in which it was handed down in the West was a little more condensed than the other. But there was no difference in its *meaning*, for any ambiguity of statement was made up for by the authoritative interpretation, or traditional commentary, which may be called by that much abused phrase, the "sense of the Church." The Nicene Creed, it should be remembered, was not *first* drawn up at the Council of Nicæa in 325. *All* the dioceses of Christendom had *inherited* the Creed in *substantially* the same shape, and with *absolutely* the same import. The 318 Bishops from all parts of the Church, who met at Nicæa to bear witness against Arius' denial of the Divinity of Christ, merely agreed upon an ancient form of the primitive Creed, hallowed by devout and immemorial usage in the Diocese of Cæsarea, which Eusebius, the Bishop of Cæsarea, who presented it to the Council, avowed he had received from his predecessors in the Episcopate, and into which, indeed, he himself had been baptized. So much of the universally inherited apostolical *credendum*, as bore upon the Person of our blessed Lord, which was the truth then assailed, was so *fortified in expression*, but not altered in meaning, as absolutely and forever to exclude all forms of Unitarian infidelity, and receive *the Imprimatur* of the first Ecumenical Council. The remainder (following the words "I believe in the Holy Ghost,") was *witnessed to and promulgated* at the Second General Council (Constantinople, 381). It was not *then drawn up*, for the entire Creed, as then *authorized*, had been in general use for an indefinite period antecedent.[5] The Creed thus ecumenically approved, a part at Nicæa, the whole at Constantinople, has ever since been received by the entire Catholic Church, as the *articulus stantis vel cadentis Ecclesiæ*, and has never been altered.[6] The Creed is, then, an unfailing witness to the inspired teaching of the Apostles, given by the *whole* Church in an age when such testimony was possible (which has long since gone by) and received by the whole Church; and hence, it is an *independent* authority, consonant of course, with Holy Scripture, and provable therefrom.

The "Athanasian Creed," or *Hymn*, composed about A. D. 430, stands on a different basis, but is at least venerable compared with all Protestant Confessions. It has never received conciliar ratification nor formal reception by the whole Church—albeit no Diocese in Christendom repudiates it or denies its definitions. Even Richard Baxter [7] could say of it: "I unfeignedly account Athanasius' Creed the best explanation of the doctrine of the Trinity that I ever read." It is simply an admirable expansion of the

---

5. See Epiphanius' "Anchorite," near the end.
6. The "*filioque*" is no proper part of the Creed. It asserts a Theological truth (see Dr. Richey's admirable monograph on the subject) in harmony with the Creed, but has never been sanctioned by any General Council, having been introduced by a local Synod in the West, with results greatly to be deplored.
7. Reasons of the Chris. Rel., Chap. IX., p. 313.

truths of the primitive Creed. And the closer we are to the heart of our Divine Human Master, the more faithfully we confess the eternal Trinity and worship the Divine Unity, the more will we understand and love that grand statement of the Orthodox Faith. The "damnatory" or *Enacting* Clauses, are hardly more a part of the Creed than the Anathemas originally affixed to the Nicene Symbol. Nevertheless they are precisely what our Saviour Himself has taught. [8] This Creed is a part of the doctrine of the English Church, and it is a matter of regret to many that the Church in the United States decided not to insert it in her Liturgy and Articles. But so far from repudiating it, she is as much bound by its doctrine as if she had retained it, since every clause is contained explicitly or by necessary implication in Holy Scripture and in the Apostles' and Nicene Creeds. Moreover, as the Bishop of Connecticut has pointed out, "That our Church accepts the Athanasian definitions is placed beyond doubt by the declaration in the Preface to the Prayer Book that we do not intend to depart from the Church of England in any essential point of doctrine; by the retention of the Preface of Trinity Sunday in the office for Holy Communion; and by the adoption of the first five Articles [which see]." [9]

A single word as to the Thirty-nine Articles. *They are not a Creed*, but a compendium of *Anti-Romish* and *Anti-Calvinistic* theology, designed for the Clergy, not for the laity. They contain a few *ambiguous* passages, but are happily susceptible of a strictly Orthodox and Catholic interpretation.

---

8. See St. Mark xvi., 16; St. John iii., 16, and viii. 24.
9. Note on Ath. Cr. Am. Ed. Brown on Art. See also Rev. F. W. Taylor's excellent monograph on the "Athanasian Creed."

It must now be shown that the Apostolic Faith is and has always been the belief of the Anglican Church.

That the Anglican Church has always held the Creed, in the same sense as she holds it to-day, is a simple matter of history. Dr. Blunt says: "The Apostles' Creed has been used in the daily Offices of the English Church as far back as they can be traced." British Bishops, beyond reasonable doubt, were present at the Council of Nicæa. At all events, the British Church not only accepted the Nicene Faith, but stands almost alone in Christendom, as a great national Church which passed through the Arian epidemic with scarce a taint of the impious plague. Withdrawn from the turmoil and strife of the rest of Christendom, the Bishops of our Mother Church clung to the primitive Faith, while the dreadful heresy which would dethrone the Son of God was making havoc of the Church in the East and even as far West as Italy and Spain. "In every city of the East and of Africa, the Arian party filled the sees, held the churches, and formed the most numerous party. The Catholics were a despised and persecuted minority."[10] Heretical Bishops, at various times, ruled the Church in Jerusalem, Antioch, Ephesus, Alexandria, Constantinople and *Rome*. [11]

In spite of the Modern Roman dogma that the Bishops of Rome are all *infallible*, Liberius, Bishop of Rome (who died

---

10. Cutt's Turning Points of Gen. Ch. Hist., p. 165.
11. This, I take it, is the meaning of Article XIX., which declares that as "the Churches of Jerusalem, Alexandria, and Antioch *have* erred, so also the Church of Rome *hath* erred." This Article does *not* say that these Churches are *now in error* (which would be, as the late Patriarch of Constantinople said, an "accusation of our neighbor, out of place in a distinguished confession"), but merely that they *have erred* in times past.

A. D. 366), became an Arian, but still governed the Church in the Imperial City. Virgilius was an heretic, and was excommunicated by the Fifth General Council (A. D. 553). Honorius embraced the Monothelite heresy, and was anathematized by the Sixth General Council (A. D. 680). The list of English Archbishops shows no such apostates as these! Various other heresies have been held by the Bishops of Rome,[12] and what one "Infallible Pontiff" has declared to be heresy, his equally infallible successors have promulgated as part of the Faith, and necessary to salvation! [See note at the end of the Chapter.]

At the Council of Sardica (A. D. 347) British Bishops were present and sided with the Orthodox party. St. Hilary, Bishop of Poitiers (A. D. 358), congratulates the "Bishops of the British Provinces" that they "have continued undefiled and unharmed by any taint of the detestable heresy." St. Athanasius, the Patriarch of Alexandria, the great champion of the Faith, in his letter to the Emperor Jovian (A. D. 363), places the British Church among the Churches loyal to the Catholic Faith. St. Chrysostom, St. Jerome and other Fathers of the fourth century, bear glowing testimony to the orthodoxy of our old British Mother. It is true that in the fifth century a Briton named Pelagius, while on a visit to *Rome*, learned a heresy which he brought back to his mother country; but the British Bishops, with the kindly assistance of two learned Bishops from Gaul, easily vanquished Pelagianism.

Indeed, no heresy touching the fundamentals of the Faith, *has ever been accepted, even temporarily*, by the Church of the British and Anglo-American race.

---

12. Cf. the cases of Cœlestius, Zosimus, Hormisdas and others.—*Bossuet c.* 30.

Our venerable sister, the Church of Rome, calls us *heretical*—not on the ground that we do not hold and profess the same old Creeds which both of us, in common with the Holy Eastern Church, have alike *inherited*, but because, forsooth, we do not accept certain *additions* to the Apostolic Faith, made on her sole authority, but not sanctioned by any General Council, not taught by the Fathers, and never accepted by the Greek Church! It matters not whether these *additions* be *true* or *false;* it is enough that they are *novelties*, absolutely and forever ruled out in advance by a decree of the Fourth General Council,[13] and therefore of no possible obligation upon Catholic Christians. How much more is this so, if some of these *additions* be found to be in themselves, contradictory; in their effects pernicious; historically untrue; and false to the witness of the Holy Ghost in the Undivided Church and in Holy Writ!

Any loyal member of the early Church would be admitted to-day to full membership in the Anglican Church, which, in matters of faith, requires of her children only what the early Church required, viz: the Creed. To be a *Roman* Catholic one must believe precisely the same, and if that were *all* that Rome requires we should be at one. As to the Faith of the Universal Church, the Anglican Church at the Reformation, made no change. Even in minor points of doctrine there was then no wide breach

---

13. The 630 Bishops at the Council of Chalcedon voted as follows with reference to the Nicene Creed: "The Holy and Ecumenical Synod decrees that it is not lawful for any man to propose, or compile, or compose, or hold, or teach to others, any different Faith. But those who presume to compose a different Faith, or to propagate, or teach, or deliver a *different Formula* to persons desirous of turning to the knowledge of the truth, from heathenism, or Judaism, or any heresy whatsoever, if they be bishops or clergymen, shall be deposed, * * * if they be monks or laymen, they shall be anathematised."

between the English and the Latin Churches, for most of the points in dispute were not, at that time, accounted essential even at Rome. Pius IV., the Bishop of Rome, in the year 1559 wrote a letter to Queen Elizabeth, in which he acknowledged the English Bible and Book of Common Prayer "to be authentic and not repugnant to truth; and that he would allow it to the English Church *without changing any part of it*, if only her majesty would acknowledge to receive it from him and by his allowance." If we Anglicans were not heretics then, we certainly are not now, for we have neither added to, nor detracted from, the *Faith* we then held.

But since then the Roman Church has added to the Faith a number of doctrines which the Undivided Church has always either disallowed or else regarded as *indifferent;* viz., the Creed of Pius IV. which carries with it the decrees of Trent, some five hundred in all; the dogma of the Immaculate Conception of the Blessed Virgin,[14] which was never believed by the early Church, or the Churches of England and the East, which St. Augustine, in the fourth century, St. Bernard in the twelfth century, and St. Thomas Aquinas, in the thirteenth century, emphatically denied; and last of all in the year of our Lord 1870, the doctrine of the Personal Infallibility of the Bishops of Rome,—a doctrine never allowed in the early Church, the Greek Church, or the English Church, and admittedly an open question among the strictest papists until fifteen years ago!!

If it be heresy to refuse assent to these novelties, then Anglican and Greek Churchmen are heretics, and so were

---

14. Promulgated in 1854.

the Apostles and Saints of old. If this be heresy, make the most of it! We are at least in good company. Oh! if Rome would confine her dogmas to the primitive Faith, that Creed of the Universal Church, which we both hold and have held, and which is still a bond of union despite our unhappy estrangement; or if she would at least leave these new beliefs optional, then, *so far as the Faith is concerned*, the three Branches of the Catholic Church, Greek and Latin and English, would be One.

A single word as to the relation of Dissenters to the Apostolic Faith. Of the hundreds of Protestant sects, very few *formally* accept even the Apostles' Creed, and none, so far as I am aware, require a belief in the Nicene Creed, even on the part of their "ordained" preachers. [15] I lay it down as a thesis, which I am prepared to maintain, that no body of Dissenters really believes the Creed. They all, from the Presbyterians to the Socinians, accept the first part of the first article, viz., "I believe in God," but some do not believe in His *Fatherhood*. Some do not believe "in Jesus Christ, His only Son, our Lord," in His miraculous Conception and Birth, His *Atoning* Death, His Descent into Hades, His Resurrection and Ascension, and in His Coming again for judgment. Some sects do not believe in the Holy Ghost; none of them believe in the *Holy Catholic Church*, in the sense in which the Church has used these words from the beginning. Few, if any, believe the Church's doctrine of the "Communion of Saints," or the "forgiveness of sins" (especially in the Nicene sense of

---

15. I refer only to the English-speaking Protestants. It is true the Irvingites retain the three Creeds, in words, though they do *not* in sense, for their interpretation of the article, "I believe in One Holy, Catholic, and Apostolic Church," is strange and unique indeed.

"One Baptism for the Remission of Sins"), or the " Resurrection of the Flesh "; and one whole sect is founded on a protest against the word "everlasting," as applied to the conditions of the future life ! !

Eliminate every article of the Creed which is rejected by one or more of the Denominations, and what remains? *A belief in God.* Yes, thank the Lord, no dissenting church has dogmatically denied *that*, however much they have denied of what God has revealed concerning Himself and His Kingdom of Grace.

No wonder that many thoughtful Dissenters, weary of a *religion of negations*, " the strife of tongues," are looking towards that ancient CHURCH which still "continues stedfastly in the Apostles' Doctrine," and "with one mouth professes the Faith once delivered to the Saints."

NOTE.—In addition to the "Infallible" Heretics, mentioned on p. 53, five Bishops of Rome (John XII., Benedict IX., Gregory VI., Gregory XII., and John XXIII.) were deposed by Western Councils, for such *freaks of Infallibility* as heresy, schism, sorcery and crime. See also Littledale's " Plain Reasons against Joining the Church of Rome," p. 160, *et Seq.*

CHAPTER VIII.

THE APOSTLES' FELLOWSHIP : WHAT SAITH THE SCRIPTURE ?

"*Episcopacy is the only form of Church order contained in the Scriptures and manifest from ancient authors;* and consequently, whether a Church should be now Episcopal or not, is a question to be settled upon considerations, not of mere *expediency*, but of deference to the model of the primitive Church, as it was constituted by the Apostles under the guidance of inspiration; so that no one ought to be accounted a '*lawful* minister in this Church, or suffered to execute any functions of the ministry, unless he hath had Episcopal Ordination.'"—*Bishop McIlvaine.*

"The history of Christianity is the history of Episcopacy. They are found united from the very first. Nor is there less evidence for the prevalence of this form of government in the primitive Church than there is of the reception of the Scriptures, or the use of the Sacraments in those times."—PALMER.

DE QUINCEY has said : "What a Church teaches is true or not true, without reference to her individual right of teaching." We have seen that the Anglican Church teaches the Orthodox Faith. We must now inquire whether she has a *right* to teach it, a right born of Apostolic Fellowship, the authority which comes of *valid Orders* and *lawful Jurisdiction*. For, as the Bishop of Quincy remarked to Mr. Moody, the revivalist: "When a boy brings us a dispatch, and we want to be sure it is genuine, we like to see 'Western Union Telegraph' on the boy's cap."

Is Episcopacy or a line of Bishops, who, by regular

Ordination, succeed to the office and commission which Christ gave the Apostles, necessary to the unity, the continuity, and the authority of the Church? Viewed *a priori*, the question resolves itself into this: Did Christ mean the Apostolic Office to be temporary or permanent? *Permanent*, beyond all shadow of doubt. Why, He promised to be with the Apostles not merely for their natural lives, but "always, even unto the end of the world." Moreover, He gave them the whole earth as their field of Jurisdiction, and bade them do what the Apostolate will not have accomplished for many years yet, viz.: Go into all the world, preach the Gospel to every creature, and baptize all nations. And how did they act? They ordained certain men, called *Deacons*, to relieve them of some of their minor duties.[1] Then they ordained *Priests* in every place where they had gathered a congregation.[2] But did they stop with that? Did they

---

1. Acts, vi.
2. Acts, xiv., 23, *et passim*. It should be remembered that *Priest* is but a shortened form of *Presbyter*. The two words are used interchangeably. The office of the Christian Minister (above the rank of Deacon) is distinctively *sacerdotal*—sacerdotal in a higher and more spiritual sense than even the Aaronic Priesthood, because of the Holy Eucharist or "Sacrifice of the New Covenant," as St. Irenæus calls it (Ir., iv., 17., 5). St. Paul speaks of himself as "*Priesting* the Gospel of God" [the word is *hierourgounta*, Rom., xv., 16], and he calls himself a *Leitourgos*. The very earliest Fathers call Presbyters *Priests*, "*Sacerdotes*," and it is only a narrow and superstitious *prejudice* which, because *priestly powers* have sometimes been abused, affects to deny the title of Priest to the Ambassadors of God and Stewards of the Mysteries of His Grace. The Anglican Church, of course, has always preserved the *identity* of the Christian *Priesthood* (as well as the identity of the Episcopate) as seen in the character of the ordination, the phraseology employed, the official titles, the functions prescribed, and the symbols of office, especially the *vestments*—of which Bp. Forbes says: "We see in the maintainance of the habits [*vestments*] the assertion of the *sacerdotal continuity* of the Church before and after the Reformation, and the denial of its identity with the purely Protestant bodies." (Int. to the XXXIX. Arts., p. XXI.) Moreover, the Latin form of the thirty-nine articles, which is of

allow their *perpetual* commission to lapse with themselves? Did they intend to leave the Church, that *Aionian Kingdom*, which the Son of God had given to them, with only the sterile Orders of Presbyter and Deacon? By no means. As the Jewish Church had its High Priest, its Priests and its Levites, so the Catholic Church was to have its *three* Orders—Apostles, Presbyters and Deacons. But if so, we must expect to find the Apostles ordaining also an Order of Ministers who rank above the lowly Deacons and Presbyters. In other words, if the Apostolic Office was to be perpetuated, we ought to find evidence in the New Testament and in the writings of the Fathers, that there were *Apostles*, or, as we now call them, Bishops, in addition to the original Twelve, but who shared their office, received the power to ordain, and inherited all the *permanent* grace and authority of the Apostolate.

The perennial ivy grows from the cathedral's foundation to the cross-topped spire, an unbroken vine; but all the way it keeps sending forth roots and rootlets, which cling to the hallowed stones and feed the growing stem, yet themselves move not on. So the Catholic Episcopate, springing from the " Root of Jesse," climbs the centuries of the Church's life, ever setting the Priests and Deacons in their hallowed place, and drawing from them the *material*, but not the *life*, of its own supernal and ever-lengthening Succession.

We have seen already that Matthias was chosen to succeed to the " Bishoprick " of Judas, to " take part of this

---

equal authority with the English form, leaves no room for ambiguity, for it uses the word *Sacerdos* for Priest; and the American Prayer Book speaks of the "*sacerdotal* functions," etc., of our Priests.

Ministry and APOSTLESHIP."³ This shows that the "Apostleship" was to continue. The charmed circle of the Twelve enlarges; St. Matthias is the "Thirteenth Apostle." Soon after another is chosen, *James*, a near relative (or "brother," as he was called in Hebrew and Greek) of the Lord. He had not at first believed in Christ;⁴ but the Lord, after His Resurrection, appeared to James.⁵ At all events James believed; and became an Apostle and the first Bishop of Jerusalem, the Head of that long line of Prelates which still rules the Mother of all Churches. St. Clement, a Priest of Alexandria, in the age next to that of the Apostles,⁶ when abundant evidence was at hand, says: "Peter, James and John did not contend for the honor of presiding over the Church of Jerusalem; but with the rest of the Apostles chose JAMES THE JUST to be BISHOP of that Church." St. Jerome, the greatest scholar of the fourth century, who spent thirty years in the Holy Land, says, in speaking of St. James, in order to show that "others besides the Twelve were called Apostles:" "By degrees, in process of time, *others also were ordained* APOSTLES by those whom the Lord had chosen." And in his

---

3. Acts, i., 25.
4. The theory that James the Lord's brother, the Bishop of Jerusalem, was one of the Twelve, seems to be fairly excluded by the assertion that "Neither did his *brethren* believe on Him" (St. John, vii., 5). Moreover, this James is specially mentioned along with Simon and Joses, in a way which precludes his being one of the Twelve (St. Matth., xiii., 55-6). Bishop Lightfoot says: "*James, though not one of the Twelve*, appears, from the very first, to have held the position of 'a bishop in the later and more special sense of the word.'"—"On Philippians" (6th ed.), p. 197. Either way, however, the Episcopacy of St. James is a strong point in favor of Catholic order, for if he was one of the Twelve, we have an instance of one of the original Apostles settling down to the work not merely of a Bishop (which they all did), but of a *Diocesan* Bishop.
5. "After that he was seen of *James*." I Cor., xv., 7.
6. A. D. 180.

biographical sketch of St. James he says: "After the passion of the Lord he (James) was forthwith ordained by the Apostles as BISHOP of Jerusalem,"[7] and that he ruled (*rexit*) the Church of Jerusalem for thirty-one years. How exactly all this agrees with the Scripture narrative, which implies throughout that James governed the Diocese of Jerusalem.

He presided at the First Council of "Apostles, Elders and brethren," held in Jerusalem, A. D. 50; he summed up the argument and pronounced the decision: "Wherefore *my sentence* is," etc.[8]

St. Paul speaks of the messengers who carried the decrees of the Council to Antioch, as coming "from *James*."[9] Indeed, when St. Paul went up to Jerusalem to attend the Council, he speaks of "*James*, Cephas, and John, who seemed to be pillars,"[10] giving James precedence over Peter and John in the Holy City. Fourteen years before, when St. Paul first went up to Jerusalem after his conversion, and spent a fortnight with St. Peter, he says: "Other of the *Apostles* saw I none save *James*, the Lord's brother,"[11] who appears always to have resided in his diocese, while the rest of the Apostles were Missionary Bishops, Apostles at large. Twenty years later, when St. Luke and others accompanied St. Paul to Jerusalem, they had an interview with the Bishop, which St. Luke describes in these words: "The day following, Paul went in with us unto JAMES, and all the Presbyters were present."[12] When St. Peter was released from prison, he

---

7. "Post passionem Domini, statim ab Apostolis Hierosalymorum *Episcopus* ordinatus."
8. Acts, xv., 13.   9. Gal., ii., 12.   10. *Id.*, 9.   11. Gal., 1., 18-19.   12. Acts, xxi., 18.

ordered that news of his escape should be carried to James. "Go show these things to *James.*"[13] Indeed, as Dr. Mines (to whom the writer acknowledges much indebtedness) puts it: "All antiquity agrees that James was Bishop of the Church at Jerusalem." Here, then, we have the fourteenth Apostle.

That St. Paul, though not one of the Twelve, was an *Apostle,* no one can doubt. Again and again he calls himself an Apostle. He stood on precisely the same ground as the original Twelve, for he was appointed and commissioned by Christ Himself. He styles himself "An Apostle not of men, neither by man, but by Jesus Christ."[11] Twice he tells us that he was "not a whit behind the chiefest of the Apostles."[15] "Am I not an *Apostle?*" says he to the Corinthians; and to Titus, he writes: "I am ordained a preacher and an *Apostle.*"

Not to prolong this part of the subject, I give a list of those who are expressly called "Apostles" in the Greek of the New Testament, in *addition* to the Twelve: Matthias, James, Paul, Barnabas, Andronicus, Junias, Epaphroditus, Timothy, Titus, Silas, and Luke. The very name *Apostle* is applied to these eleven men, by God the Holy Ghost. Moreover, they are seen doing the same work as the Twelve, and are constantly mentioned by the Fathers and early historians as Apostles or Bishops ordained by the Apostles.

For example, history and tradition bear witness to the fact that the Apostle Timothy was the first Bishop of Ephesus, and the Apostle Titus the first Bishop of Crete,

---

13. Acts, xii., 17.   14. Gal., i., 1.   15. II Cor., xi., 5, and xii., 11.

being ordained and appointed thereto by the Apostle Paul. The epistles of St. Paul to Timothy and Titus not only accord with this statement, but are irreconcilably absurd on any other supposition, for they show that these men were left by St. Paul not only with power to do such things as all Presbyters could do, but also to *superintend* the whole work of the Church in their respective jurisdictions—to give order concerning the doctrine which the Presbyters were to preach; to rectify all deficiencies; to ORDAIN Presbyters in all the cities; to examine into the qualifications of candidates for the Priesthood and the Diaconate, being careful to "*lay hands* suddenly on no man;" to have charge of promoting faithful Priests and Deacons; to settle the liturgical and sacramental systems on a complete and uniform basis, prescribing "supplications, prayers, intercessions and EUCHARISTS,"[16] for all men, for kings, etc.; to *discipline the laity;* to enforce obedience to the moral law; to regulate marriage; to have a special care over the setting apart of widows and virgins as Sisters or Deaconesses; to enforce the Creed or "form of sound words," and after one or two warnings, to excommunicate "a man that is an *heretic.*" And whence came all this authority and power? St. Paul tells us, for he says to his "son Timothy:" "Stir up the *gift of God* which is *in thee* BY THE PUTTING ON OF MY HANDS."[17]

---

16. See the Greek.
17. II. Timothy, i., 6. The assertion here made that Timothy received the gift "BY (*dia*) the putting on" of St. Paul's hands, is not weakened (as some have claimed) by the expression, in I. Tim., iv., 14: "The gift that is in thee, which was given thee by prophecy, WITH (*meta*) the laying on of the hands of the *presbytery.*" The assumption that this implies the right of Priests (Presbyters) to ordain, is wholly unwarranted. For it is clear that in the ordination of St. Timothy, mentioned in II. Tim., i., 6., *St. Paul himself was the consecrator*

I leave it to any candid reader to say whether the work of Timothy and Titus was not clearly and incontrovertibly the work of a Bishop in the Church of God ? Besides the original Twelve and the eleven who are called Apostles in the New Testament, twenty-three in all, there are many more who are called " companions, fellow-laborers," etc., who seem to have done the same work, and who, though not expressly called Apostles in the Bible,

---

["By the putting on of MY hands"]. If the reference, in I. Tim., iv., 14, be to the *same* ordination, then the expression, "WITH the laying on of the hands of the Presbytery," merely implies that certain men were *associated* with St. Paul in the act of ordination which he performed. Now, who were these men ? "The 'Presbytery,'" says Dr. Blunt, "has been understood by St. Chrysostom, Theodoret, Oecumenius, Theophyloct, Suicer, and all the best commentators, ancient and modern, to designate the *College of Bishops*"—i. e., the Apostles who assisted St. Paul in the consecration of Timothy to the Apostolic Episcopate, according to the rule which afterward universally prevailed, that at least *three* Bishops should take part in the ordination of every Bishop. The Apostles, it should be remembered, often called themselves *Presbyters*, for the greater includes the less. As late as A. D. 107, St. Ignatius speaks of the "Apostles" as "the Presbytery of the Church."

If, on the other hand, we take the view that, while the act mentioned in II. Tim., i., 6, was the ordination of Timothy to the Episcopate, the act mentioned in I. Tim., iv., 14, was his previous ordination to the *Priesthood*, what then? Why, we may hold that the ordination which was undoubtedly performed by St. Paul as Bishop, was accompanied by the laying on of the hands of some Priests, as a token of their assent to the act—as has been customary in Western Christendom since the fifth century—though it would be an isolated instance, so far as we know, in the Eastern and Early Church. It must be remembered also that St. Ambrose, St. Hilary, and St. Jerome among ancient, and *Calvin* and many others, among modern interpreters, make the phrase, "of the Presbytery," refer to the *Office* to which Timothy was ordained:—"Neglect' not the gift of THE PRIESTHOOD (*Presbyteriou*) that is in thee, which was given thee by prophecy, with the laying on of the hands." Here is what Calvin says of it:

"Paul speaks of himself as having laid hands upon Timothy without any mention of any others having united with him. 'I put thee in remembrance that thou stir up the gift of God which is in thee by the putting on of my hands.' His expression, in the other epistle, of 'the laying on of the hands of the Presbytery,' I apprehend not to signify a company of Elders, but to denote the ordination itself; as if he had said, Take care that the grace which thou receivedst by the laying on of hands, *when I ordained thee a Presbyter*, be not in vain."—Calvin's "Institutes," Book IV., end of Chap. iii.

are so called by the early Christian writers. For example: Dionysius, Gaius, Aristarchus, Archippus, Antipas (the "faithful martyr"), Crescens, Euodias, Linus, Clement, Mark, Judas, and the "Angels" of the Seven Churches in Proconsular Asia. These eighteen (to mention no others) should, therefore, be added to the twenty-three given above, as clergymen of the Early Church who ranked above the Presbyters and Deacons, who were associated with the Apostles, called Apostles by the Fathers, and rated in history and tradition as Apostolic Bishops. Nor is there in the New Testament a single word which implies the "parity of the ministry," or makes against a genuine and permanent Apostolic Episcopacy.

CHAPTER IX.

PRIMITIVE EPISCOPACY AND ITS OFFICIAL TITLES.

"Christ and His princely race."
—*Lyra Apostolica*, p. 67.

BEFORE presenting the evidence for Episcopacy in the writings of the Fathers, it is necessary to make a remark touching the use of the words Apostle, Bishop, Presbyter, and Deacon, in the New Testament.

It has been shown that the Apostolic Church had a threefold Ministry: (a) The supreme and permanent order of Apostles, including both the original Twelve and those others who, as St. Jerome says, "were by degrees in process of time,[1] ordained Apostles by those whom the Lord had chosen." (b) The order of Presbyters who were ordained in "every city." (c) The order of Deacons, an

---

1. Some disingenuous controversialists have claimed this passage, as going to prove that Episcopacy was not primitive, because, forsooth, does not St. Jerome say that it arose "by degrees" and "in the process of time?" They take care, however, not to put the whole passage before their readers, for that shows that the phrase, "by degrees and in the process of time," means as occasion demanded *during the lifetime of the Apostles*, for it is distinctly affirmed that those others who were ordained Apostles, were ordained by *those whom the Lord had chosen*, *i. e.*, the Twelve; and if by them, certainly during their lifetime. St. Jerome's words are: " Paulatim vero, tempore procedente, et alii ab his quos Dominus elegerat, ordinati Apostoli." If successors of the Apostles were ordained by the Apostles, and during the lifetime of the Apostles, then it is by *Apostolic Authority* that the Church has always been *Episcopal*.

account of which is given in Acts vi. That these three distinct orders by whatever names called, existed in the Apostolic Church, and have existed ever since, is as certain as that the Church has existed at all.

Some people, however, have stumbled at the apparent confusion of names by which these orders were called. But in the first place it should be borne in mind that a higher order always includes the lower,[2] so that an Apostle could call himself a "Presbyter,"[3] or even a "Deacon."[4] Indeed, Christ Himself, the great Head of the Church, is called an Apostle, a Bishop, a Priest, and a Deacon.[5] But on the other hand, a lower order could not appropriate a title which belonged to an higher order. Now it is not denied that the term Deacon is the distinctive appellation of the lowest order, Apostle of the highest order, and Presbyter of the intermediate order. But the term *Bishop* (which means "Overseer") was not at first exclusively appropriated to one order; but was used in its literal rather than its technical sense. Accordingly the Presbyters are often called Bishops, as being Overseers or Pastors of a congregation, although their *Order* was always clearly distinguished from the order of the Apostles, to whom gradually the title of Bishop became limited. How this came about would be easy to surmise even if we had no positive evidence. The word Apostle means *one who is sent;* and as, one by one, those who had received their

---

2. As St. Hilary expresses it, "In the Bishop are contained all other orders." "Nam in Episcopo omnes ordines sunt, quia Primus Sacerdos, hoc est Princeps, est Sacerdotum."
3. 1. S. Pet., v., 1; II. St. John, i., 1; III. St. John, i., 1 (Greek).
4. Acts, i., 17, 25; xx., 24; I. Cor., iii., 5; II. Cor., iii., 6, and vi., 4 (Greek).
5. Heb., iii., 1; I. Pet., ii., 25; Heb., v., 6; Rom., xv., 8 (Greek).

commission *directly* from Christ ("As My Father hath *sent Me, even so send I you*,"[6])—those "adamantine Martyrs and Athletes" of the Early Church, went up to God in chariots of fire; their humble successors felt naturally enough, that there was a certain propriety in limiting to *them* the name of *Apostle*, and contented themselves with the title of *Bishop*[7] by which the Apostles, the commissioned chief pastors of the Church, have ever since been known. As an holy Father has said: "*Apostoli sunt Episcopi*"—the Apostles are the Bishops. All this, I say, might be readily surmised, to account for the change of name; and the writer begs to say that he conceived this explanation long before he stumbled upon those Patristic authorities which positively assert the same. Theodoret, a Syrian Bishop, a disciple of the great St. Chrysostom, writing about the year 440, says: "The same persons were in ancient times called indifferently, Presbyters or Bishops, *at which time those who are now called Bishops, were called Apostles.*" In his commentary on First Timothy, iii., 1, after making the same statement, he adds: "In process of time, the name of Apostle was left to those who were in the strict sense *Apostles* [*i. e.*, sent directly by Christ Himself], and the name of Bishop was confined to those who were anciently called Apostles." The same thing is said by St. Jerome, St. Hilary, St. Chrysostom, and St.

---

6. St. John, xx., 21.
7. "The name Bishop hath been borrowed from the Grecians, with whom it signifieth one which hath principal charge to guide and oversee others. The same word in ecclesiastical writings being applied unto Church governors, at the first unto all, and not unto the chiefest only, grew in short time peculiar and proper to signify such episcopal authority alone as the chiefest governors exercise over the rest."—*Hooker.*

Clement, who was a Priest and teacher in Alexandria in the year 189.[8]

It must be remembered that this gradual change of *name* involved no change in the character of the *office*.[9] If we in the American Church should gradually introduce the custom of calling our Bishops, Presidents or Superintendents, it would not alter their office nor affect their Apostolic functions. We have already, whether wisely or not, changed several of the *titles* used in our Mother Church of England, without affecting the position or work of those to whom the title belongs. We call our Primate "the Presiding Bishop," but his office is none the less that of Primate. We call our Episcopal Coadjutors by the synonymous term, "Assistant Bishops," and our Ecclesiastical *Synods* by the less technical and less correct designation of "Convention."

I have dwelt thus at length upon what is a very simple matter, the change of a name (a matter of philology rather than of Ecclesiastical order), because controversial opponents of the divine institution of Episcopacy have a

---

8. Bingham, in his "Orig. Ecc., II., 2, 1," quotes also an ancient but unknown writer who called himself Ambrose, who speaking of those who were ordained to succeed the Apostles, says. "They thought it not becoming to assume to themselves the name of *Apostles*, but dividing the names they left to Presbyters the name of Presbytery, and they themselves were called *Bishops*."

9. I cannot forbear to quote here a striking passage from "Mine's Pres. Clerg. Looking for the Church, page 413." Speaking of St. Timothy's ordination as Bishop of Ephesus, he says: "We care not by what name you call him—Priest, Presbyter, Bishop, Suffragan, Superintendent, Ruler, Governor, Evangelist, Missionary, Moderator, Primus-Presbyter, Apostle, Assistant of the Apostle, Messenger, Prelate, Angel, Antistes, Princeps, Præses, Præpositus, Archon, Proestus, or Prefect (as Calvin styles James in the Church at Jerusalem)—*call h m by what name you please;* write it in Latin, Greek, or Hebrew; read it forward; read it backward; it comes to the same thing; Timothy succeeds to the powers and prerogatives of Paul."

bland way of saying "Episcopacy is an innovation. All learned and pious Episcopalians have *now* been forced to admit that in the early Church there was no difference between Bishop and Presbyter!" Who ever denied it? Theodoret, Chrysostom, Hilary, Jerome, and Clement were "Episcopalians," and they pointed it out a thousand years before the first non-episcopal church was founded! But just as long as the Presbyters were called Bishops, just so long *were the Bishops called Apostles*. The Orders were distinct, and remained unchanged.

In some localities the name Apostle lingered as the official title of a Bishop, a good many years after the death of St. John, as is apparent in the "*Didache*," or "Teaching of the Twelve Apostles," and in occasional passages in the early Fathers.[10] The two names, Apostle and Bishop, shade off into each other. While Eusebius says: "It is recorded in history that Timothy was the first *Bishop* of Ephesus, and Theodoret and others call him "the *Apostle* of the Asiatics;" the eloquent and scholarly Chrysostom blends the titles and unifies the truth when he calls him "THE APOSTLE AND BISHOP OF EPHESUS."

---

10. The *Didache* or Teaching of the Twelve Apostles, recently discovered by Bryennios, the Metropolitan of Nicomedia, was *probably* written early in the second century. It still calls the Pastors "bishops," i. e. overseers, but it speaks also of an order of APOSTLES (called also "*Prophets*" and "*High Priests*"), who appear to be sort of *Missionary Bishops*, whose duty it was to make brief visitations of the various parishes. I quote from Chapter XI: "And with regard to Apostles and Prophets, do with them according to the ordinance of the Gospel. Let every *Apostle* who cometh to you be received as the Lord." Says the editor of the "Church Times:" "As the *Teaching* disposes of the Baptistic heresy with one barrel, so it brings down Independency with the other; for while it assumes that Bishops (*i. e.*, Presbyters) and Deacons constituted the ordinary stated ministry, it speaks of *Apostles* and Prophets visiting the local churches from time to time, and it directs them to be 'received as the Lord.' It also declares that they are 'HIGH PRIESTS;' it demonstrates that there was an order of *Apostles* and prophets *other than the Twelve*."

CHAPTER X.

PRIMITIVE EPISCOPACY AND THE TESTIMONY OF THE APOSTOLIC FATHERS.

"If I know anything of Church History, it is that Episcopacy is a divine institution."—*Bishop Wordsworth.*

"All over the earth, from India to Spain, the Episcopate was a definite organization. It is impossible to account for this hierarchical uniformity without pre-supposing an original Divine institution. If we consider the difficulty of the transmission of intelligence, the rarity of the occasions of communication, the deep-rooted ethnical peculiarities of the varying tribes which were converted to Christianity, we can in no way account for it save on the supposition of the threefold ministry being a part of the original constitution of the Christian Church."—*Bp. Forbes.*

AMONG all the early Christian writings, including those which the Church has selected from the rest and declared to belong to the Canon of Holy Scripture, we will look in vain for anything like an argument in defense of Episcopacy. I fancy I hear some reader exclaim : "Well! well! how did that happen ?" Why, simply because *Episcopacy was not an open question.* No one thought of sitting down to write a treatise to prove that the Bishops were the successors of their predecessors (the Apostles), and that the polity of the Church was Episcopal, any more than of laboring to prove that the Roman Empire was governed by the Emperor, or that a human being has a head on his shoulders! It was precisely the same as in the case of Infant Baptism : no Council ever legislated the Episcopate into being or decreed that infants should be christened. Nobody was wild and presumptuous enough to challenge these primitive and God-given institutions. But Councils—Ecumenical and Provincial—canons, sermons, treatises, commentaries and epistles by the score, allude to Episcopacy as primitive and universal, always *assuming* it as a matter of course—a much stronger proof, by the way, than volumes of *defense*, which would imply that it was at least *questioned* in some quarters.

The Church, wherever it spread, from India to Britain, from Thrace to Ethiopia, from Babylon to Spain, was always and everywhere Episcopal. To argue that it was anything else—*e. g.*, Papal or Congregational—is just as absurd as if the American Congress, in the face of the Constitution and the laws, and in defiance of history, should argue that "these United States" were not designed to be a Republic, but an Absolute Monarchy, or, on the other hand, an Anarchy, having no government at all. And yet nothing is more common than to hear well-meaning people say (as was remarked recently by a Doctor of Divinity in the Presbytery of Philadelphia[1]) that the Church of the New Testament was *Presbyterial* in its order and polity. Presbyterial! So it was, if *you ignore the* APOSTLES who had the oversight of the Presbyters. So, too, is the Anglican Church Presbyterial—IF you leave

---

1. See "The Independent," February 12, 1885, p. 4. Dr. Bacon, a Congregational minister, addressing the Presbytery, said: "The nearest reproduction, in modern times, of the Church polity of the New Testament, seems to me to have been in the original type of the Presbyterian Church, as instituted by John Calvin, of Geneva." Calvin himself, however, was not so sure of it, otherwise he would never have used the strong language he did in favor of Episcopacy (see his commentary on Titus, Ch. I, v. 5, and Instit. lib. 4, Ch. 4 and 12). Nor would he have tried so hard to get Apostolic Orders from the English Church (see Strype's Life of Archb. Parker, pp. 140 and 141)

out the HOUSE OF BISHOPS! England would be a Republic, were it not for the *Crown;* and Russia, an Anarchy, but for the fact that it happens to be governed by the *Czar.* The early Christians were Quakers forsooth, but with the somewhat important difference that they had the Ministry, the Sacraments, and the Divine Liturgy. The early Church was *Diaconal,* but for those venerable *Presbyters* who out-ranked the Deacons. In like manner the early Church was *Presbyterial,* but for the stubborn fact that *over the Presbyters was an order of Chief Pastors, divinely commissioned unto the end of the world.* Now in all candor, I ask, is it reasonable in judging the polity of a Church, to leave out of consideration the most notable, primitive, permanent, and authoritative part of its system? Nevertheless this amazing process—be it sophistry or paralogism—is gone through with by everyone who can see Presbyterianism or Congregationalism in the Church of the New Testament.[2] Moreover, as the original Twelve did not die until they had ordained scores of Apostolic Bishops to succeed them, this rational (!) process must be followed up by the logical legerdemain of those who (as one has said with a pardonable pun), " can *translate* Jerome, Chrysostom, Augustine, and even Clemens and Ignatius, by the hair of the head, over to the side of Presbyterianism!"

We must not expect to find a settled *Diocesan* Episcopacy all at once—with mitres and crosiers, Archdeacons, Examining Chaplains, and Standing Committees, which are but the insignia and impedimenta of the office. The

---

2. You might as well say that a three-story house is only *two* stories high, because you are not willing to look *high* enough to see the upper story.

AUTHORITY. 75

Apostles held what may be called a roving commission, as Bishops at large. The world was the joint Province of their Jurisdiction. It was only gradually that it was parcelled out among them and their fellow-laborers. Of the thirty men who are actually called *Apostles*[3] in the New Testament, at least fifteen appear to have settled down to a sort of local jurisdiction, as Diocesan Bishops, viz: St. James, in Jerusalem[4]; Titus, in Crete[5]; Epaphroditus, in Philippi[6]; Timothy in Ephesus[7]; succeeded by Onesi-

---

3. I include here the seven who are called "Angels" of the Seven Churches, *Angel* being a *poetic synonym of Apostle*, in exact keeping with St. John's literary and mystical style. *Angel* in Greek means *messenger*, one who is sent; and *Apostle* means precisely the same, and is sometimes translated *messenger*, as in Phil., ii., 25. In the Angels of the Seven Churches no candid scholar can fail (as Archbishop Trench says) "to recognize the Bishops of the several Churches. So many difficulties, embarrassments, improbabilities, attend every other solution, which all disappear with the adoption of this, while no others rise in their room, that were not other interests, often, no doubt, unconsciously, at work, it would be very hard to understand how any could ever have arrived at a different conclusion." Thiersch, one of the greatest of German scholars, says: "What are the Angels of the Seven Churches but *Superior* Pastors, each at the head of a congregation, and at least similar to the later Bishops. The ancients looked on them as Bishops. Of all the Church Fathers who touch upon the matter, *not one thinks of any other interpretation.*"—Quoted in Timlow's "Plain Footprints," Chap. ix., *which see.*

4. "[Jacobus] ab Apostolis, Hierosalymorum Episcopus ordinatus," St. Jerome, Scr. Eccl., c. 2. See also Euseb., ii., 23.

5. See Titus, i., 1, *et passim;* Euseb., iii., 4; St. Chrys. on Tit., i., 4 and 5; Theod. on I. Tim., iii., 1; St. Jerome, Catal, Scr. in Tit. The ancient tradition in Crete is that he lived till the age of 94 in Gortys, his see city. The cathedral of the island is dedicated to him.

6. "Epaphroditus was called the 'Apostle' of the Philippians, because he was entrusted with the *Episcopal* government; for those whom we now call *Bishops*, were more anciently called *Apostles.*" Theod. on Phil., ii., 25; and see Theod. and St. Chrys. on Phil., i., 1. Also St. Jerome, who calls him the Apostle of the Philippians, and says: "*Erat Compar Officii,*" *i. e.*, with St. Paul.

7. See Epists. to Tim., *passim.* St. Jerome says: "Timotheus a Paulo *Ephesiorum Episcopus* ordinatus" "Timothy was ordained Bishop of the Ephesians by Paul." See the authorities cited above concerning Titus. The Acts of the Gen. Coun. of Chalcedon are referred to by Bishop Wordsworth, as the crowning evidence.

mus[8], (the "Angel of the Church in Ephesus ;") St. John (who also himself made his home at Ephesus, perhaps doing the work of a diocesan, between the Episcopates of Timothy and Onesimus, but certainly returning to Ephesus after his banishment to Patmos, and laboring as a sort of Archbishop ; for Clement of Alexandria[9] tells us that he " used to make journeys to neighboring Gentile territories, to ordain Bishops in some, and in others to set in order whole Churches "); the Angel of the Church in Smyrna who was either St. Polycarp,[10] or possibly his predecessor; the Angel of the Church in Pergamos, the successor of Antipas; Carpus, the Angel of the Church in Thyatira ; and the three who presided over the Churches of Sardis, Philadelphia, and Laodicea. St. Peter also remained for a long time as Bishop of Antioch. Indeed St. Chrysostom speaks of St. Ignatius as succeeding St. Peter in Antioch.[11]

---

8. Onesimus was at least Bishop of Ephesus, ten or twelve years later, for he is lovingly mentioned as such by Ignatius, in his letter to the Ephesians, chap. vi., written before 107 A. D.
9. See *Quis Div. Salv.*, c. 42.
10. See letter of Ignatius to "Polycarp, Bishop of the Church of the Smyrneans." Tertullian says he was consecrated Bishop of Smyrna by St. John (See Praes. Her., 32). Irenaeus, who had often conversed with him, says the same. See also Euseb., iv., 14, Jerome, and others.
11. The Roman Catholic theory that St. Peter went to Rome, A. D. 40, and was Bishop of Rome for 25 years, is demonstrably absurd. His residence at Antioch must have been much later, for at that time the Church there was under the leadership of its founders, the Apostles Paul and Barnabas. (Acts, xi., 19, *et Seq*. Moreover, St. Ignatius, who succeeded him in Antioch, could not have done so in A. D. 40, as he was then but 10 years old. To borrow the words of Canon Farrar: "As late as A.D. 52, St. Peter was at Jerusalem, and took an active part in the Synod of Jerusalem (Acts, xv., 7); and he was then laboring mainly among the Jews (Gal., ii., 7, 8, 9). In A. D. 57, he was traveling as a Missionary with his wife (I. Cor., ix., 5). He was not at Rome when St. Paul wrote to that Church, in A. D. 58; nor when St. Paul came there as a prisoner in A. D. 61, nor during the years of St. Paul's imprisonment, A. D. 61–63, nor when

During the latter part of the first century, St. John alone of the original twelve survived, but many other Apostles, Angels, Bishops, or High Priests (as they were sometimes called) were still alive, who had been ordained by him or his peers. There was St. Clement, the Bishop of Rome, the "fellow-laborer" of St. Paul, who had been ordained by him or by St. Peter. There was St. Ignatius, that glorious Apostle, who had sat at the feet of the beloved John, the true successor of St. Peter in Antioch; while the venerable Polycarp, the friend of St. John, was still ruling his diocese in the spirit of his master, till past the middle of the second century. These are the earliest witnesses to the antiquity and authority of Episcopacy. They bridge over the so-called gap between the Church of the New Testament and the Church of the second century. Let us hear their testimony.

St. Clement, the companion of St. Paul, the Bishop of "the Church sojourning at Rome," wrote a letter to the Church at Corinth, not later than A. D. 97. In it he clearly teaches that there are "diverse orders in the Church," which he likens to the ranks of officers in the Roman army. "All," says he, "are not generals, nor commanders of a thousand, nor of a hundred, nor of

---

he wrote his last Epistles, A. D. 66 and 67. If he was ever at Rome at all, which we hold to be almost certain, from the unanimity of the tradition, it could only have been very briefly before his martyrdom. And this is, in fact, the assertion of Lactantius (about A. D. 330), who says that he first came to Rome in Nero's reign; and of Origen (about A. D. 254), who says that he arrived there at the close of his life; and of the *Praedictio Petri*, printed with the works of St. Cyprian. His 'Bishopric' at Rome probably consisted only in his efforts, about the time of his martyrdom, to strengthen the faith of the Church and especially of the Jewish Christians." (*Early Days of Christianity*, 1., 117.) See also the "The Petrine Claims at the Bar of History."—*Church Quarterly Review*, April, 1879.

fifty."[12] Speaking of the duties of the clergy and laity, he uses language which shows that the Christian Ministry was *threefold:* " His own peculiar services are assigned to the HIGH PRIEST, and their own proper place is prescribed to the *Priests,* and their own special ministrations devolve on the *Levite;* while the *layman* is bound by the laws which pertain to laymen."[13] He also says : " The Apostles knew through our Lord Jesus Christ that contentions would arise about the office of the Episcopate ; and for this reason, being endued with perfect foreknowledge, they appointed those already mentioned, *and handed down a succession,* so that when they should depart, other approved men should take their office and ministry."[14]

Our next witness is St. Polycarp, that grand old Bishop and Martyr. Born while St. Paul and St. Peter were still alive, he was for more than thirty years contemporary with his master, St. John, and survived him by half a century, having, as he told the Roman Governor, served Christ " eighty and six years." He is portrayed to us by his pupil, St. Irenæus, the Bishop of Lyons, in a passage of charming simplicity but tantalizing brevity : " I could describe the very place in which the blessed Polycarp sat and taught ; his going out and his coming in ; the whole tenor of his life ; his personal appearance ; how he would tell of conversations he had held with John and with others who had seen the Lord ; how he would make men-

---

12. Chap. 37.
13. Chap. 40. In like manner, says St. Jerome (in his *Epist. ad Ev.*), "What Aaron and his sons and the Levites [*three orders*] were in the Temple, that let the *Bishops,* and *Presbyters,* and *Deacons,* claim to be in the Church."
14. Chap. 44.

tion of their words, and of whatever he had heard from them respecting the Lord."[15]

Again Irenæus says of him : "Polycarp also was not only instructed by the Apostles, and conversed with many who had seen Christ, but *was also by Apostles in Asia, ordained Bishop of the Church in Smyrna*, whom I also saw in my early youth, having always taught the things which he had learned from the Apostles, and *which the Church has handed down*, and which alone are true."[16]

A single Epistle of St. Polycarp has come down to us of the genuineness of which there can be no doubt. It is written as by a Bishop, surrounded by his "*Corona Presbyterorum.*" "Polycarp and the Presbyters with him to the Church of God sojourning at Phillippi." The Epistle is beautiful and breathes the spirit of a St. John. Its chief evidential value, however, as to the Episcopate, is to be found in the fact that this holy and apostolic man sets the seal of approval to the teachings of St. Ignatius, that devout and stalwart Episcopalian, the Bishop of Antioch. "The Epistles of Ignatius," says he, "written by him to us, and all the rest of his Epistles which we have by us, we have sent to you as you requested. By them ye may be *greatly profited;* for they treat of faith and patience, and *all things that tend to edification in the Lord.*" Let us appeal then to St. Ignatius.

He was born about A. D. 30. Tradition has assigned him the honor of being the "little child" whom Jesus placed in the midst of the Apostles.[17] He succeeded St.

---

15. From the *De Ogdoade* of Irenæus. 16. Adv. Her., iii., 3, 4. 17. St. Matt, xviii., 2.

Peter as Bishop of Antioch,[18] the capital of Syria, and so he alludes to himself not only as the Bishop of Antioch, but as "the Bishop of Syria." A vivid account of his martyrdom (written probably about A. D. 110), says that in the year A. D. 98, "Ignatius, the Disciple of John the Apostle, a man in *all* respects of an *Apostolic* character, governed the Church of the Antiochians," and that he had done so for many years. The story of his bold confession before the Emperor Trajan, in Antioch, A. D. 107, his arrest, his journey (like St. Paul's) to Rome, and his glorious martyrdom in that city, which is "drunken with blood of martyrs," is familiar to all. On that memorable journey he was permitted to tarry quite a while at Smyrna, of which the venerable Polycarp was the Bishop, and whither the Bishops of Ephesus, Magnesia, and Tralles, accompanied each by several Priests and Deacons, came to comfort him, or rather be comforted by him, and to receive the Martyr's benediction. While in Smyrna he wrote four letters ; to the Ephesians, the Magnesians, the Traillians, and the Romans. Also at Troas, where he was detained a few days, he wrote three letters ; to the Philadelphians, to the Smyrnæans, and to Polycarp, their Bishop. There are eight other letters extant, purporting to have been written by St. Ignatius, but as their authenticity is doubtful, I pass them by. But these seven genuine letters of the Apostolic Bishop, Saint and Martyr— *every one ought to read.* And I leave it to any candid reader whether such letters could possibly have been

---

18. He is quoted from and mentioned with approval by Justin Martyr, Irenæus, and Origen (who styles him "Ignatius, the second Bishop of Antioch, coming after Peter") ; by Chrysostom, Jerome, Theodoret, Gelasius, etc.

written to leading Churches in the east and as far west as Rome, *unless* Episcopacy had been the universal polity of the Church, and believed by such competent witnesses as these personal friends of St. John, to be primitive, God-given and necessary. Notice, then, a number of extracts which I have collected from the short and uncorrupted form of the Epistles, which even the most critical scholars allow to be genuine and authentic.

In his Epistle to the Ephesians he speaks of having seen their "Bishop, Onesimus," and blesses God for having granted them "such an excellent Bishop."[19] He mentions also one of their Deacons and several Presbyters, and exhorts them, saying : " Be ye subject to the Bishop and the Presbytery " [*i. e.*, the whole body of the Presbyters].[20] He lays great stress upon the universality of the Episcopate : "For even Jesus Christ, our inseparable Life, is the manifest Will of the Father ; *as also Bishops, to the uttermost bounds of the earth, are so* BY THE WILL OF JESUS CHRIST."[21] "Wherefore," he goes on to say, "it is fitting that ye should run together in accordance with the will of your Bishop, which thing also ye do; for your justly renowned Presbytery, worthy of God, *is fitted as exactly to the Bishop as are the strings to the harp.*"[22] What a diocese that must have been ! "Let us, then," he continued, "be careful not to set ourselves in opposition to the Bishop."[23] "For we ought to receive every one whom *the Master of the House sends to be over his Household*, as we would receive Him that sent Him. It is clear, therefore, that we should look upon the Bishop, even as the Lord Himself ;[24] and

---

19. Chap. 1.   20. Chap. 2.   21. Chap. 3.   22. Chap. 4.   23. Chap. 5.
24. Cf. our Lord's words to the Apostles: "He that receiveth you receiveth ME," St. Matt., x., 40, and St. John, xiii., 20.

indeed Onesimus himself greatly commends your good order in God, and that ye all live according to the truth, and that no *sect* has any dwelling place among you."[25]

In his Epistle to the Magnesians, he says : "I have had the privilege of seeing you through Damas, your most worthy Bishop, and through your worthy Presbyters, Bassus and Apollonius, and through my fellow-servant, the Deacon Sotio, whose friendship may I ever enjoy, inasmuch as he is subject to the Bishop as to the grace of God, and to the Presbytery as to the law of Jesus Christ."[26] The Bishop of the Magnesians, although a *young* man, was, by virtue of his Episcopal Office, exalted above all the rest, whether clergy or laity, and just as St. Paul had written to the young Bishop of Ephesus, some fifty years before, "Let no man despise thy youth," so now Ignatius writes to the Christians in Magnesia : "It becomes you also not to treat your Bishop too familiarly on account of his youth, but to yield him all reverence, *having respect to the Power of God the Father, as I have known even holy Presbyters do,* not judging rashly from the youthful appearance of THEIR BISHOP."[27] A Bishop, then, though a young man, is entitled to the homage of his *Presbyters*, though "holy" and venerable. And this is the teaching of a saint who was living while our Saviour was still on earth, the companion of St. John, and for more than forty years the Bishop of the city where the disciples were first called Christians. Again he says : "Let nothing exist among you that may divide you ; but be ye united with your Bishop, and them that preside over you."[28] "Neither do anything without the Bishop and Presbyters."[29] "Your

---
25. Chap. 6. 26. Chap. 2. 27. Chap. 3. Cf. I. Tim., iv., 12. 28. Chap. 6.
29. Chap. 7.

most admirable Bishop, the well-compacted spiritual crown of your Presbytery, and the Deacons who are according to God."[30] [Various persons] 'salute you, along with Polycarp, the Bishop of the Smyrnæans."[31]

In his Epistle to the Trallians, whom he says he salutes "in the *Apostolic* character," he speaks of " Polybius, your Bishop who has come to Smyrna."[32] " Let all reverence the *Deacons* as the appointment of Jesus Christ, and the BISHOPS as Jesus Christ, Who is the Son of the Father, and the *Presbyters* as the Sanhedrim of God and assembly of the Apostles. APART FROM THESE THERE IS NO CHURCH."[33] Nor was there any thing new or startling to those early Christians in this statement, for he immediately adds: "Concerning all this, I am persuaded that ye are of the same opinion."

In his Epistle to the Romans he says: " God has deemed me, *the Bishop of Syria*, worthy to be sent," etc.[34] " Remember in your prayers the Church in Syria, which now has *God for its Shepherd instead of me*. Jesus Christ alone will *oversee* it."[35] Strange words for Ignatius to have used if he were only one among the many equal (!) Presbyters in the great metropolis of Antioch, with its two hundred thousand inhabitants. The fact is, no one but one who is, at least in theory, an Episcopalian, can read the letters of Ignatius without either becoming a Churchman or else bidding farewell to reason, logic, and common sense.[36]

In his letter to the Philadelphians he speaks of them as

---

30. Chap. 13.   31. Chap. 15.   32. Chap. 1.   33. Chap. 3.   34. Chap. 2.   35. Chap. 9.
36. If any one doubts this, let him see how Dr. Miller, the champion of Presbyterianism, undertook to find Presbyterianism in St. Ignatius (!). In all the world of controversy, religious, political, philosophical, scientific, literary, Dr. Miller's exploit with Ignatius is unparalleled for sophistry, audacity, and unconscious suicide. I advise every reader to get a copy of Mine's " Presbyterian Clergyman Looking for the Church" (Dutton, N. Y.), and read chapter xxiii.,

"in unity with the Bishop, the Presbyters and the Deacons, who have been appointed according to the mind of Jesus Christ."[37] "If any man follows him that makes a *schism* in the Church, he shall not inherit the Kingdom of God."[38]

In his Epistle to the Smyrnæans he says: "See that ye follow the Bishop even as Jesus Christ does the Father, and the Presbytery as ye would the Apostles, and the Deacons as being the institution of God. Let no man do any thing connected with the Church without the Bishop. Let that be deemed a proper Eucharist which is administered either by the Bishop or by one to whom he has entrusted it. Wherever the Bishop shall appear, there let the multitude also be; even as wherever Jesus Christ is, there is the *Catholic Church*. It is not lawful without the Bishop [*i. e.*, without his authority] either to baptize or to celebrate the Holy Communion * * * so that every thing that is done may be secure and valid."[39] "It is well to reverence both God and the Bishop."[40]

In his Epistle entitled "Ignatius, who is called Theophoros, to Polycarp, Bishop of the Church of the Smyrnæans," he bids his Episcopal brother: "Let nothing be done without *thy* consent."[41] "My soul be for theirs who are submissive to the Bishop, to the Presbyters and to the Deacons; and may my portion be along with them in God."[42]

So much, then, for the testimony of the Apostolic Bishop of Antioch, which comes to us ratified and endorsed by the Angel of the Church in Smyrna.

---

especially pp. 454 to 465, on "Dr. Miller's extracts from Ignatius, something odd." That chapter alone is worth ten times the price of the book. See also Dr. Bowden's patient and exhaustive reply to Dr. Miller: "The Apos. Orig. of Epis." Hall's "Epis. and the Pap. Suprem," and "Kip's Double Witness," pp. 70 to 71.

37. In the dedication.
38. Chap. 3. 39. Chap. 8. 40. Chap. 9. 41. Chap. 4. 42. Chap. 6.

CHAPTER XI.

THE WITNESS OF THE FATHERS—CONTINUED.

"And drink the untainted fount of pure antiquity."
—*Lyra Apostolica*, p. 154.

"If I might leave one request to the rising generation of clergy * * * it would be, In addition to the study of Holy Scripture, which they too studied night and day, *Study the Fathers*."—*Dr. Pusey*.

IT should never be forgotten that Gibbon, the keen skeptical historian of the Decline and Fall of the Roman Empire, although he ignores the spiritual authority which the Bishops derived from the Apostles, nevertheless freely admits (for he could not deny it) that " the Episcopal form of government [by which he meant organized *Diocesan* Episcopacy] appears to have been introduced *before the close of the first century;*" that its "advantages" were "obvious and important;" that it "had acquired at a *very early period* the sanction of *antiquity;*" that "Bishops, under the name of *Angels*, were already [*i. e.*, before the end of the first century] instituted in the seven cities of Asia;" and that "'*Nulla Ecclesia sine Episcopo*'—no Church without a Bishop—has been a *fact* as well as a maxim, since the time of Tertullian and Irenæus." Gibbon moreover declares that "after we have passed the difficulties of the *first century*,[1] we find *the Episcopal form of government universally established*, until it was interrupted by the republican genius of the Swiss and German reformers."[2]

The learned French Protestant, Guizot, says: "*The Apostles themselves* appointed several *Bishops*. Tertullian, Clement of Alexandria, and many fathers of the second and third century do not permit us to doubt this fact."

The "Learned Grotius,"[3] himself a Presbyterian, through force of circumstances, was candid enough to give up the attempt to invalidate Episcopacy. Like many of the continental reformers, he regretted that the Church of Holland had lost the Apostolic Ministry. He was as familiar with the Fathers as most Protestants are ignorant of them; and this is what he says of their evidence for Episcopacy: "To reject the supremacy of one pastor above the rest is to condemn the whole ancient Church of folly or even of impiety." "The Episcopacy had its commencement *in the times of the Apostles*. All the *fathers, without exception, testify to this*. The testimony of *Jerome*[4] alone is sufficient. The catalogues of the Bishops, in Irenæus, Socrates, Theo-

---

1. *I. e.*, before the death of St. John. And what after all are these "difficulties of the first century"? Why, as I have shown, the gradual transition from the general Missionary Episcopate of the Apostles to the local jurisdiction of their successors, together with the gradual change of name, which I trust was made clear in Chapter IX. But call these *natural* processes "the difficulties of the first century," if you please; they are a thousand times less than our Papal and Presbyterial brethren have to encounter, when they try to fit their respective systems on the Early Church.

2. These quotations from Gibbon are all taken from the Dec. and Fall, chap. xv., and from his notes on that chap., 110, 111, 112.

3. A. D. 1583 to 1645.

4. Jerome! And yet he is the one whom Dr. Miller and others, by bold misquotations from his Epistle to Evagrius, would metamorphose into a Presbyterian. Can it be that such have ever read that Epistle? We will have a taste of it ere long.

doret, and others, all of which begin in the Apostolic age, testify to this. To refuse credit in a historical matter, to so great authorities, and *so unanimous among themselves*, is not the part of any but an irreverent and stubborn disposition. What the *whole Church* maintains, and was not instituted by Councils, but was *always held*, is not with any good reason believed to be handed down by any but APOSTOLIC AUTHORITY."[5]

Not one *bona fide* quotation can be adduced from any Father or Council of the Early Church which makes against Episcopacy. *We Churchmen do not begin to realize the strength of our position.* Some of us are frightened by the timid and treacherous utterances of our own sick and disloyal comrades; or are for yielding up the Citadel of God, whose walls can stand the artillery of hell, because, forsooth, the sham batteries of a Dr. Miller, or the spiked guns of some roving Monsignor are directed against us. It does us good, once in a while, to " walk about Zion, and go round about her, and tell the towers thereof, and mark well her bulwarks." We shall at least be able to show our wandering brothers that we have better reasons for staying in the dear old homestead than they ever had for leaving it. There is to-day a widespread feeling among thoughtful Dissenters which is often expressed in some such way as this: " Churchmen, after all, are no fools!"

For some strange reason, Apostolic Succession is a stumbling-block to many. And yet Apostolic Succession rests on a stronger historical basis than the Canon of Holy

---

5. For Grotius' testimony in full, see his Annotations on the *Consultations of Cassander*, his comments on Acts, xiv., and *Testimonies concerning him* appended to his *De Veritate Religionis Christianæ*.

Scripture itself. During the first thousand years of the Christian era, there were several instances of Churches which, though they had the Creed, had never seen a complete copy of the New Testament; but all the while not one single instance of a Church without Bishops, Priests, and Deacons. If any one doubts this, let him try for himself to answer this, as yet *unanswered*, challenge which the "Judicious Hooker" made in the year 1594, to those who had set up a non-Episcopal Ministry: "A very strange thing sure it were, that such a discipline as ye speak of should be taught by Christ and His Apostles in the word of God, and no Church ever have found it out, nor received it till this present time. * * * *We require you to find out but one Church upon the face of the whole earth, that hath been ordered by your discipline or hath not been ordered by ours, that is to say, by Episcopal regimen, since the time that the blessed Apostles were here conversant.*"[6]

---

6. Pref. to Eccl. Pol., § 4. Cf. also the challenge of Bishop Jewell, first made at St. Paul's Cross, Nov. 26, 1559; repeated March 31, 1560. "If any learned men of all our adversaries, or if all the learned men that be alive, be able to bring any one sufficient sentence out of any old Catholic Doctor or Father, or out of any old General Council, or out of the Holy Scriptures of God, or any example of the Primitive Church, whereby it may be clearly and plainly proved; * * * that the *Bishop of Rome* was then called an Universal Bishop, or Head of the Universal Church; * * * I promised then that I would give over and subscribe unto him." (Bp. Jewell's Works, I, p. 20, Ed. Parker Soc.), quoted in Dr. Huntington's admirable little book, "The Ch. Idea," p. 71. I cannot forbear to quote here the strong language of Mines (Pres. Clerg., p. 341): "Episcopacy existed wherever the Church existed, and the world has again and again been challenged to produce one single Church in all Europe, Africa, or Asia, which in the first, the second, the third, the fourth, the fifth, or the sixth century, was for one moment Presbyterian. When Presbyterians demand of Episcopalians a chain of Bishops from [to-day] back to the days of the Apostles, Episcopalians produce it—link after link, name after name—back to the hands of St. Thomas in Syria, St. John in Ephesus, St. James in Jerusalem, St. Mark in Alexandria, St. Peter and St. Paul in Rome. But when Episcopalians ask Presbyterians to produce, not a succession of Churches reaching beyond Luther and Calvin and a

I shall now give a few extracts from the early Fathers, which will corroborate what we have already learned from the Bible, and from SS. Clement, Polycarp and Ignatius. The unknown author of that beautiful treatise, the "Epistle to Diognetus" (about A. D. 130), who calls himself a "Disciple of the Apostles," says: "The tradition of the Apostles is preserved,"[7] which he could not have said, had the then universal Episcopacy of the Church been contrary to their teaching. Hegesippus, who was born about A. D. 100 — *Vicinus Apostolorum temporum*, as St. Jerome calls him[8] — wrote a Church History, which was familiar to Eusebius and St. Jerome, but which has since been lost. He traveled over a large part of the known world for the express purpose of ascertaining the teaching and practice of the Apostles, as retained in the Churches which they founded. Eusebius has preserved a few fragments of his writings,[9] in which "he declares of himself, that as he had made it his business to visit the Bishops of the Church, so he had found them all unanimous in their doctrines; and that the same books of the Law, the same Gospel and Faith * * * had been constantly preserved along with *the Succession of the Bishops in all the Churches.*" Moreover he says: "The first heretic was Thebusis, who was disappointed in his expectations of a Bishopric."

---

gulf of a thousand years, but one poor, single, solitary Church, in a world full of Churches, that in the first, or the second, or the third, or the fourth, or the fifth century, was bona fide *Presbyterian*; they return the writ with *non est inven us;* it cannot be found." [The futile attempts to find it among the Chaldees are well known.]

7. Chap. 10.
8. De Scrip., c. 22, "Near the time of the Apostles."
9. Euseb. Ecl. Hist., IV., 22, as quoted by Bowden, Letter VII.

Dionysius, the wise and holy Bishop of Corinth, who lived to A. D. 176, wrote a number of letters, fragments of which are preserved by Eusebius[10]—one to the Athenians, in which he speaks of the martyrdom of their Bishop, Publius (early in the century), and mentions his successor, Quadratus;[11] one to the Churches in Crete, in which he praises Philip, their Bishop; one to the Churches in Pontus, in which he mentions Palma, their Bishop; one to Pinytus, the Bishop of the Gnosians, in which he urges him not to enforce celibacy upon his clergy,—to which the ascetic Bishop replied, attempting to justify his course.[12] All of which shows, as indeed do all incidents and allusions in the literature of the Early Church, that the Episcopal polity prevailed. He also wrote a letter to Soter, the Bishop of the Church in Rome.

St. Irenæus (A. D. 120 to 202) had been a disciple of St. Polycarp. Leaving the East he accompanied Pothinus, a companion and equal of St. Polycarp, on a mission to Gaul, and settled in the city of Lyons. Pothinus was a Bishop, ordained by St. John or by one whom St. John had ordained—which is of interest to us, as it is generally supposed that the old British Church derived its Orders, in part at least, from this source; and at all events a successor[13] of Pothinus in the See of Lyons was one of the

---

10. *Id.*

11. This Quadratus, the second or third Bp. of Athens, A. D. 120, "was," says Dr. Mahan (Ch. Hist., p. 114), "a disciple of the Apostles, many of whose miracles he had seen with his own eyes. * * * Becoming Bishop of Athens, he labored with great success in re-establishing the Church which in that part of Greece had fallen into decay." He also wrote a calm and able defence of Christianity, which he presented to the Emperor Hadrian, who reigned from A. D. 117 to 138.

12. See again Bowden's seventh letter.

13. Viz: Etherius, thirty-first Bishop of Lyons, who, with Virgilius, Bishop of Arles, ordained Augustine.

consecrators of Augustine, the first Archbishop of Canterbury.

After the martyrdom of Pothinus in the dreadful Lyonnese persecution of A. D. 177, Irenæus, who was the leading Presbyter of the Gallic Church, was made Bishop of Lyons, and seems to have exercised a sort of Primacy over the Churches of Gaul.[14] Himself a Bishop, and the pupil of a Bishop whom St. John had loved and ordained, he was certainly in a position to know the polity of the early Church. Let us hear him

He says: "The tradition of the Apostles is manifest throughout the whole world; and we are in a position to reckon up those who were, *by the Apostles, ordained Bishops in the Churches, and the Succession of those men to our own time.* If the Apostles had known hidden mysteries, they would have delivered them, especially to those to whom they were also committing the Churches themselves. For they were desirous that those men should be very perfect and blameless in all things, whom also they were leaving behind *as their successors,* delivering up *their own place of government* (magisterii) *to these men.*"[15]

He speaks also of "those to whom the Apostles did commit the Churches;"[16] and again: "The *Bishops* to whom the Apostles did commit the Churches."[17] In one place he calls Bishops "Presbyters," but he distinguishes them from ordinary Presbyters, just as we would to-day, by describing them as Presbyters who have the Apostolic or Episcopal succession. These are his words: "Obey the Presbyters who are in the Church, *those who,* as I have

---

14. Eus., v. 23. 15. Adv. Haeres, iii., chap. 3, § 1. 16. iii., chap. 4, § 1.
17. v, chap. 20, § 1.

shown, *possess* the SUCCESSION FROM THE APOSTLES, those who, together with the *Succession of the Episcopate*, have received the certain gift of truth, according to the good pleasure of the Father. But [it behooves us] to hold in suspicion others who depart from the *primitive Succession* and assemble themselves together in any place whatsoever, either as heretics of perverse minds or as schismatics." [18]

Our next witness is Polycrates, whose testimony is thus summed up by Dr. Cutts : [19] " Polycrates, Bishop of Ephesus, writing A. D. 196, says that at that time he himself had been sixty-five years a Christian. He was, therefore, born about thirty years after the death of St. John, and

---

18. iv., 26, § 2. The whole passage is too long to quote, but is valuable as showing the good Bishop's holy horror of breaking "the Fellowship of the Apostles." After comparing *heretics* to Nadab and Abihu (Lev., x., 1 and 2), he likens Dissenters or such as "exhort others against the Church of God," to Korah, Dathan, and Abiram (Num., xvi., 1-33); while as to schismatics, or "those who cleave asunder and separate the unity of the Church," he likens them to *Jeroboam* (I. Kings, xiv., 10). Irenæus also gives what he calls the "Successions of the Bishops" in the Church at Rome, choosing this "very ancient and universally known Church," because "it would be very tedious in such a volume as this to reckon up the Successions of all the Churches." The list is as follows: "The blessed Apostles [SS. Peter and Paul] committed into the hands of Linus the Office of the Episcopate. Of this Linus, St. Paul makes mention in his Epistles to Timothy [II. Tim., iv., 21]; to him succeeded Anacletus; and after him in the third place from the APOSTLES [observe the *plural*. Irenæus knew nothing of St. Peter's having any exclusive right in Rome] Clement was allotted the Bishopric. This man, as he had seen the blessed Apostles, and had been conversant with them, might be said to have the preaching of the Apostles still echoing in his ears, and their traditions before his eyes. Nor was he alone in this, for there were many still remaining who had received instructions from the Apostles." (And here I must put in a word to thoughtful readers. Is it *possible* that these early Bishops and others who had been *taught by the Apostles* would have maintained *Episcopacy*, unless the Apostles had so taught them ?— *sit verbum sat sapienti.*) "To this Clement succeeded Evaristus," and so he gives the names down to Eleutherius, who, says he, "does now in the twelfth place from the *Apostles* hold the inheritance of the *Episcopate.*"

19. Turning Points in Gen. Ch. Hist., p. 121.

was contemporary with Simeon of Jerusalem, Ignatius, Polycarp, and others, disciples of the Apostles. He, writing about the time of keeping Easter, appeals to the tradition of *former Bishops* and martyrs. * * * Among others, he mentions Polycarp, Bishop of Smyrna and Martyr; Thraseas, Bishop of Eumenia and Martyr; Sagaris, Bishop of Laodicea and Martyr; seven Bishops of his own kindred, and great multitudes of Bishops who had assembled with him to consult about the Easter question."

Clement of Alexandria, during the Episcopate of Demetrius (about A. D. 185), likens the Orders of Bishop, Priest, and Deacon to the ranks of the blessed Angels. He also says there are many rules, some of which relate to Presbyters, others to Bishops, and others to Deacons.[20] He alludes to St. John's ordaining Bishops in various cities of Asia;[21] and he calls Bishop Clement of Rome "an Apostle."

Tertullian, a Presbyter of the Church in Carthage (born A. D. 135, died A. D. 217), uses these words : "*The Chief or Highest Priest, who is the* BISHOP, *has the right of giving Baptism, and after him the Presbyters and Deacons, but not without the Bishop's authority.*"[22] Speaking of the Churches in the regions where St. John labored, he says: "The Order of the Bishops, when traced up to its original, will be found to have *John* for its author."[23] The heretics of his day he boldly challenges in these words : " Let them

---

20. Pedagogue, Chap. xii.
21. Quis Div. Salv., Chap. 42.
22. Quoted by Dowden, Let. vi.
23. "Ordo tamen Episcoporum ad originem *recensus*, in *Johanem* stabit *auctorem*," Adv. Mar., IV., 5.

produce the original of their Churches, let them show *the Order of their* BISHOPS, *that by their Succession deduced from the beginning,* we may see whether their first Bishop had any of the APOSTLES or Apostolic men, who did likewise persevere with the Apostles, for his *Ordainer and Predecessor!* For thus the Apostolical Churches hand down their records; as the Church of Smyrna from Polycarp, whom John the Apostle placed there; the Church of Rome from Clement, who was in *like manner*[24] ordained by Peter; and so the other Churches can produce those *constituted in the Bishoprics by the Apostles, and so regarded as transmitters of the Apostolic seed.*"[25] He also calls a Bishop's seat " the *Apostolic Chair."*

The profound and versatile Origen, in the beginning of the third century,[26] also bears witness to the divine authority of Episcopacy. In one of his Lectures he asks: " If Jesus Christ, the Son of God, be subject to Joseph and Mary, shall not I be subject to the *Bishop who is ordained of God to be my Father?* Shall I not be subject to the Presbyter who by divine appointment is set over me?"[27] Speaking of the duties common to all people, he adds: " Besides these general debts, there is a debt peculiar to *Deacons,* another to *Presbyters,* and another to *Bishops,* which is the greatest of all, and exacted by the Saviour, of the whole Church, who will severely punish the non-payment of it."[28]

---

24. Tertullian, by the way, like all the Early Fathers, knew nothing of the *Bishop of Rome* being appointed to any higher or different office than the rest of the Bishops.
25. De Praescrip. Haeret., c. 32. 27. Quoted in Bowden's 5th Letter.
26. He was born A. D. 186. 28. Quoted by Cutts, p. 122.

Time would fail me were I to attempt to set before you the testimony of Firmilian, the Bishop of Cæsarea, A. D. 233 ; of St. Cyprian, Bishop of Carthage, A. D. 248, that Saint, Scholar, Apostle and Martyr, who, if not the first, was at least the deepest and clearest expounder of the *philosophy of the Episcopate*, as the unifying principle of the Church, and as being itself an UNITY[29] *in which all Bishops throughout the world do equally participate;*[30] and of St. Ambrose, St. Jerome,[31] and St. Augustine, and especially

---

29. "Episcopatus *unus* est, cujus a singulis in solidum pars tenetur."—*De Unit, Eccl.*
30. St. Cyprian, writing to Cornelius, the Bishop of Rome, says: "This is and ought to be our chief care and study, that we maintain the *unity* which was delivered by our Lord, and His Apostles to *us their Successors.*"
31. Although St. Jerome again and again asserts the universality and Apostolical authority of Episcopacy, Presbyterians lay great store by his letter to Evagrius. Yet after reading it with care, I can find nothing in it which can be used against Episcopacy. He was writing to rebuke a certain person who undertook to rank a Deacon above a Presbyter. His whole argument amounts merely to this: That in the New Testament (as we have seen) the terms Bishop and Presbyter are used interchangeably, and that the Apostles sometimes call themselves *Presbyters* (which of course proves nothing, as they also call themselves *Deacons*). He asserts that the elevation of one Presbyter above another was a "remedy against schism," but he tells us elsewhere that it was done by the authority of the Apostles, and as early as A. D. 57. He does *not* say, as some Presbyterians claim, that in Alexandria the Presbyters *ordain* one of their number to be their Bishop, but that they only *nominate* him ("Nominabant")—quite a different thing. Finally, it is in this very letter which Presbyterians quote certain passages from, that St. Jerome lays down the real distinction between a *Bishop* and a *Presbyter* in a way which neither Presbyterians nor Roman Catholics can endure: it is the exact theory of the Greek and Anglo-Catholics: "What doth a Bishop do, which a Presbyter may not do, ORDINATION EXCEPTED?" Then he proceeds: "Wherever there is a Bishop, whether at *Rome* or at *Eugubium* [which was a very insignificant diocese], whether at Constantinople or Rhegium, whether at Alexandria or Tanis, he is of the *same validity, and of the same Priesthood.* Neither the power of wealth nor the weakness of poverty can make a Bishop more exalted or more depressed; *but they are* ALL SUCCESSORS OF THE APOSTLES. * * * That which Aaron and his sons, and the Levites were, in the Temple, *that let the Bishops and Presbyters and Deacons claim to be in the Church.*" Surely if our Presbyterian brethren can find any "crumbs of comfort" in the Epistle of St. Jerome to Evagrius, they are most welcome to them. Such as they be, they are the largest crumbs of the sort that fall from the Patristic board.

the testimony of Eusebius,[32] who, by order of the Emperor, had all the records of the Empire put at his disposal for the great task of writing a history of the first three centuries of the Church.

Such, in brief, is the history of the early Patristic evidence for the Catholic Episcopate. There is nothing to offset it. It cannot be gainsaid nor denied.

I cannot leave this branch of my subject without reiterating the maxim quoted above : "Study the Fathers." Study them for the intrinsic value of their writings, and for their unimpeachable witness to the facts of primitive Catholicity.

The Christian Church, though at the start she contained "not many wise men after the flesh,"[33] though she was "unto the Greeks foolishness,"[34] nevertheless soon made herself felt in the world, not only as a religious, but as an intellectual power. Then were laid the foundations of the first institutions of Christian education. The Catechetical School of Alexandria—founded by St. Mark and adorned by Athenagorus, Pantaenus, Clement, Origen—the Cathedral Schools of Antioch and Edessa, with others, became strong centers of religion and learning, and were the parents of the parish and public school, the germ of the Christian college, university, and theological seminary. Then began that long procession of Christian scholars—men of saintly lives, who added to their virtue knowledge.

---

32. "Eusebius, the historian of the early Church, who lived in the latter part of the third and early part of the fourth centuries, derives the Bishops of all Churches from the Apostles. He gives exact and authentic catalogues of the Bishops who presided in all the principal cities of the Roman Empire, and from the Apostles down to his own time.—*Cutts.*

33. I. Cor., i., 26. 34. I. Cor., i., 23.

Then shone forth the Churchly piety of an Ignatius ; the Scriptural and Theological devotion of an Irenæus ; the chaste, philosophical acumen of a Justin Martyr ; the cogent and fervid logic of a Tertullian ; the prodigious and inexhaustible and unparalleled learning of an Origen ; the unconquerable, enthusiastic, triumphant Faith of an Athanasius ; the pious, practical, and beneficent ecclesiasticism of a Cyprian and an Ambrose ; the stern, towering, indefatigable talent of a Jerome ; the supreme, universal, immortal excellence of an Augustine ; and the hallowed genius and consecrated eloquence of a Chrysostom. And thence onward to our own times, the natural succession of Catholic Scholars runs side by side with that other and diviner succession—to which they have ever paid the homage of consentient and supporting testimony — the "Apostolic Succession" of Bishops in the Church of God.

CHAPTER XII.

IF THE PRIMITIVE CATHOLIC CHURCH WAS NOT EPISCOPAL, WHAT WAS IT?

"*Nulla Ecclesia sine Episcopo.*"

"It is evident unto all men, diligently reading Holy Scripture and Ancient Authors, that from the Apostles' time there have been these orders of Ministers in Christ's Church, Bishops, Priests and Deacons."—*Preface to the Ordinal.*

"Controversy may beat against these words, like waves against a rock, but it will never move them."—Bp. Chas. Wordsworth's "Outlines of the Christian Ministry," p. 137.

A LEARNED priest of the American Church, who was for many years a Presbyterian minister, has often remarked to the writer : " O, when I was a Presbyterian, and used to read the Fathers, I had to resort to most ingenious *explanations;* but as soon as I began to read them from a Church standpoint I found *nothing to explain—*it was all plain sailing." He reasoned thus with himself: I have always read the Fathers with the assumption that the primitive Church was Presbyterian, and by hook and by crook[1] have managed to explain away the difficulties. But why not make the experiment of reading them from an Episcopalian standpoint? So, beginning with the New Testament, he read all the ancient Christian writings, and found (as we have seen) that Christ gave a perpetual commission to His Apostles, that they ordained not only Deacons and Presbyters, but others who were called *Apostles;* that Timothy and Titus were appointed to an office

---

1. See Appendix to this Chapter.

and work, including the right of *ordaining*, as clearly Episcopal as the office and work of the Bishop of New York or of Minnesota; that when St. John wrote to the Seven Churches there was some *one* at the head of each Church who was responsible for the faith and practice of that Church and those who were teachers in it; that the Fathers constantly alluded to the three orders of the ministry, those in the first order being "Successors of the Apostles," and *all equal*, whether at Rome or elsewhere; that those writers who had actually sat at the feet of the blessed Paul, or Peter, or John, were as stanch Episcopalians as those who lived later; that the Church, as it appears on the pages of history, was always Episcopal, and believed itself to have been so by divine ordering; and that *assuming* the Catholic Church to have started *Presbyterian*, it is impossible to assign any date when it became *Episcopal*, or to account for the fact that no protest was made at a revolution so radical and gigantic.

To the Churchman it is all clear enough—the historic Church was Episcopal because it was born so, the Apostles being the Bishops (as the Fathers testify): there was no break, no imaginary change to account for, nothing to explain away. But with the Presbyterian, how is it? Alas! he must in the first place set aside the Saviour's promise to be with His *Apostles* until the end of the world. Then he must prove that the Apostolate was confined to the original Twelve,[2] Holy Scripture to the contrary notwith-

---

2. I have heard Dissenters boldly assert that the Eleven did *very wrong* to choose Matthias, and that God set aside their action by appointing St. Paul to take the place of Judas (!), and that there could, by no possibility, be more than *twelve* Apostles—although, at the very least, twenty-three (23) are called "Apostles" by the Holy Ghost in the New Testament. "But," the Presbyterians argue, "the Apostles worked *miricles*, and no one can be an Apostle unless he can

standing; that SS. Timothy and Titus and the "Angels" of the Seven Churches were not Bishops; in short, that the Apostles left no successors, although the Fathers constantly assert that they did. And having proved all this, he must needs show how his primitive Presbyterian Church did afterwards become Episcopal, and how it got the firm belief that it had always been so.

If Christ had meant His Church to be Presbyterian, St. John would have known it, and so would his friends, the Bishops of Antioch, and Smyrna, and their friend, the Bishop of Lyons, and the rest. Or, to reverse the process, the Church of the third century, which was nothing if not Episcopal, must have known whether the Church of the second century was Episcopal or not; and the Church of the second century must have known whether the Church of the first century was Episcopal or not; and the venerable Bishops and teachers who were associated with St. John in the latter part of the first century must have known whether or not the Church was Episcopal from the start. We have had their testimony. There is no break in the chain.

Take the admission of Gibbon and of all candid scholars

---

show the same signs of his Apostleship." But if that argument proves anything, it proves too much; for the early *Presbyters* worked miracles, and the Deacons, too—notably, SS. Stephen and Phillip. *Ergo*, nobody can be a Presbyter or a Deacon unless he can work miracles; or even a layman, for that matter. The miraculous powers of the Early Apostles and elders and brethren belonged to the Pentecostal outpouring of the Holy Ghost, and were not a part of their *permanent office*. A Presbyterian minister once challenged the late Bishop Doane to prove his Apostleship by drinking prussic acid! I am not informed whether that venerable Apostle stooped to notice the impious taunt, but certainly he might have replied: I accept the challenge on the condition that you, Mr. Minister, will prove yourself to be even a layman by doing the same thing. For it is written: "These signs shall follow *them that believe;* In my name shall they cast out devils, * * * and *if they drink any deadly thing, it shall not hurt them,*" etc. (St. Mark, xvi., 17 and 18.)

that the Church was universally Episcopal at the close of the first century. How shall we account for it? Well, it either started so, or else if it started Presbyterian, the early Presbyterians abandoned it so *soon*, so *unanimously*, so *universally* as to show that Presbyterianism was regarded as a stupendous failure—so *soon* that the change was made before the Apostles were cold in their graves; so *unanimously* that not a single Priest or layman lifted his voice against the usurpation of those who made themselves Bishops ; so *universally* that not a single " Presbytery," nay, not one solitary isolated congregation, in the forests of Britain, in the mines of Spain, in the valleys of Gaul and Italy, on the deserts of Africa, or the fertile banks of the Nile, on the Islands of the Mediterranean, in the cities of Greece, on the sands of Arabia, on the prairies of Babylon, in the jungles of India, or on the hallowed hills of Galilee and Judea—not one poor single solitary Presbyterian Congregation survived to witness against Episcopal usurpation and say like Job's messenger : " I, even I only, am escaped alone to tell thee."

If you strain out the gnat of primitive Episcopacy, you have got to swallow a camel larger than the wooden horse of Troy, viz., this : *The assumed Presbyterianism of the Apostolic Church, in one generation, unanimously and universally changed to Episcopacy*, an Episcopacy, too, which knew nothing of any change, but always supposed itself to have been primitive and Apostolic ! I can only murmur the trite maxim of Horace :

Credat, Judæus, Apella,
Non ego!

And yet every Dissenter swallows this "camel," which is a necessary postulate of all non-Episcopal systems.

Let there be no dodging of the issue. At an early date the Church was Episcopal. If it was founded so, well and good; if not, what was it originally, and when and how did it change? It was not originally Presbyterial, for it is absurd to talk of the "parity of the ministry," when the two lower orders of Priests and Deacons were subject to the oversight of the Apostles. While the Apostles lived, therefore, the Church was undeniably Episcopal. But after their death? Well, as has been shown, there was no break. The post-Apostolic Episcopate is dovetailed into the Episcopate of the Apostles. But waiving this, and passing over that numerous company of men who were also called Apostles, suppose we grant, for the sake of argument, that after the death of all the original Twelve, about A. D. 100, the whole Church was *Presbyterial*—say for ten years, or, to be generous to a fault with historic facts, say fifty years—how on earth was the unanimous and universal change then made to Episcopacy? It is as if the United States should suddenly become a monarchy, and yet not one state, not one county, not one town, not one man—be he congressman, soldier, or private citizen—utter a word of protest, and not a single allusion to so revolutionary a change be made by any friend or foe, citizen, or foreigner, in contemporary and subsequent history.

I ask our Presbyterian friends, using the word to include all Christian bodies which have lost the Apostolic Succession: Would it be possible for one of your presbyters in every synod, presbytery, conference, or association in your denomination, to usurp to himself the office and functions of a Bishop, involving the sole right to ordain and confirm, the care and oversight of all the ministers in his district, etc., and this spontaneously in all parts of your denomination, even in distant countries, without any opportunity for concerted action; and yet not a solitary voice be raised in protest, and not a single line left to show that such a change had taken place? You would say : " *The idea is preposterous*—the bare attempt in *one* Presbytery would raise a tempest in a tea-pot, and we should never hear the last of it ! " And yet you believe, and would have us believe, that precisely that very thing was done throughout the whole Catholic Church, and that, too, in an age when Apostolic tradition was fresh, universal, and most highly esteemed.

Revolutions do not take place in that way. Had the Early Church been Presbyterial (and, by the way, the sorriest compliment one can pay Presbyterianism is to call it the *primitive* polity, for if so, those early Presbyterians showed no love for it)—had the early Church, I say, been Presbyterial, we should have seen evidence of it in the New Testament, which we do not; then gradually in *some* quarters, but not possibly in *all* quarters, some ambitious presbyters might have attempted to lord it over God's heritage (although ambitious clerics are not the kind that court martyrdom, and the early Bishops were the first and most conspicuous mark for the persecutor), and some at least would have been unsuccessful in their attempted usurpations, as they would be to-day if they tried it in any Presbyterial denomination. Moreover, the thing could not be " done in a corner; " it would have been known; it would have been commented on ; it would have raised a commotion, as all *real* changes, innovations, "developments," even trifling ones, have done ever since. Take, for example, the "Papacy." It was not primitive; it was opposed in its germination and in every stage of its growth; and it has never yet been accepted by four out of the five great Patriarchates of the Catholic Church. Observe: A new order is created above the Bishops; it takes many centuries for it to effect even a *partial* usurpation; it makes a tremendous stir; it splits the Catholic Church into *two*, and at length into *three* divisions.[3] And yet Presbyterians would have us believe that a far more radical revolution—one which destroyed the "primitive Presbyterian Church," by adding the "new and man-made order of Bishops"—was carried, not in one Patriarchate or portion of the Church, but throughout the whole world, without any stir or opposition, without leaving a document or a tradition of any part of the transaction, and all within a few years of the death of St. John!!

Is it reasonable—I submit—is it reasonable? Nay, is it not rather an insult to logic and common sense? How much wiser, how much easier to accept the simple, natural fact, that the historic Church is Episcopal, because it started so.[4]

---

3. We might say *four*, including the "Old Catholics," and also charge it with being the real cause of the nearly 400 Protestant sects.

4. "There is no doctrine or tenet of the Christian religion in which all Christians in general have, for the space of fifteen hundred years, so unanimously agreed, as in this of Episcopacy. In all ages and times down from the Apostles, and in all places, through Europe, Asia, and Africa, wheresoever there were Christians, there were also Bishops. Even where Christians differed in other points of doctrine or custom, and made schisms and divisions in the Church, yet did they all remain unanimous in this, in retaining their Bishops."
—JABLONSKY, quoted by Rev. Wm. A. Rich, in "The Examination Examined."

APPENDIX TO CHAPTER XII.

DESPERATE EXPEDIENTS TO GET RID OF THE BISHOPS OF
THE EARLY CHURCH.

ONE desperate expedient was to *assume* that each early Bishop was only a *Pastor* over the one "Presbyterian Church" in the city, as James in Jerusalem, Ignatius in Antioch, Onesimus in Ephesus, Dionysius in Alexandria, Cyprian in Carthage, Cornelius in Rome, etc. They take care not to mention *Titus* in Crete; for there were *one hundred* cities in Crete, and Titus was commanded to "ordain Priests in *every city*"—queer work for a Priest who was simply Pastor of one parish! But how is it with the others? Poor St. James! What an "overworked Pastor" he must have been! And what a monstrous "meeting-house" he must have had to preach in! When he was "installed" over his pastoral charge, there were more than 3,000 members of his congregation; a few days later (see Acts, iv.) 5,000 more were added in a day; and we read: "The Lord added to the Church *daily*," "Believers were more added," "multitudes—both of men and women," "the number of the disciples multiplied in Jerusalem *greatly*, and a great company of the Priests were obedient to the faith." About twenty years later, St. James and all the *Presbyters* of Jerusalem [the "Ruling Elders," who composed the "Session," forsooth], said to St. Paul: "Thou seest, brother, how many *thousands*"—literally, how many *tens of thousands*—" myriads "—" of Jews there are which believe" (Acts xxi., 20). Why, some *Presbyterian* scholars have admitted that there must have been, at that time, 50,000 Christians in Jerusalem. And considering that their Churches or places of worship were *small* (mostly in private houses), with daily services, weekly Eucharists, and thorough pastoral care, there must have been at least fifty congregations, and fifty to one hundred clergy under St. James. Jerusalem was a great city; the Jews had more than 325 Synagogues in it. These facts speak for themselves.

And so with *Ignatius* in Antioch, a city of over 200,000 inhabitants. He had many ministering Priests and Deacons under him, and his jurisdiction extended so far outside the city, that he calls himself " the Bishop of Syria."

As to *Onesimus*, the Bishop of Ephesus, he succeeded to St. Timothy, who was certainly not a mere *Pastor*, but an *Apostolic Overseer*. And the idea of only *one* parish in Ephesus, which fifty years before had a goodly number of *Presbyters*—not " Ruling Elders," but such as had the duty and power to "*feed* the Church of God," i. e., Priests and Preachers—is simply absurd.

As to Alexandria, why, there were several parishes or Churches there while St. Mark was still alive (see Euseb. II., c. 17), and the Nicene Council alludes to it as an "*Ancient* custom " that the " Bishop of Alexandria " should have metropolitan jurisdiction " over all Egypt, Lybia, and Pentapolis." And St. Jerome says: "At Alexandria, from Mark the Evangelist down to the times of the Bishops Heraclas and Dionysius, the Presbyters always nominated as Bishop one chosen out of their own body and placed in a higher grade."—JEROME, *Ad Evag.*

The same is true as to St. Cyprian in Carthage, where were many thousands of Christians, and where Geisericus found "the Bishop and a very great multitude of clergy" (*maximam turbam clericorum*), and these, not "Ruling Elders," for their Bishop, Cyprian, calls them "Glorious Priests"—*gloriosis sacerdotibus*. A few years later we have the names of the *Cathedral* and ten of the Churches of Carthage. While Cornelius, the Bishop of Rome, had under him, at that time, forty-six Presbyters and seven Deacons, besides sub-deacons, lay-readers, etc. (See Euseb., VI., c. 43.)

"The earliest Bishops of Rome, we have no hesitation in affirming, were diocesan Bishops. We learn from Tacitus that in Rome, in the persecution under Nero, 'a vast multitude' were apprehended, and convicted of the crime of being Christians. Had that vast multitude, in that vast city, but a solitary Presbyter, a simple parish Bishop, to minister to them and to watch over their souls? And if there were many—how did it come to pass that twelve of them in succession, from Linus in the time of the Apostles, to Eleutherius in the time of Irenæus, attained so marked a pre-eminence that the names of those twelve alone were thought worth recording?"—(From p. 70 of an excellent little pamphlet on Episcopacy, entitled "The Examination Examined," by Rev. Wm. A. Rich, Priest in the Diocese of Albany.)

Many Presbyterian scholars, seeing the absurdity of this notion, have advanced the theory that the Bishops of the early Church were merely the "Moderators of the Presbyteries" [Sic]. I think it would be a surprise to those venerable Apostles now in Paradise, if they could hear of it. Well, call them "Moderators," if you will ; but *Moderators* who held a *life* position, as those early "Moderators" did, who, like Timothy and Titus, ordained *alone* (which no Presbyterian Moderator ever thought of doing) ; who tried and deposed Priests and Deacons ; whose office (to which, by the way, they were always set apart by a *new* Ordination) exalted them, even though *young* men, like Timothy or Damas, over the heads of the *holy seniors;* who were the *unifying* and *governing* power, each in a given district, including some central city and the adjacent country ; who claimed to be "Successors of the Apostles ;" who called themselves "Bishops " ; who did everything which a Bishop does to-day, and which a Moderator does *not* do—*such* a "Moderator," I say, by whatever *name* you call him, is a BISHOP and an APOSTLE.

"That which we call a rose,
By any other name would smell as sweet."

CHAPTER XIII.

A FEW FRAGMENTS THAT REMAIN TOUCHING APOSTOLIC SUCCESSION.

"It is as impossible for an impartial man to doubt whether there was a succession of Bishops from the Apostles, as it would be to call in question the succession of the Roman Emperors from Julius Cæsar, or the succession of Kings in any other country."—*Archbishop Potter, of Canterbury.*

"The doctrine of Apostolical Succession is indeed established by the plain sense of Holy Scripture; but the presumption also in its favor derived from its history is singular and overwhelming. Other doctrines develop slowly; this starts forth at once. Other doctrines find their first formal statement in Fathers removed by a century or even more from apostolic times; this is enunciated and enforced in the most emphatic words by those who had been taught by the Apostles themselves. Other doctrines have been disputed from time to time, and have worked their way to acceptance by the gradually elaborated balance and combination of opposite truths; this one held undisputed and absolute possession of men's beliefs throughout the Church for fifteen hundred years."—HADDAN ON APOSTOLICAL SUCCESSION.

THERE are still several lines of argument in defense of primitive Episcopacy, which I have not even hinted at, but which are incontrovertible and all point the same way.

Such are the Canons enacted by the Early Church, not to *create* or *introduce* Episcopacy, but to guard it as an Apostolic trust, and hand it down to the ages to come, particularly the "Apostolic Canon" requiring three Bishops to take part in the ordination of every Bishop. This ancient custom, which was made binding on the whole Church by the Council of Nicæa, both shows how important was the preservation of the Episcopal Succession in the estimation of the Fathers, and is also a guarantee that the Succession has not been lost through the ages. Apostolic Succession is not a *chain* consisting of a *single row* of links—although that would be strong enough—but rather an intricate *network* such as no spider ever wove, and *no one* strand of which is essential to the continuity of the whole. To prove it, take a net of wire rings and strands, each ring representing a *Bishop*, and the interlacing strands his sacramental connection with those who ordained him, and with those whom he, in conjunction with others, ordained ; extend it so as to represent one century or eighteen centuries of the Church's life ; then apply a galvanic current at one end of the net ; of course it will be felt at the other. Take out a ring here and there ; nay, cut and slash the wire strands, and break the rings by the score, the circuit will still be unbroken. So it is with the Catholic Episcopate. Invalidate it here and there, *if you can;* the error will be rectified in a few years. "If you can," I say, but *can you?* Try it and see. Put your finger on *one single Bishop* of the Catholic Church—Ancient or Modern, Greek, Latin, or Anglican—and *prove* that his consecrators were not Bishops, that his orders are *nil;* *prove* it, I say, or even throw a fair degree of suspicion on it, if you can, and then—*what?* Why, console yourself with the thought that you have done no harm ; and even could you have demolished an hundred Episcopal links, instead of [not even] *one*, the Apostolic Succession would still be intact ; just as surgeons sometimes apply a ligature to the *femoral artery*, and then find that the almost unnoticed *collateral* circulation proves sufficient to nourish the limb in every part. In our Mother Church of England the Archbishops of Canterbury have been the chief Consecrators of Bishops for 1300 years. And yet (to make the wildest concession imaginable), suppose that every one of them—from St. Augustine to Dr. Benson—was an impostor, a mitred layman, the Anglican Succession would still be unimpaired, and Anglican orders as valid as before. As a recent writer has said : " The first Canon of the most ancient body of Canons in the Christian Church —called the *Apostolic* Canons[1]—requires that a Bishop shall be consecrated by two or three Bishops, thus recognizing the *collective* idea from the start, and the larger of these numbers, *three*, has been the express requirement of all subsequent canonical legislation on the subject.

It has always been maintained in the Anglican Church, and in every branch of it to this day, though not so strictly in the Roman branch, nor has *any* Anglican consecration *ever* taken place with less than *three* Bishops uniting in the act. This gives a threefold guarantee of *validity* to every Bishop consecrated. It is an open and public guarantee. As each of the three consecrators must himself have been consecrated by three others, the second step has a *ninefold* guarantee, and so on by geometrical progression. This is

---

1. Another of these Apostolical Canons says: "Neither do we permit the laity to perform any of the offices belonging to the Priesthood; as, for instance, neither the sacrifice, nor baptism, nor the laying on of hands, nor the blessing, whether the smaller or the greater, for 'no one taketh this honor to himself, but he that is called of God.' For such sacred offices are conferred by the laying on of the hands of the Bishop. But a person to whom such an office is not committed, but he seizes upon it for himself, he shall undergo the punishment of Uzziah."

somewhat reduced by the same Bishop acting in two or more consecrations. It is, on the other hand, *increased* by the fact that very often four or more Bishops join in a consecration, thus greatly *multiplying* the threads of connection with the past. Take, for instance, the case of the present Bishop of Albany. He was consecrated by *five* Bishops, and, tracing up the lines of their consecrators, it will be found that every Priest ordained by Bishop Doane combines in himself the transmission of the spiritual gift through no less than *sixty-nine* Bishops of the American Episcopate, including the whole of the four (*one* Scottish and *three* English) consecrations with which our American succession begins; and *besides* these includes *four* Bishops of the English and Colonial Churches—Spencer, Medley, Fulford, and Staley—besides the *three* Scottish and *six* English with whom our succession began, or *eighty-two* Bishops in all. And this is in less than one century. The same rule, having prevailed in every part of the Catholic Church from the beginning, must everywhere have produced the same result. It is as sure and as simple as the multiplication table. It leaves no room for doubt.

Take our American Church, for instance. Is it conceivable that a man should be received by all the clergy and laity of a diocese as a Bishop who had *never been consecrated?* And that, too, when the sole ground on which he *could* be received was that he *had* been consecrated! Is it *conceivable* that a man would be received into the House of Bishops, and sit and vote there unquestioned, while as yet he had *never been consecrated?* And that, too, when the sole right to a seat rested on the fact that he *had* been consecrated, and those among whom he sat *must* have certainly known whether *they* had consecrated him or not! And as these consecrations are things of *public local notoriety*, the stealing in of any unconsecrated man, and his universal recognition, both by the clergy and laity of a diocese, as well as by the House of Bishops, is a *moral* impossibility. The same is true of every Province and Provincial Synod in Christendom.

The fact of consecration, therefore, is as certain as any human event can be. And in every such consecration there is the *personal contact* of the *consecrators* and the *consecrated*, and each consecrator imparts to the consecrated that which *he himself already possesses*—a part in that One Episcopate of the Catholic Church, of which each validly consecrated Bishop has an undivided share. No one can say of such an act that the consecrators undertook to *give* what they *had not got themselves*. And the requirement of three or more consecrators in each consecration produces, not a single chain composed of single links, the failure of any *one* of which would break the line; but it gives a multitudinous web of validity, so widespreading and comprehensive that the loss of one thread here and there— even if it could be *proved* (as it can *not*)—would have no effect at all on the general result." [2]

The Apostolic Succession is thus vastly more certain than that of the Jewish High Priests, nor can any King in all the world be half so sure that he is the heir of his ancestors, as can the Bishops of the Church that they are the lawful inheritors of the office and commission of the Blessed Apostles. " The official lives of two Bishops of our own Church, Bishops White and Smith, extending

---

2. Rev. J. H. Hopkins, D. D., in Am. Ch. Rev., Jan., 1885.

over nearly a century, suggests that the chain of Episcopal Succession has not so many links as is often imagined, and (from such imagination) argued that it is quite incredible that there should be no missing link in that chain. Thirty-six of such lives carry us back to the Apostolic age ; and when it is furthermore considered that the rule has always prevailed of requiring at least three Bishops to unite in the consecration of another, it will readily be seen that so far from there being a high degree of probability against the continuance of a lineal succession in the Episcopate, there is scarcely the least ground for the opinion that it could have failed even if we had not ample documentary evidence to the contrary." [3]

Another argument is to be found in the homage which all early schismatics paid to Episcopacy ; for they resorted to desperate expedients in order to get the Apostolic Succession. For example, when the Roman *Presbyter*, Novatianus, started his schism, about A. D. 250, he is said to have invited three country Bishops to his house, where he dined them, and wined them, and made them *drunk*, and then forced them to go through the sacriligious form of ordaining him a Bishop. And yet, like all schismatics, his ostensible aim was to *purify* the Church ! In like manner, Fortunatus, who headed a schism in Carthage, during the Episcopate of good St. Cyprian, got himself ordained by Privatus, an *excommunicated* Bishop, assisted by several of his kind, whom St. Cyprian calls "false bishops." A few early sects who were unable to get even the shadow of a succession, set up a man-made

---

3. The Rt. Rev. H. A. Neely, D. D., Bishop of Maine, Convention Address, 1884.

ministry with *imitation bishops*, like the "Tulcan bishops," who for a while drew the Episcopal revenues of Scotland, or like the so-called "bishops" of the *Danish* Lutherans, and the Methodist Episcopalians.

Another argument might be found in the occasional allusions to the polity of the Church, which are made by pagan writers, and by the early opponents of Christianity. *Fas est ab hoste doceri.*

Or, take the two or three instances where a disappointed priest undertook to play the bishop. Early in the fourth century, Colluthus, a Presbyter at Alexandria, separated from his Bishop and undertook to ordain certain men to the priesthood. Whereupon a council of all the Bishops in Egypt was held in Alexandria, A. D. 324, by which the ordinations above mentioned were declared null and void, on the ground that Colluthus not being a Bishop, but only a Priest, had no power of ordaining. Those whom he had laid his hands on, pretending to make them Priests, were declared to be simply laymen, and, having been reconciled to the Church, lived thereafter in lay-communion.[4]

In the same century, Aërius, a Presbyter who was disappointed at not being made a Bishop, apostatized from the Faith, denied the Divinity of Christ, and, as St. Jerome says, "is reported to have added also some *dogmas of his own* [sic], saying that there ought to be no difference between a Presbyter and a Bishop."[5] He was well answered by Epiphanius, who called his novel theory "an outrageous and senseless doctrine"— *dogma furiosum et*

---

4. See Athanasius' Works, Vol. I., pp. 134 and 193.
5. "*Propria* quoque addisse dogmata nonnulla, dicens Presbyterum ab Episcopo nulla differentia debere discerni."

stolidum. The Churchmen of his day regarded him as a "mad man."

Finally, take the history of the Ancient Councils, especially the Six General Councils, which brought together in all 1,630 Bishops from all parts of the Universal Church; study them with care. It is all one way: There is no popery and no parity in any of them.

Such is a part of the evidence of antiquity as to the divine order and polity of the Catholic Church. Well does Archbishop Potter say: "There is such a multitude of unexceptionable witnesses for this fact, as can scarce be produced for any other matter of fact, except the rise and progress of Christianity; so that whoever shall deny this may with better reason reject all histories whatever." Apostolical Succession is a historical fact. And Macaulay, who is often quoted against the doctrine, said: "Whatever may be the doctrine, there can be no question of the historical truth." And here I close the testimony of antiquity, lest it be said of me, as of another: *Utetur in re non dubia argumentis non necessariis.*[6]

---

6. "In an affair which admits of no doubt, he uses superfluous arguments."

CHAPTER XIV.

THE ANGLICAN CHURCH AND THE "FELLOWSHIP OF THE APOSTLES."

"O, mother of our sinful land,
By kings and saints of yore
Called to Brittania's savage strand
From Syria's distant shore."
—*Lyra Apostolica,* p. 173.

IN assigning reasons why we Anglo-Saxons should be *Anglo-Catholics* instead of either *Roman*-Catholics or *anti*-Catholics, I have shown that the primitive Church had certain definite marks which must be retained in essential continuity by any Church which would justly claim the allegiance of thoughtful and pious men. These marks, as laid down in the Bible and as apparent in the early Church, are Baptism, the Doctrine of the Apostles, the Fellowship of the Apostles, the Breaking of the Bread, and the Prayers—in other words, the New Birth, the Orthodox Faith, the Apostolic Ministry, the Eucharist, and the " Divine Liturgy " (as Early Christians used often to call the Church's most solemn prayers).

Now, if the Anglican Church be a true and pure branch of the Catholic Church, it must be found to possess all these things, and if any of them have ever, even for a short time, been lost or impaired, they must have been lawfully restored. I cannot see that any one of these things was ever lacking in the Christianity of England, though at times some of them have been somewhat *clogged* in their use and operation. But I dwell at length on the Apostolic Fellowship, which inheres in the Catholic Episcopate, because it, and it alone, has the power to remedy all defects; or, as St. Paul said to the first Bishop of Crete, to "set in order the things which are wanting."[1]

No reader is asked to take for granted the conclusions to which this course of argument may ultimately lead; but only to follow candidly and without prejudice the process of interrogating the Bible and history to find the essentials of Catholicity, and then to see whether the An-

---

1. In this connection the eloquent words of the late Bishop of Ohio are certainly apropos: "Deprive the Church of her ministry, and all her other agencies of good, except under a special Providence, must wither away; then zeal for the truth languishes and dies, because the constituted channel of its nourishment is cut off; agents and efforts of religious usefulness cease, because the voice of those whom God has ordained to summon and animate them to duty is not heard; * * * the Bible is not sought for, because the commissioned expounders and enforcers of its truths are not; Christianity, with all her lovely retinue of virtues and benefits, withdraws from the abodes of men, because her cause is not pleaded; her solemn feasts are not celebrated: her *altars* are not honored; her law is not published; her blessings are not proclaimed. Thus the day is turned into night, and the garden of the Lord into a wilderness and solitary place. Nothing, in such a condition, could bring back the sun and the rain and the dew—nothing restore Christianity, with * * * the Bible, the Sanctuary, the daily oblation, and all that is precious in heavenly grace, but the reinstatement of that ministry of reconciliation, by which, in the beginning of the Gospel, the world was so rapidly and wonderfully planted with its blessings.

"If any ask, why such connection; it is enough at present to answer—'*So is the will of God*.' It might have been otherwise. But He who ordained that the earth should have no day but by the shining of the sun, hath alike ordained that the world shall have no spiritual light but by reflection from His Church, and His Church no power of reflection but by the agency of her ministry, to which is committed the word of reconciliation, and which, like the mystic lamps of the Tabernacle, He hath set up in the midst of the sanctuary."—The Rt. Rev. Dr. McIlvaine, The Christian Ministry, p. 15.

glican Church has retained them. If we find that she has not, and that some other religious body has—be it the Tridentine Church or the Salvation Army—then let us yield gracefully, and say with the converted Epicurean:

> "Nunc retrorsum
> Vela dare atque iterare cursus,
> Cogor relictos."

Thus far we have seen that the Anglican Church has always continued steadfastly in the primitive theory and practice of Holy Baptism, and in the Orthodox Catholic Faith. Has she also kept fellowship with the Apostles through the Apostolic ministry which Christ ordained? I answer: Our Mother Church, from her infancy among the Britons to this day, has never for one hour known what it is to be without her Catholic Episcopate.

The actual date of the introduction of Christianity into Britain has no bearing on the authority of our Church. The oldest Church is that of Jerusalem, followed by the various dioceses and provinces of the East. The Church in Rome was for a long time only an Oriental mission, working among the Greeks and Jews of the Metropolis. It was in Greek that St. Paul wrote his letter to the Roman Christians, and Greek was for two centuries the official and liturgical language of the Church in Rome. No one dreamed of such a thing as that the struggling community of Christians in Rome was in any sense the Mother and Mistress of all Christendom. There is, moreover, strong ground for believing that Christianity was introduced into Britain as early, if not earlier than into Rome. Indeed, there is some evidence that the Church got a foothold in Britain five years before it was planted in Rome; so that Rome, instead of being our Mother, would really be only a *younger* sister, and—more's the pity!—not a very loving one at that. As Hore says (in his "Eighteen Centuries of the Church in England," p. 191): "It has been asserted that the foundation of the British Church was prior in date to that of the Roman: Cf. Crackenthorp, *Def. Eccl. Angl.*, p. 23. '*De Brittannica Ecclesia nostra liquidum est fuisse illam aliquot ante Romanam annis fundatam.* * * * *Disce Romanam ecclesiam, Britannicæ nostræ non matrem sed sororem, atque sororem* INTEGRO QUINQUENNIO MINOREM.'"[2]

Linus, whom St. Paul ordained as the first Bishop of Rome, was a Briton, and is with good reason believed to have been converted to Christianity in Britain before ever he came to Rome. His father, Caractacus, a petty British king, and his grandfather, Bran, a Druid, were carried to Rome, together with his sister, Claudia,[3] and lived in the imperial palace. St. Paul says (Phil., iv., 22): "All the saints salute you, chiefly those that are of Cæsar's household;" and again (II. Tim., iv., 21): "Eubulus greeteth thee, and Pudens, and *Linus*, and Claudia." For the whole story about these royal British Christians and their relation to St. Paul, see Hore's Eighteen Centuries, and Jenning's *Ecclesia Anglicana*.

The evidence that St. Paul, after his journey into Spain (See Rom., xv., 24 and 28), made a brief visit to Britain,

---

2. As to our British Church, it is clear that it was founded some years before the Roman. * * * Learn, then, that the Roman Church is not the Mother of our British Church, but the sister, and that, too, a sister *fully five years younger*.

3. Clement, the third Bishop of Rome, speaks of "most holy Linus, the brother of Claudia."

although not regarded conclusive by some scholars, is pretty strong, and at least proves the great antiquity of the British Church.

Gildas, the first Briton whose writings are extant (sixth century) says that Christianity dawned on Britain as early as A. D. 61.

Fortunatus, a poet of the sixth century, says St. Paul "passed over the ocean to Britain." Theodoret (b. 386, Bishop of Cyprus 410) says that "St. Paul, at the time of his journey into Spain, brought salvation to the islands lying in the ocean;" that he went to Spain, and thence carried the Gospel to other nations; and he expressly states that some of the *Apostles* preached to the *Britons*. He says: "Our fishermen and publicans, and *he who was a tent-maker*, carried the evangelical precepts to all nations; not only to those who lived under the Roman jurisdiction, but also to the Scythians and the Huns; besides to the Indians, *Britons*, and Germans."

St. Jerome (b. about 340) says that St. Paul went from one ocean to another, that he preached the Gospel in the western parts, *as far as the earth itself.* Britain was regarded as the extremity of the western world.

Eusebius (b. about 290) says that some of the *Apostles* crossed the ocean to those islands which are called *British*.

Origen, who flourished A. D. 197, says: "The power of the Saviour reached as far as Britain."

Tertullian (b. about 135) says: "There are places in Britain inaccessible to Roman arms, which are subdued to Christ."

Justin Martyr (b. about 100) says that Christianity existed in every country known to the Romans.

And St. Clement, the third Bishop of Rome, the "fellow-laborer" of St. Paul, says that St. Paul preached the Gospel to "the *utmost bounds of the west.*"

"There can be," says Hore, "no reasonable ground for doubting that the British Church was not only of very ancient, but also of Apostolic foundation. A Roman Catholic writer, not generally very favorable to the Anglican Church, whose testimony on that account is the more valuable, readily admits this: 'It is probable,' he says, 'that Christianity was disseminated over parts of England during the Apostolic age. *This was universally believed by our ancestors.* * * * The documents on which the history of the first conversion of England depends, approach much nearer than those of the ancient Romans to *historical certitude.*'" [4]

The old legends about St. James and Joseph of Arimathea going to Glastonbury, cannot be looked upon as historical, but are valuable as showing the general belief that Christianity was on British soil in the first century; and there is good reason to believe that the church in Glastonbury was the first building ever *erected* for *Christian* worship.

While much obscurity hangs over the early history of our Church in Britain, there can be no doubt that it was very ancient, that it was independent of *foreign control,* that it received help from Gaul in the second century; and as Gaul received its Christianity from *Ephesus* and not from Italy, the British Church was very *Oriental* in its ways, and on that account had, and has to this day, several

---

[4]. Butler's Book of the Church, quoted in Hore's Eighteen Centuries, pp. 8-9.

points of difference from the Western Churches which were more intimately associated with Italy.

If, as we are whirled across the country, we look out of the car window every few minutes, and each time see the landscape covered thick with snow, we feel sure that the snow has fallen all along the line. So, from the few glimpses that we get of the early British Church, we see that it was *Episcopal*, and are *sure* that in the brief intervals between these glimpses, the Apostolic Ministry ever spread the white vestments of its divine and gracious office over the rugged surface of that ancient Church.

After the Diocletian persecution, A. D. 303, in which our Proto-martyr, St. Alban, suffered for the truth, many Roman soldiers stationed in Britain, became interested in Christianity, and at least learned to respect it—among whom was the Military Governor, Constantius, the father of the Emperor Constantine. Constantine, thanks to his residence in Britain, was favorable to the religion of Christ, and became the first *Christian* Emperor. In the year 314 he summoned a Council of Bishops at Arles, and among those who were present and signed the decrees of the Council, were three Bishops from our own Church, accompanied by a Priest and a Deacon. They were *Restitutus, Bishop of London, Eborius, Bishop of York*, and *Adelphius*, who was Bishop probably of *Caerleon on Usk* (the modern St. Davids, of which, at this writing, the Right Rev. Dr. Jones is Bishop).

It is uncertain, but, on the whole, highly probable that British Bishops were present at the General Council of Nicæa, A. D. 325. At all events, they were *invited*, and they accepted the doctrinal decrees of the Council. Bishop Restitutus and probably some other Bishops attended the Council of Sardica, A. D. 347. And at the unfortunate Council of Rimine, a number of British Bishops were present, and so independent were they that, as is recorded by Sulpicius Severus, they thought it *unbecoming that Britons* should accept the generous offer of the Emperor to defray their expenses from the public treasury, with the exception of three who were in straitened circumstances. *"Britannis indecens visum est; repudiatis fiscalibus, propriis sumptibus vivere voluerunt."* [5]

Thus our Mother Church, with the Sacrament of Holy Baptism, with the Orthodox Faith, with the Apostolic Ministry of Bishops,[6] Priests, and Deacons—and of course also with the Holy Eucharist and a truly Catholic Liturgy —flourished until, in the fifth and sixth centuries, the Pagan Saxons invaded the Island and drove the native Christians from the Eastern parts to the hill country of the West, chiefly Wales and Cornwall. Theon, the Bishop of London, and Thadioc, the Bishop of York, held their Sees manfully till A. D. 587; and then, when their flocks were scattered and a host of heathen wolves were in the fold, " when London sacrificed to Diana, and Westminster to Apollo," they also fled and followed their brethren to Wales, where their Church still lives.

---

5. "To Britons it seemed unbecoming [to have their expenses paid], so, declining the public bounty, they preferred to live at their own expense."

6. See Haddan and Stubb's " Councils and Ecclesiastical Documents " (Vol. I., pp. 3–21).

CHAPTER XV.

ANGLO-CATHOLICISM ; OR, THE MAKING AND ESTABLISHING
OF THE PRESENT NATIONAL CHURCH OF ENGLAND.

"It is of paramount importance to remember the *organic identity* of the Church of England before and after the Reformation."—*Bishop Forbes.*

FROM the year 587, when the Archbishops of London and York fled to Wales, to the year 597, when Augustine, the Apostle of the Anglo-Saxons, first set foot in Canterbury, Christianity was almost totally extinct in England proper. In Wales, Cumberland, and Cornwall, however, our dear old Church was still strong, and numbered more bishops and clergy than she does to-day in those same parts. Moreover, her daughter,[1] the Church of Ireland, and her grand-daughter,[2] the Church of Scotland, were in

---

1. Ireland was converted mainly by St. Patrick, a native of North Britain, the son of a clergyman, ordained by French Bishops, A. D. 441. He fixed his See at Armagh, which is to this day the Primal See of the Irish Church. He also ordained the first Bishop of the Isle of Man. He was on intimate terms with the Bishop of Rome; but was as free from all Romish error as his successor, the present Archbishop of Armagh. The Bishop of Rome found it harder to usurp dominion over the Irish Church than any other in Western Europe, and was not even allowed to confer the "pall" on any Irish Archbishop till A. D. 1151.

2. Scotland was mainly converted by an *Irish* missionary, St. Columba, in A. D. 565, though British missionaries had preached the Gospel in the South of Scotland more than a century before, especially St. Ninian, who also aided in evangelizing Ireland. "The first legate (from Rome) that ever appeared in Scotland was John of Crema, in the year 1125, before which time there is no trace to be met with of any *Papal authority* in this country."—C. I. Lyon, quoted in Coit's "Early Hist. Christianity in Eng.," p. 157.

full and loving communion with their British Mother. These three Churches of the Celtic race, Catholic, independent,[3] full of missionary spirit, knew nothing even of that *mild form* of Latin tyranny and Roman centralization which were then to be found in Western Europe. As the learned jurist, Blackstone, puts it : " The British Church, by whomsoever planted, was a stranger to the Bishop of Rome, and all his pretended authority." (Com. iv., 8.)

Ethelbert, King of Kent, the foremost of the Saxon Kings, had married a Christian princess, Bertha, a daughter of the King of Paris. She brought with her a Gallic bishop (Luidhard, the Bishop of Senlis) and staff of clergy who maintained Christian worship in an old British church for some twenty-five years before the arrival of Augustine. She was thus the *first* missionary to the Saxons, and but for her, Augustine's mission would have been of very doubtful success. Gregory himself, the Bishop of Rome, who sent Augustine to England, said that " next to God, England was indebted to *her* for its conversion." The Venerable Bede declares that the Saxon King had heard of Christianity from his wife before the coming of Augustine ; and William of Malmsbury testifies that the exemplary life of Bishop Luidhard, the Queen's chaplain, had silently allured the King's heart to the knowledge of Christ.

I have no wish to disparage the good work done by Augustine or any other Italian missionaries in converting the Anglo-Saxons to the religion of Christ. But observe : In the first place, had *they* done *all* the work, it would

---

3. Dr. Lingard (Romanist) says of the Britons: "The *independence* of their Church was the chief object of their solicitude."

not have made the *English* Church a part of the *Italian* Church, much less have committed it in advance to doctrines and practices which were then undreamed of even in Rome itself. The distinctive Romish errors were then unknown. Mariolatry was not yet in its infancy; no one believed in the "Immaculate Conception" or had ever heard of it; the Sacrament of the Altar was administered in *both* kinds; Transubstantiation was not taught; and although political considerations made the Bishop of Rome very powerful and much respected, yet so far from his having any *supremacy*, there was at that time far more danger that a sort of "papacy" or universal supremacy would be attached to the Bishops of *Constantinople*, one of whom, the Patriarch John, had just then assumed the title of *Universal Bishop,* which is still retained by his successors. Gregory, however, the Bishop of Rome, begged the other Patriarchs (viz., the Bishops of Alexandria, Antioch and Jerusalem) not to allow such a title to the Patriarch of Constantinople; nor would he allow himself to be called by such a "proud, superstitious, profane and *blasphemous* name" "contrary to the *Gospel* and the *Canons.*" "Whoever," says he, "calls himself a Universal priest, or desires to be so called is the *forerunner* of *Anti-Christ.*" The Patriarch of Alexandria replied that he had given up calling John by that title, "as you have commanded me" (*sicut jussistis*), and in his letter he addressed Gregory himself as "Universal Pope;" whereupon, with true Catholic humility, Gregory wrote again: "I beg that you will not speak of my commanding, since I know who I am and who you are. *In dignity you are my brother*, in character my father. * * * I pray your most sweet holiness to address me no more with the proud appellation of 'Universal Pope,' since that which is given to another beyond what reason requires, is subtracted from yourself. If you style me Universal Pope, you deny that you are at all that which you own me to be universally.[4] Away with words which puff up vanity and wound charity." In his letter to John he declares *Christ* to be the "Head of the Universal Church."

How absurd, therefore, is the idea that Gregory and Augustine sought to commit the Saxons to anything resembling Modern Romanism. When Augustine tried to bring the British Bishops—seven of whom he met under the "Oak" of Herefordshire—to acknowledge the Bishop of Rome, it was not as being "the Pope" in the *modern* sense of that perverted title (which was common to *all* Bishops for 850 years),[5] but as having a certain primacy of honor, or at the most only a metropolitical jurisdiction which Augustine wished to extend as far as possible. Indeed, as late as 1100, Pascal II. claimed to be Head of the Church only within the bounds of *Europe*.

Gregory, however, was a strange compound; as one has said, "He was the last of Rome's good Bishops, and the first of its bad ones." While he disclaimed any right to supremacy, he nevertheless did much to build up the Roman power in Spain and Gaul; and also, in direct violation of the Canons of the General Councils which he had

---

4. The Bishop of Alexandria was then and is to this day officially styled, "The Pope and Patriarch of the Great City of Alexandria," etc. Pope (Latin *Papa*) means only *Father*, and corresponds exactly to our Episcopal title, "Father in God."

5. Indeed, it was as late as A. D. 1070, that Hildebrand, the Bishop of Rome, decreed that he alone should be called *Pope*. See Coit's Earl. Hist. Christianity in Eng., p. 170, note.

sworn to maintain, he presumed to give Augustine authority over the British Bishops. They, of course, repelled his interference with courteous dignity and catholic authority.

Augustine was ordained Bishop by Aetherius, the Bishop of Lyons (who derived his orders through Pothinus from St. John) and by Virgilius, the Bishop of Arles (who derived his through Trophinus from St. Paul), and was constituted Archbishop of Canterbury. Gregory conferred on him the *pall*, a white woolen scarf with purple crosses, which was at that time only a mark of *favor*, conferred with the consent of the Emperor, and *not*, as it afterwards became, a badge of submission to Rome.

But whatever were the claims, admissible and inadmissible, which Gregory might have made to a primacy over the Christianity of the British Isles, provided he had been the author of it, we must remember that only *a small part* of the work of planting Christianity there was done by the Italian Church. Wales, Cornwall, and Cumberland, with many Bishops and thousands of clergymen, were not indebted to Rome; Ireland and Scotland were converted by Celtic missionaries, *and so was the larger part of England proper;* I mean the Anglo-Saxons. All that Augustine and other Italian missionaries did was to sow the seed in Kent, which was already prepared for it by Queen Bertha and Bishop Luidhard (and even in this a large share of the work was done by the Gallic missionaries who accompanied Augustine as *interpreters*), and in Wessex, and indirectly also in East Anglia. All the rest of England was converted by Celtic missionaries, indirectly from Wales, and directly from Ireland and Scotland, with a little help from France.

One gift, however, the Roman missionaries gave to England, and that was the genius of thorough organization, centering in the See of Canterbury. Augustine was consecrated Archbishop of Canterbury in 597. After him came five Archbishops who ruled only a part of the Saxon Christians, as the larger portion of them were of the Celtic obedience.

Meantime, the two schools of Christians in the Heptarchy were being drawn nearer together, and at length agreed to unite under one Archbishop. Accordingly they received Theodore, a Greek, born in the city of Tarsus, the birthplace of St. Paul. Under him the English Church was welded into one compact organism, long before England was a nation, or had any central government.

Theodore, as being a member of the Greek Church, was acceptable to the British party, who prided themselves on their Oriental Origin ; and as having been ordained by the Bishop of Rome, was acceptable to the Italian party. The magnitude and beneficence of his work cannot be too highly appreciated. He held the first general Synod of the *Saxon*[6] Church at Hertford, A. D. 673 ; he subdivided dioceses ; he was instrumental in introducing the Greek parochial system with resident clergy in each parish ; he introduced ten very important canons of Ancient Councils, which he had brought with him from the East ; he arranged to a large extent the financial system of the English Church ; in fact, he established a united Church in England, pure, Catholic, independent — *the same* which God has preserved through all the vicissitudes of the ages

---

6. Before the Saxon Invasion there had been at least twelve such Synods, under the British Archbishops of London, of whom there were fifteen.

to this day; a Church which was *never established by the State*, or by any act of Parliament, *for it antedates the State itself by a hundred and fifty years* ;[7] and can more properly be said to have *established the State*, than to have been *established by the State*. Archdeacon Churton has said of Theodore : " He found the Church divided, and left it united ; he found it a missionary Church scarcely fixed in more than two principal provinces ; he left it what it will ever be, while the country remains in happiness and freedom, the Established Church of England."

In 874, the Welsh Church acknowledged the Archbishop of Canterbury, and by the year 1200 had become fully united with the English Church, bringing in the line of Apostolic Succession of the old British Bishops, and those of Gaul, and of *Jerusalem*, the See of St. James, which the second General Council called "The Mother of All Churches."

---

7. "The unity of the Church in England was the pattern of the unity of the state; the cohesion of the Church was for ages the substitute for the cohesion which the divided nation was otherwise unable to realize. * * * It was to an extraordinary degree a national Church; national in its comprehensiveness as well as in its exclusiveness. Englishmen were in their lay aspects Mercians or West Saxons; only in their ecclesiastical relations could they feel themselves fellow-countrymen and fellow-subjects."—Stubb's Constitutional History, Vol. I., Chap. viii., "The Anglo-Saxon Church."

CHAPTER XVI.

THE ENGLISH CHURCH NEVER THE ROMAN CHURCH.

"The only logical basis of Anglicanism is the maintenance of the IDENTITY."
—*Bishop Forbes.*

IT is a great mistake to suppose that, before the Reformation, the Church in England was the *Roman* Church, and after the Reformation the *English* Church. It was always the same English Church from the time England received Christianity, and long before the English were a nation. Its legal name was the English Church—*Ecclesia Anglicana*—and neither its name nor its organization, nor the essentials of its faith and worship, have ever been changed. In the reign of King Alfred, the Church of England leased a piece of property to the Crown for 999 years. A few years ago the term of the lease expired, and the property reverted to the present Church of England as being the identical corporation which leased the land a millennium before.

But all this is not to deny that during the Middle Ages, the English Church became corrupt in many ways; and by a series of successful encroachments on the part of the Bishop of Rome, backed by the "Forged Decretals," by the superstition of the times, and by the vices of some of the kings, was gradually brought, to a considerable [1] extent, under the yoke of Italy. Thus a reformation became necessary in order to free and purify the English Church. Let me illustrate :

Napoleon the Great extended his imperial usurpation over the kingdom of Prussia ; but Prussia was still Prussia, and retained her own government and royal succession. By and by Prussia freed herself from Napoleon's tyranny. Did that make her a new nation ? Was she not the same old kingdom that she was before ? Or, to bring the matter nearer home, here in North America are two sister Churches, the Church in the United States, and

---

1. Says the Rev. Wm. A. Rich, in "The Examination Examined:" "In England, 'from before King John'—say, from the Norman Conquest—'to the Reformation,' papal encroachments by degrees reached the point where they became intolerable. But never at any time did the papal sway in Britain attain such proportions that we can rightly speak of it as *absolute*.

Plainly it was not absolute when the Norman William laid down the law that no papal legate should set foot on English soil without the royal permission.‡

Nor when his son William Rufus (as the ancient chronicler, Matthew Paris, relates) declared that no Bishop or Archbishop of the English Church was subject to the Pope.§

Nor when the statute *De Asportatis Religiosorum* (35 Edw. I,) was enacted, forbidding that the revenues of monasteries and other religious houses, held by papal ecclesiastics, should be carried out of the kingdom.‖

Nor when by the statutes of Provisors (25 and 38 Edw. III., 13 Rich. II., and 2 Henry IV.) it was ordered that any English ecclesiastic obtaining from the Pope a nomination to any benefice, abbey, or priory in the realm of England, shall be outlawed. 'And any man may do with him as with an enemy of our Sovereign Lord the King and his realm.'¶

Nor when the celebrated statutes of Præmunire were enacted (27 Edw. III., and 16 Rich. II.), restraining all British subjects from appealing to the Papal authority or attempting to act under it.**

Nor when the Parliament of 1399 declared that "in all time past the crown and realm of England had been so free that neither Pope nor any other outside the realm had a right to meddle therewith."††

‡ Stubbs' Constitutional History, I., p. 310.
§ Quoted in Wordsworth's "Theoph. Ang.," p. 162.
‖ Gibson's Codex, p. 1222. ¶ Gibson's Codex, pp. 74, 81, 83 and 87.
** Gibson's Codex, pp. 80, 86. †† Stubbs, iii., 293.

the Church in Canada. Suppose our "Presiding Bishop" should, by a system of shrewd and unscrupulous aggression—such as bribing the Governors of Canada, and circulating skillfully forged documents which deceived many of the Canadians into believing that our Presiding Bishop really had an ancient and divine right to the obedience of all Canadians—usurp dominion over the Canadian Church. Suppose the Canadian Church was thus forced, against her own interests and honor, to submit to this foreign interference, but all the while kept up a *protest*, maintained her old *name*, and her own *prayer book*, and her own *succession* of bishops, and her own diocesan and Provincial Synods, would she really cease to be the same old Church of Canada? And if after a time she should find out that she had been originally *independent*, and so should simply decide that the great American Bishop had no just authority over her, and should find herself strong enough to resist his interference, would that make her a new or different Church? Would it sever her historic continuity? Would it break her fellowship with the Apostles? Not at all. Now, this was precisely the case of our own Church, as she was gradually brought under the dominion of the Bishop of Rome—struggling manfully the while against his usurpation, and at last throwing it off. Surely there was no making of a new Church. If a man is enslaved and escapes from bondage, he is the *same* man; if he is taken sick and recovers, he is the *same* person; if a chariot gets covered with mud, and is washed, it is the *same* chariot.

In the Arabian tale, "Sinbad the Sailor," after his fifth voyage, was living on an island, when a monster, called the "Old Man of the Sea," dropped down upon his shoulders, and rode poor Sinbad almost to death. By and by Sinbad made the Old Man drunk with wine, and, throwing him off, was free again. Sinbad the Sailor was Sinbad the Sailor before the Old Man of the Sea mounted him; he was Sinbad the Sailor while the Old Man of the Sea was on his back; and he was the same Sinbad the Sailor after he had cast him off. Our Church, in like manner, was on an Island. The *Old Man of the Papal See* [forgive the *paronomasia*] jumped upon our Church and rode it like a beast of burden. Like Sinbad, we threw him off; we bathed and refreshed ourselves; but (thank God) we remained the same old Catholic and Apostolic Church, without losing our Orthodox Faith, our Apostolic Succession and Fellowship, our historic continuity, our lawful Sacraments and Worship, or our divine jurisdiction and authority.

Until the Norman Conquest (A. D. 1066), the Bishop of Rome had very little authority over the English Church. In the seventh century, Wilfrid, the Archbishop of York, was the first English Churchman to appeal to Rome. The Roman Bishop sustained him, and pronounced eternal anathemas on all who should refuse to abide by his decision. But he was dealing with *Englishmen*, not with the effeminate races of Southern Europe. The King of Wessex convened a synod which ruled that Wilfrid's *appeal to Rome* was a *public offense*, and cast him into prison. At the same time, the Archbishop of Canterbury refused to notice a summons from the Bishop of Rome to attend a council.

After Wilfrid had been set at liberty, and allowed to

return to his diocese, through the kindly mediation of the Bishop of London, he again appealed to Rome on the same question—the division of his diocese. For this second offense against the authority of the English Church he was deposed and excommunicated, and the sentence of the Bishop of Rome was set at naught.

When St. Cuthbert was Archbishop of Canterbury, his friend Winfrid ("St. Boniface"), an Englishman who had converted a large part of Germany, advised him to bring the English Church under the authority of Rome, as he claimed he had done with the Church in Germany.

In the first place, this proves that the Church was *not* already in submission to Rome; and, in the second place, when St. Cuthbert—pleased with the idea—called a council of the English Church, at Clovesho, A. D. 747, and proposed, as an entering wedge, that difficult cases in the English ecclesiastical courts should be referred to Rome, "the Council refused to compromise the dignity of the Church, and the Archbishop was declared the Supreme head."

In the eighth century, when the great controversy about "image worship" was agitating the whole Church, the Bishop of Rome declared in favor of the *semi-idolatry;* but the English, so far from owning his supremacy, stood out boldly against his decree, and, in company with the Gallican Church, sided with the Greeks.

The Bishop of Rome, of course, as being the foremost Prelate and the only Patriarch in the West, was justly respected for his office, and accorded a primacy of honor. But Roman ambition was leading to the gradual submission and subjugation of the leading provinces and dioceses of Europe ; and during the unhappy reign of Offa—the most powerful of the Saxon Kings—the Bishop of Rome, like the camel in the fable, got his front feet within the door of the English Church. Offa was a very cruel and licentious king, and being at variance with the Archbishop, he determined to elevate the diocese of Lichfield into an archbishopric in his own kingdom. Accordingly, by offering the Bishop of Rome a vast *bribe*, which he was base enough to accept, he succeeded in getting the "pall" for the Bishop of Lichfield (which, however, remained an archdiocese for only fifteen years). In bestowing the pall, the Bishop of Rome made the first notable aggression on the liberties of the English Church. He insisted that Offa should receive two Roman legates, and allow them, in spite of the protest of the Primate, to hold a council in England. It was a small thing in itself, but a *bad precedent*.

The second aggression was brought about in this way : Offa, toward the end of his life, to atone, forsooth, for his grievous crimes, established a tax of one penny a year on every family in his kingdom, to be sent to Rome. This was the beginning of "Peter's Pence" (A. D. 855).

The part played by that wicked King Henry VIII. in freeing the Church of England from Roman tyranny, is thus well offset by the fact that an equally wicked king was the means of opening the way for that tyranny seven hundred years before.

Meantime, the "False Decretals," which were forged about A. D. 836, claiming that Christ had constituted Rome the Head of the Church, etc., were doing their pestilent work throughout Europe, and opening the way for further encroachments on the divine liberties of the Anglo-Catholic Church.

All scholars, Roman and Protestant, now admit that these decretals were only a "clumsy forgery." Doctor Fulton, in a thoughtful and suggestive note, says of them: "They might well be called the most prodigious disgrace of Christian literature, of which a history, and a complete translation, would be the most crushing reply to the modern Papal pretensions."[2]

Just before the Norman Conquest, two men, Robert and Stigand, claimed the Archbishopric of Canterbury. Robert, like Wilfrid four hundred years before, appealed to Rome, being the second English Bishop to do so. The Bishop of Rome sustained him, but the English Church scorned the foreign prelate's interference, and Stigand remained Archbishop.

It is not strange that the Bishop of Rome favored William of Normandy in his conquest of England, for it seemed sure to bring the English Church under Roman dominion. Stigand and many of the Saxon bishops were removed by William and Normans put in their places. Lanfranc was made Archbishop of Canterbury; and was, by the way, the first English bishop to teach the doctrine of Transubstantiation. Both William and Lanfranc, however, resisted Rome in many ways. William was the only king in Europe who dared stand out against Gregory VII., the most powerful of all Roman bishops. He refused to do fealty for his kingdom; and he allowed the payment of "Peter's Pence" only as a voluntary *alms*, not

---

2. Am. Ch. Review, Jan., 1885, p. 293.

as a right. When Gregory summoned all the English bishops to a Council, and threatened William with the "Wrath of St. Peter" unless they came, not a single bishop obeyed the summons. When he declared all the *married* clergy of the English Church excommunicated, unless they put away their wives, the English Church held a Council, A. D. 1076, and refused to allow the new regulation except in the case of the cathedral and collegiate clergy, who were required to put away their wives.[3] When the Bishop of Rome summoned Archbishop Lanfranc to Italy, on the penalty of deposition and "severance from the grace of St. Peter," if he did not arrive within four months, Lanfranc took no notice of the threat, and nothing was done. Rome's power, though still increasing, was far from complete. Urban II., the Bishop of Rome, A. D. 1100, declared that the Archbishop of Canterbury ought to be treated as an *equal*, and called him "the *Pope* and Patriarch of another world."

The Council of Clarendon, A. D. 1164, forbade all appeals to Rome without the King's consent. Surely every one is familiar with the bold anti-Roman stand taken by Rich, the Archbishop of Canterbury, 1234 ; by Grostete, the Bishop of Lincoln, 1235 ; and by Sewell, the Archbishop of York, 1265, against whom Rome fulminated a vain and unheeded excommunication.

Italian aggression reached its climax in the reign of King John (1199-1216), when John placed the whole

---

3. English clergy (except the monastic orders) were generally married up to A. D. 1102. After that, though prohibited by law, it was still common, provided they paid a special tax to the king. They were never required to take a *vow* of celibacy. See Hore's Eighteen Centuries, p. 136; and Jenning's *Eccl. Ang.*, pp. 76-7. The civil law forbidding the marriage of the clergy was not repealed till long after the Reformation, in the reign of James I.

realm at the feet of the Bishop of Rome, which, of course, he had no right to do. The whole country rose against him, clergy, barons, people, calling themselves "The Army of God and the Church." "It was," says Hore, "the army not only of the barons against the King, but of the Church against the Pope." On that memorable 15th of June, 1215, they forced the King to sign *Magna Charta*, which was the work of Stephen Langdon, the Archbishop of Canterbury, and the first article of which declares: "THE CHURCH OF ENGLAND shall be free, and have her rights entire and her liberties uninjured."[4] The Bishop of Rome was, of course, in a fury. He swore: "By St. Peter, this outrage shall not go unpunished;" declared the charter null and void; and commanded the Archbishop to excommunicate the barons—which, however, the patriotic Churchman refused to do. The Roman usurper had stretched his power too far; it snapped; the charter remained; the Archbishop required the new King, Henry III., to sign it; it has since been ratified thirty-two times, and, despite its Roman nullification, has ever since been a part of the fundamental law of England.

Two reforms were now necessary:

(a) To free the English *State* from the Roman claim of sovereignty; and

(b) To free the English *Church* from the Roman claim of supremacy.

The freeing of the State was accomplished in 1365, when the king, clergy, lords, and commons declared that John had no right to make England a fief of Rome, and forbade the payment of Peter's pence.

---

4. "In primis * * * quod Anglicana Ecclesia libera sit, et habeat jura sua integra, et libertates suas illaesas."

The freeing of the English Church was a long and hard process. Various laws had from time to time been enacted against the Roman usurpation; and in 1351, the "Statute of Provisors" (followed by the statutes of "Præmunire," in 1353, 1365, and 1393), left scarce a vestige of the Roman Bishop's power in our Church. The *legal* freeing of our Church by these famous statutes of the fourteenth century is not sufficiently appreciated. By them the Bishop of Rome was forbidden to appoint to any bishopric or other Church dignity in England. If he did so, the benefice was declared vacant, and the right of nomination lapsed to the king. These statutes also prohibited carrying any suits to the Roman court; and forbade, under penalty of confiscation of property and perpetual imprisonment, any one to procure from Rome, or elsewhere outside of England, any appointments, bulls, excommunications, or the like.

Thus, *in theory*, the Roman yoke was cast off, but practically two things were needed in order to carry out the theory: First, the removal of the *popular superstition* that, after all, the Bishop of Rome had a sort of divine right over all churches; and, secondly, a king bold enough and strong enough to break with the Triple Tyrant, and say:

"That no Italian priest shall tithe or toll in our dominions."

As to the first, the illusion was dispelled, the prestige of Rome broken, by the vices and quarrels of the Bishops of Rome; by the removal of the Roman Court to Avignon, where for seventy years the Bishops of Rome were mere puppets of the French kings; and by the fifty years of "rival popes," cursing and excommunicating each other. The Council of Pisa (1409) deposed and excommunicated both of them, and elected a third bishop of Rome. The Council of Constance (1415) deposed the wicked John XXII., and the Council of Basle (1431) deposed Eugenius IV. These "Reforming Councils," as they are called, asserted the superiority of a Council to the Bishop of Rome. For a while it looked as if the whole Western Church might be reformed on Anglican principles. All Europe clamored for a reformation. Over 250 books were written by Western Ecclesiastics pleading for the correction of Roman abuses.

The fall of Constantinople (1453) sent a host of learned Greek Churchmen to the West, and opened the eyes of English Churchmen to the fact that the Greek Church got on well enough, as it had from the beginning, without submitting to the Roman Pontiff; while the revival of Greek learning opened patristic treasures long forgotten, and the increased study of Holy Scripture was bearing fruit in a widespread longing for light and liberty.

It was only needed that a bold king should take the first step.[5] In the providence of God Who maketh even the wrath of man to praise Him, Henry VIII. was the man for the hour.

As to Henry's character, we need not trouble ourselves. It was about as bad as it could be, while his confiscations of our Church property make him the greatest *Church-*

---

5. "If any man will look down along the line of early English history, he will see a standing contest between the rulers of this land and the Bishops of Rome. The Crown and Church of England, with a steady opposition, resisted the entrance and encroachment of the secularized ecclesiastical power of the Pope in England. The last rejection of it was no more than a successful effort after many a failure in struggles of the like kind."—*Manning* "*On the Unity of the Church.*"

robber that ever lived. God, however, used him like Cyrus of old.

After the King's quarrel with the Bishop of Rome, Parliament and Convocation passed stringent laws against Roman interference. The *experimentum crucis* was made, the " Gordian Knot " was cut in June, 1534, when the following resolution was submitted to the bishops of both provinces in Convocation assembled : *"Resolved that the Bishop of Rome has no greater jurisdiction conferred on him by God, in this kingdom, than any other foreign bishop."* [6]

All the bishops, with the single exception of Fisher, Bishop of Rochester, assented to the proposition ; the clergy and the Universities of Oxford and Cambridge agreed with the bishops, and the King and Parliament gave the governmental sanction. Thus our Mother Church reasserted her ancient Catholic independence. The English bishops in taking their oath of office were no longer allowed to speak of the Bishop of Rome as "the Pope," but simply as "the Bishop of Rome," and " fellow brother," —"as the old manner of the most ancient bishops hath been." [7]

All that was done in the way of reform, however, under Henry VIII., and his son Edward VI., was undone under Queen Mary, 1553 to 1558. Mary was a sincere and bigoted Romanist, and succeeded in bringing Parliament and Convocation to rescind the recent acts against the supremacy of the Bishop of Rome, to restore the Latin language, etc.

---

6. ' Quod Romanus Episcopus non habet majorem jurisdictionem sibi a Deo collatam in hoc regno quam aliusquivis externus Episcopus."—*Journal of Convocation.*

7. Heart's Eccl. Recs. quoted in Colts " Early Hist.," p. 171.

This *second* subjugation of the English Church to Rome, achieved in a few weeks and lasting less than five years, was a sort of miniature reproduction of the previous usurpation which extended over several centuries. It was equally unjust, and was as justly abolished.

Mary illegally removed and put to death a number of the bishops, and in fact burned to the stake some 280 persons for their religious opinions. Still nothing was done to break the continuity of the English Church. Pole, a cousin of the Queen, was elected Archbishop of Canterbury, but would not be consecrated while his predecessor in office, the reforming Archbishop, was alive. The day after Cranmer's execution, Pole was consecrated by several English bishops.

When Elizabeth came to the throne, she as a good Catholic, used all her influence to save the English Church, on the one hand, from being permanently enslaved to Rome, and on the other, from losing any of the essentials of true Catholicity. We have already seen that our Church at the Reformation invented no new doctrines, but merely retained the three Creeds, the Bible and the general beliefs of the Early Church. Did she also at this crisis in her history, keep the *Apostolic Succession,* and her lawful *jurisdiction?* In other words: Is the Anglo-Catholic Church to-day (a) a *Protestant Sect?* (having neither ministry nor jurisdiction), or (b) a *schism?* (having the ministry but no jurisdiction), or (c) A CATHOLIC CHURCH — having not only the Faith, Sacraments, and worship, but also that Apostolic Fellowship which comes of *valid orders* and *lawful jurisdiction?*

CHAPTER XVII.

ANGLICAN ORDERS.

"As the Reformation did not find the English bigoted *Papists*, so neither was it conducted in such a manner as to make them zealous *Protestants.*"—Macaulay's Essays, "Burleigh and His Times."

IN this sentence Macaulay, despite his inability to understand theology or appreciate ecclesiastical movements, stumbles on an important truth, viz.: that between Papist and Protestant stands the true Catholic ; and to make English Christians *true Catholics* as distinguished from both Papists and Protestants, was the object of the English Reformation. Queen Elizabeth struck the key-note of Anglo-Catholic independence when she replied to those English bishops who requested her to continue the arrangements which Queen Mary had made with Rome : " Our records show that *the papal jurisdiction over this realm was usurpation. To no power whatever is my crown subject save to that of Christ the King of Kings. I shall, therefore, regard as enemies, both to God and myself, all such of my subjects as shall henceforth own any foreign or usurped authority within my realm.*"

All the bishops, except Bonner of London, attended the Coronation of Elizabeth, January 13, 1559. The Archbishop of Canterbury had breathed his last within a few hours of Queen Mary's death. Nine other bishops had died. Indeed, out of the twenty-seven dioceses of our Church, thirteen were canonically vacant,[1] fourteen were canonically filled. Of the fourteen bishops, nine were deprived of their sees for refusing to take the oath to the new Queen; five were favorable to reform, together with several suffragan Bishops; moreover, there were the Irish bishops, who, almost to a man, accepted the Reformation.

Of course, ordination by one bishop, though irregular, would have been valid,[2] but no such desperate expedient was necessary.

The first thing to be done was to elect, confirm and consecrate a new Archbishop of Canterbury. The Dean and Cathedral Chapter petitioned the Queen to allow them to elect an Archbishop in the room of Archbishop Pole, lately deceased. To their request the Queen granted the usual *Conge d' elire*, as follows:

"The Queen, to her beloved in Christ, the Dean and Chapter of the Metropolitan Church of Canterbury, greeting:—

"On your part, a humble supplication has been made to us, that, whereas the aforesaid Church, by the natural death of the Most Reverend Father and Lord in Christ, the Lord Reginald Pole, Cardinal, the last Archbishop

---

1. Turberville of Exeter, Morgan of St. David's, Bourne of Bath and Wells, Heath of York, and probably also Scott of Chester were *intruders* thrust into the sees uncanonically by Queen Mary, while the lawful occupants of the sees were still living. I do not take them into account.

2. The first Roman Catholic bishop in the U. S. A., Dr. Carroll, had but *one* consecrator, the titular Bishop of Ragal, Dr. Walmsley, who appears to have had only the same uncanonical consecration himself. See Hook's Preface to Life of Bp. Hobart, p. 25. The Swedish and the "Old Catholic" Episcopates also come through a single bishop

thereof, is now vacant and destitute of the solace of a pastor, we would be graciously pleased to grant to you our fundatorial License to elect another Archbishop and Pastor. We, favourably inclined to your prayers in this matter, have thought fit to grant you this License. Requiring that you may elect such a person Archbishop and Pastor, who may be devoted to God, and useful and faithful to us and our kingdom.

"In testimony of which thing, etc., witness the Queen at Westminster, the 18th day of July, 1559."[3]

The Dean and Chapter then, "according to the ancient manner and laudable custom of the aforesaid Church, anciently used and inviolably observed," chose the devout and scholarly Matthew Parker, Priest and Doctor of Divinity, August 1st, 1559. Parker had been ordained to the Priesthood according to the Latin Pontifical. On the 6th day of the following December, the Queen issued letters patent to six bishops, as follows :

"Elizabeth, by the grace of God, of England, France, and Ireland, Queen, Defender of the Faith, etc., to the Reverend Fathers in Christ, Anthony, Bishop of Llandaff; William Barlow, sometime Bishop of Bath, now elect of Chichester ; John Scory, sometime Bishop of Chichester, now elect of Hereford ; Miles Coverdale, sometime Bishop of Exeter ; John, Suffragan, of Bedford ; John, Suffragan, of Thetford ; John Bale, Bishop of Ossary, greeting :—

"Whereas, the Archiepiscopal See of Canterbury being lately vacant by the natural death of the Lord Reginald

---

3. *Roll's Patents*, 1 *Eliz.*, p. 6, and *Rymer*, vol. 15, p. 536, quoted in Bailey's "Defence of Holy Orders in the Church of England."

Pole, Cardinal, last and immediate Archbishop and Pastor of the same, upon humble petition of the Dean and Chapter of our Cathedral and Metropolitan Church of Christ, at Canterbury, we, by our letters patent, have granted to the same, license to elect for themselves another Archbishop and Pastor of the See aforesaid ; and the said Dean and Chapter, by virtue of our aforesaid license obtained, have elected for themselves and the Church aforesaid, our beloved in Christ, Matthew Parker, D. D., as Archbishop and Pastor. We, accepting that election, have granted to the said election our royal assent and also favor, and this by the tenor of these presents we signify to you: Requiring and strictly commanding you by the faith and affection in which you are held by us, that you, or at least four[4] of you, would effectually confirm * * * the aforesaid election, and consecrate the said Matthew Parker, Archbishop and Pastor of the Church aforesaid, and perform and execute all and singular other things which belong in this matter to your pastoral office, according to the form of the statutes set forth and provided. * * *

" In witness whereof, we have caused these our letters to be made patent.

" Witness ourselves at Westminster, the sixth day of December, the second year of our reign."[5]

Every precaution was now taken that the new Archbishop-elect — the successor of Archbishop Pole, the sixty-eighth Archbishop in unbroken line from Augustine —

---

4. It is a civil law in England that an Episcopal Ordination must be performed by an Archbishop and at least two bishops, but if no Archbishop takes part, then by at least four bishops, as was the case in Parker's Consecration.

5. *Parker's Register*, vol. I., p. 3; and *Bull's Chapel*, quoted by Bailey, p. 7.

might be validly and lawfully ordained. On the 9th day of the same month, in the church of "St. Mary-le-Bow," Dr. Parker's election was regularly confirmed, open challenge being made for any one to show reason why the elect should not be consecrated. No objection was made. Accordingly, on Sunday, the 17th of December, 1559, in the chapel of the Archiepiscopal Palace at Lambeth, the solemn and sacramental ceremony of Consecration was performed in the presence of bishops, bishops-elect, priests, royal commissioners, noblemen, and commoners.

O what a scene was that! And how memorable the act which saved to England's venerable Church that ministry of grace and power, which Christ had ordained !

The chancel of the chapel was beautifully adorned. At the east end stood the altar, at the north side of which was placed the Bishop's throne. At six o'clock in the morning the procession entered the west door of the chapel — the Archbishop-elect, vested in scarlet cassock and hood, with four wax torches borne before him, and accompanied by the four bishops, who were to unite in the laying on of hands, viz.: William Barlow, Bishop of Bath and Wells; John Scory, Bishop of Chichester ; Miles Coverdale, Bishop of Exeter, and John Hodgkins, Bishop Suffragan of Bedford. Of these four bishops, two had been consecrated according to the Latin form of the old English Ordinal in the days of Henry VIII., and two according to the English form of the Ordinal during the reign of Edward VI.

Weighing my words with care, I affirm there can be no more doubt that these four prelates were lawful Catholic bishops, than that Anselm or Augustine, Ignatius or St. John were partakers of the Apostolic ministry.

Morning Prayer is now said by Andrew Peerson, chaplain of the Archbishop-elect. The Bishop of Chichester ascends the pulpit, and taking as his text: "The elders who are among you I exhort who am also an elder," he preaches (as the old Lambeth register has it) "not inelegantly." Now the Bishops withdraw to vest for the Holy Communion, and return, the Archbishop-elect in the surplice of a priest, Bishop Barlow, the Celebrant, with the archdeacons of Canterbury and Lincoln, who serve at the altar as deacon and sub-deacon, in gorgeous copes of silk. After the Gospel the candidate is presented; the Queen's mandate for the Consecration is read; the oath of office is administered;[6] the people are bidden to pray for the can-

---

6. In the oath, after declaring that the Queen is the only "Supreme Governor of Thys Realme, as well in spirituall or ecclesiastical things or causes, as temporal," come the words: "And that no foreign prince, person, prelate, State or potentate, hath, or ought to have, any jurisdiction, power, superioritie, preeminence, or authoritie ecclesiasticall or spirituall within this realme." It should be remembered that Elizabeth never took the title of "Head of the Church." Henry VIII. took it, but convocation allowed it only with this qualification: *As far as the law of Christ alloweth.* It was abolished in 1553 and never revived.

The oath of supremacy has long been abolished. The present oath of allegiance runs thus: "I swear that I will be faithful and bear true allegiance to Her Majesty Queen Victoria, her heirs and successors, according to law."

Even Henry VIII. distinctly repudiated any claim to *spiritual* authority, such as pertains to Episcopal and Sacerdotal functions. All that Elizabeth claimed was the *ancient* privileges of the Christian Kings of England. The title of the law of I. Eliz. shows this: "An act to restore to the Crown the *ancient* jurisdiction over the estate, ecclesiastical and spiritual, and abolishing all *foreign* powers repugnant to the same." And Elizabeth distinctly declared: "The Crown challenged no superiority to define, decide, or determine any article or point of the Christian faith or religion; or to change any right or ceremony before received and observed in the *Catholic Church.*" Says Bp. Forbes: "The Crown is no more the head of the Church in England than of the [Presbyterian] kirk in Scotland."

Article XXXVII. says: "We give not to our Princes the ministering either of God's word, or of the Sacraments; * * * but that only prerogative which we see to have been given always to all godly Princes, in Holy Scripture, by God Himself," etc.

didate; Bishop Barlow sings the Litany, the choir responding. After the usual questions and answers, and special prayers, the four bishops lay their apostolic hands on the head of the kneeling priest, *each one of them* saying in English the ancient words of Consecration; and Dr. Parker rises a bishop in the Church of God, and is vested in the episcopal robes. No part of this important transaction was done in a corner. After the service the Archbishop gave a reception in his palace; and that night he made the following entry in his private diary, which is still preserved in the library of Corpus Christi College, Cambridge:

"Seventeenth December, in the year 1559, I was consecrated Archbishop of Canterbury. Alass! Alass! O Lord, to what times hast thou preserved me? Lo, I am come into deep waters, and the storm hath overwhelmed me. O Lord I am oppressed, undertake for me, and with thy mighty spirit strengthen me. For I am a man, both of a short time and weak," etc.

On the first of January, the new Archbishop was enthroned in the cathedral, after which he was placed in possession of the temporalities of his see, and summoned to his seat in the House of Lords.

I know of no event in Anglo-Catholic history better certified than the Consecration of Parker. I give here a list of the chief documents which prove the fact of his Consecration:

"*a.* The register of the act in the archives of Lambeth, written in the same hand as the registers of Cranmer and Pole, and attested by the same notaries public as Pole's own record.

b. A contemporary copy of part of this register in the State Paper Office.

c. Another contemporary copy of the register in the library of Corpus Christi College, Cambridge.

d. Parker's autograph note-book, in the same library, mentioning his Consecration on December 17, 1559.

e. The casual mention of the fact, as an item of news, in the contemporary MS. diary of Henry Machyn, preserved in the British Museum.

f. The contemporary MS. "Zurich Letters," testifying to the same fact, and but lately discovered.

g. The conduct of Bishop Bonner, in his suit against Horne, Bishop of Winchester, in which the *fact* of Parker's Consecration itself was allowed by Bonner.

h. The precise dove-tailing of the event into the long and intricate series of civil (not ecclesiastical) documents required by the State in evidence of Parker's right to his barony, revenues, seat in the House of Lords, and coercive jurisdiction in his province.

i. The manner in which contemporary writers, such as Camden, Holinshed, etc., take the matter as notorious and undisputed."

Against all this overwhelming evidence one, and only one, attack has been made, that known as the "Nag's Head Fable," which must be briefly and candidly noticed.

In the year 1604, forty-five years after Parker's Consecration in Lambeth Chapel, a wily Jesuit, named Holywood, published a pamphlet in which he claimed to have been told by one Thomas Neal (then fourteen years dead) that he, peeping through a key-hole in the "Nag's Head" tavern, in Cheapside, saw Scory lay his hands on Parker, and some others, who in turn laid their hands on him [7] and thus all made each other bishops!!

The story is absurd on the face of it; but, like the Jewish fable that the disciples stole the body of Jesus while the watch slept, it is the best that ingenious malice has been able to devise against the fact of Parker's Consecration. The Earl of Nottingham, and others, however, who had attended the Consecration at Lambeth, were still living to bear witness against this " tale of foolery."

I cannot forbear to transcribe here, from Bailey's " Defence of Holy Orders " (p. 30), the quaint and graphic record of the effect of the fable on King James I. as given by William Hampton, in 1721 :

" In the beginning of King James his reigne, there came out a book under the name of Sanders with the story of the Nag's Head Ordination. This book made a great noyse, and was wonderfully cried up by the Roman Catholics as sapping the whole Reformation at once by destroying the Episcopacy. This book was shewed to King James, and upon his reading of it, it stratled [sic] him. Upon this he called his Privy Council and showed it to them, and withal told 'em that he was a stranger among 'em, and knew nothing of the matter, and directing himself to the Archbishop who was present, My Lord (says he), I hope you can prove and make good your ordina-

---

[7]. Here is one mani'est absurdity, for Scory himself had been consecrated, Aug. 30, 1551, by Archbishop Cranmer and two other bishops.

Romanists, of all others, are debarred from questioning Bishop Scory's orders, for he is one of the reforming Bishops, who was "reconciled" during the Roman usurpation under Queen Mary; and, at the time of the Queen's death, was actually serving as a Suffragan or Co-adjutor Bishop under Bonner, the Romanizing Bishop of London. The fact is attested by Bonner in his own register.

tion, for by my sol, man (says he), if this story be true we are no Church. The Archbishop replied, he had never heard the story before, but did not question but he could detect the forgery of it, and by examining the Lambeth register could prove Archbishop Parker's ordination. At another Privy Council upon the same account, the old Earle of Nottingham was present, and when it was debated the old Earle stood up and told the King and Council, he could give them full satisfaction as to that matter upon his own personal knowledge, for (says he) Archbishop Parker's ordination made a great noyse about towne that he was to be ordained such a day in Lambeth Chappel, which drew a great deale of company thither, and out of curiosity I went thither myself, and was present at his ordination, and he was ordained by the form in King Edward's Common Prayer Book. I myself (said he) had the book in my hand all the time, and went along with the ordination, and when it was over I dined with 'em, and there was an instrument drawn up of the form and order of it, which instrument I saw and read over Some time after (I being acquainted with the Archbishop and being at Lambeth with him) he told me he had sent that instrument to Corpus Christi College in Cambridge to be laid up in their Library *in perpetuam rei memoriam*, and sayes the old Earle, I believe it may be in the Library still if your Majesty please to have it searched for.

"By my sol, man (says ye King), thou speakest to the purpose, we must see this instrument, and this puts the thing out of dispute. Upon this a messenger was sent, the instrument found and brought to ye king, he shewed it and had it read in Council, and desired the old Earle of Nottingham to look upon it, and see if he could remember whether it was the original instrument which was drawn up at the ordination. The Earl perusing of it declared it was ye original he saw and read when Archbishop Parker was ordained. The King upon this addressing himself to several Popish Lords who were then present in Council, my Lords, sayes he, what do you now think of ye matter? They all declared their abhorrence of the forgery of ye Nag's Head ordination, and several of 'em upon it left the Popish Communion, and came over to ye Church of England, declaring that Church was not fitt to be trusted with their souls who would invent and abett such a notorious falsity. For truth of this I witness my hand."

"Wm. Hampton, rector of Worth, 1721."

I would add that, while unscrupulous controversialists still make use of this fable, all candid Roman Catholic scholars long since abandoned it, Lingard,[8] Charles Butler, Canon Tierney, etc. Indeed we are indebted to Roman

---

8. Lingard's repudiation of the fiction is as follows:

"To this testimony of the register [of Abp. Parker's consecration] what could the champions of the Nag's Head story oppose? They had but one resource, to deny its authenticity; to pronounce it a forgery. But there was nothing to countenance such a supposition. The most experienced eye could not discover in the entry itself, or the form of the characters, or the color of the ink, the slightest vestige of imposture. * * * If external confirmation were wanting, there was the archbishop's diary, or journal, a parchment roll in which he had been accustomed to enter the principal events of his life, and in which, under the date of the 17th of December, 1559, is found:

"'Consecratus sum in archiepiscopum Cantuariens. Heu! heu! Domine Deus, in quæ tempora servasti me!'

"Another confirmation to which no objection can be reasonably opposed occurs in the Zurich letters, in which we find Sampson informing Peter Martyr, on the 6th of January, 1560, that Dr. Parker had been consecrated Archbishop of Canterbury during the preceding month."—Lingard's "History of England," vol. vii., note G.

Catholic writers for some of the ablest defences of Anglican Orders ever written — e. g. Courayer, Colbert, Bossuet, Affre (Archbishop of Paris) and Cardinal de la Luzerne.[9] It should also be remembered that the Bishop of Rome, Julius III., ordered Archbishop Pole to absolve and reconcile bishops and priests ordained in Edward VI.'s time, but not to re-ordain them. Pius IV. also agreed to recognize all the reforms under Elizabeth, if only she would recognize his supremacy. After she declined to do so, he requested the Council of Trent to declare English Orders invalid, which the council expressly refused to do. Horly, Archbishop of Paris, and Innocent XII., Bishop of Rome, advised James II. to have the non-juring English bishops keep up the Apostolic succession in England, which they certainly would not have done, had they not believed in Anglican Orders. Richard Selden, a Roman priest, wrote as follows.

"I myself lately for my own satisfaction, searched the registers, and I found clearly, that Archbishop Parker was sufficiently, truly, and canonically ordained and consecrated."[10]

Archbishop Parker, of course, ordained many bishops, but as he was always assisted by two or more bishops, even had he never been ordained himself (and there is no ordination in history more certain than his), our Orders would still be valid.

For the benefit of any who may still choose to be skep-

---

9. Du Pin, De Girardin, and Beauvoir, in their correspondence with Archbishop Wake (1718), fully acknowledged Anglican Orders. See Dr. Pusey's Irenicon, pp. 215-16.

10. Selden's "*De Spiritibus Pontificii*," quoted in Bailey's Df. of Holy Ord., p. 9.

tical on this subject, and especially any Roman Catholic brother who may chance to read this sketch, I would call attention to one important fact in the post-reformation history of the Anglo-Catholic Church. Early in the seventeenth century a Roman Catholic Bishop, Marc Antonio de Dominis, Archbishop of Spalato, conformed to the English Church, and was appointed Dean of Windsor. He took part in ordaining two English bishops, George Monteigne, of London, and Nicolas Felton, of Ely, from both of whom the eight bishops derived their Orders, who survived the seventeen years of persecution under the commonwealth, and handed down the succession from 1660 to the present time. Observe also that every one of these eight bishops inherited the Irish succession as well, from George, the Bishop of Derry, Hampton, the Archbishop of Armagh, and Murray, the Bishop of Kilfenora. No loss of continuity has ever been alleged against either the Irish or the Italian Succession, so that, even if we waive the old English Succession, there is no possibility of invalidating the present Anglo-Catholic Episcopate.[11]

---

11. The following extract from that admirable tract on "Anglican Orders and Jurisdiction" (Church League Press, 18 Liberty St., New York), will explain this more fully:

"At the restoration of Charles II., in 1660, after Episcopal government had been suspended for seventeen years under the Commonwealth, there were eight prelates of the Anglican Church still surviving. From these the existing line is derived, and it is convenient, therefore, to narrow the inquiry to the validity of their succession. They were Juxon of London (at once translated to Canterbury), Frewen of York, Duppa of Winchester, Wren of Ely, King of Chichester Skinner of Oxford, Warner of Rochester, and Roberts of Bangor.

"All of these, except King and Frewen, were consecrated by Archbishop Laud with sometimes four, and sometimes five, co-consecrators. The two others raised to the mitre while Laud was in prison, were severally consecrated by Juxon with three other Bishops, and by Williams, Archbishop of York, with four others, including Duppa.

"Laud and Williams were consecrated within a week of each other, one by six

The *American* Episcopate comes through four bishops ordained, one by three Scottish bishops, and three by the Archbishop of Canterbury, with the canonical number of assisting bishops.

In the case of the English *Colonial* Bishops the same care has been taken. The Anglican Church, therefore, has "continued steadfastly in the Apostles' Fellowship." Her two hundred and twenty-five bishops to-day, bearing the Saviour's commission to the uttermost parts of the earth, and inheriting his promise, "Lo, I am with you always even unto the end of the world," are, with the twelve apostles and all their successors in the Catholic Episcopate, a perpetual "witness of His Resurrection," fulfilling the Saviour's prophesy: "Ye shall be witnesses unto Me * * * *unto the uttermost part of the earth.*" (Acts, i., 8.)

Behold the "Father of Waters" as he pours his flood into the southern gulf. In that mighty current are blended the rain-drops that fell on the plateaux of the north, upon the Alleghany Hills, and among the mountain ranges that lie towards the setting sun. So the Anglo-Catholic Episcopate draws its potent and beneficent authority from St.

---

bishops, the other by five of those six. Among them were George Monteigue of London, and Nicolas Felton of Ely, who had been consecrated in 1617 by Marc Antonio de Domonis, Archbishop of Spalato, assisting Abbot of Canterbury, and four others. Another of their consecrators was Field of Llandaff, one of whose consecrators was George, Bishop of Derry; and a fourth was Howson of Oxford, who derived, through Morton of Durham, from Hampton, Archbishop of Armagh. Morton and Bancroft of Oxford (who had been consecrated by William Murray of Kilfenora) were amongst Duppa's consecrators.

"Thus in the present line of Anglican prelates, three successions meet, the Italian, the Irish, and the English. No allegation of loss of continuity is urged against the two former, and thus, even if the third be imperfect, the cord is unbroken.

"That the English strand is as perfect as the two others is easy of proof."

James in Jerusalem,[12] from St. John in Ephesus, from SS. Paul and Peter in the west. And as the rain which feeds the river is from above," so the grace of Holy Orders *flows down* to us by way of the Orient and Italy, by way of Gaul and Britain of old — Hebrew and Greek, Roman, Celtic, and Saxon, it comes from above, and swells that " River, the streams whereof shall make glad the City of God."

---

12 St. David, Archbishop of Wales in the sixth century, was consecrated by the Patriarch of Jerusalem.

APPENDIX TO CHAPTER XVII.

PIUS IV. AND THE ENGLISH REFORMATION.

IT is asserted in almost every history of the Anglican Church that Pius IV. agreed to recognize the English reformation, provided that his own supremacy should be acknowledged. This concession on his part is valuable as showing that our Church had lost nothing which even in the estimation of Rome, is essential to a true Church.

Hore, in his "Eighteen Centuries of the Church in England" (p. 348), says: "Pope Paul IV. having died on August 18, 1559, was succeeded by Pius IV. The new Pope sent his nuncio with a letter to the Queen, announcing his approval and willingness to accept the new Prayer Book, as well as the Communion in both kinds, if only the Queen would acknowledge his supremacy."

Jennings, in his excellent "*Ecclesia Anglicana*" (p. 319), says: "Convinced that nothing was to be gained in England by hostility to the throne, Pius made friendly overtures to Elizabeth. We have it on good authority that he offered to sanction the Prayer Book of 1559, provided the English Church recognized the supremacy of Rome."

Cutts, in his "Turning Points of English Church History" (p. 237), says: "A new Pope, Pius IV., in 1560 addressed to her (Elizabeth) a letter of very different tenor, making overtures for a reconciliation. He offered that, on condition of her adhesion to the see of Rome, the Pope would approve of the Book of Common Prayer, including the Liturgy or Communion Service and the Ordinal. Although his Holiness complained that many things were omitted from the Prayer Book which ought to be there, he admitted that the book nevertheless contained nothing contrary to truth, while it certainly comprehended all that is necessary for salvation. He was therefore prepared to authorize the book if the Queen would receive it from him and on his authority."

Blunt, in his historical introduction to the Prayer Book (p. xxxv.), says: "It is worth notice, however, that the Book of Common Prayer as thus revised in 1559 was quietly accepted by the great body of Romanist laity; and also that the Pope himself saw so little to object to in it that he offered to give the book his full sanction if his authority were recognized by the Queen and the kingdom." And he quotes Sir Edward Coke as saying that the Pope, Pius IV., " before the time of his excommunication against Queen Elizabeth denounced, sent his letter unto her Majesty, in which he did allow the Bible and Book of Divine Service, as it is now used among us, to be authentic and not repugnant to truth. But that therein was contained enough necessary to salvation, though there was not in it so much as might conveniently be, and that he would also allow it unto us without changing any part, so as her Majesty would acknowledge to receive it from the Pope, and by his allowance, which her Majesty denying to do, she was then presently by the same Pope excommunicated.

And this is the truth concerning Pope Pius Quartus, as I have faith to God and men. I have oftentimes heard avowed by the late Queen her own words, and I have conferred with some Lords that were of greatest reckoning in the State, who had seen and read the Letter, which the Pope sent to that effect, as have been by me specified. And this upon my credit, as I am an honest man, is most true." Blunt moreover gives a list of authorities, viz.: "The Lord Coke, his speech and charge, London, 1607. See also Camden, Ann, Eliz., p. 59, ed. 1615. Twysden's Historical Vindication of the Church of England, p. 175. Validity of the Orders of the Church of England, by Humphrey Prideaux, D. D., 1688. Bramhall's Works, ii., 85, ed. 1845. Bishop Babington's Notes on the Pentateuch ; on Numbers, vii. Courayer's Defence of the Dissertation on the Validity of English Ordinations, ii., 360, 378. Harrington's Pius IV. and the Book of Common Prayer, 1856."

Our own Van Antwerp, in his very readable and comprehensive "Church History" (vol. iii., p. 144–5), gives the same story.

The following extract from Butler's "Historical Memoirs of the Catholics" (Lond., ed. 1822, vol. i., ch. 22, § 9, p. 280), is especially valuable, as coming from a learned *Roman* Catholic:

"In May, 1560, he (Pius the fourth), sent Vincentio Parpalia * * * to the Queen with a letter, most earnestly but respectfully entreating her to return to the bosom of the Church. On this occasion, Parpalia, if we are to credit Camden, was instructed by the Pope to offer to the Queen, that the Pope would annul the sentence of Clement, his predecessor, against her mother's marriage, settle the liturgy by his authority, and grant to the English the use of the sacrament under both kinds.

"Parpalia reached Bruxelles; from that place he acquainted the English ministry with the object of his mission, and proceeded to Calais. The propriety of admitting him was debated in the royal council and determined in the negative

"The conciliating Pope was not disheartened; at a subsequent time he deputed the Abbe Martenengo to the Queen, to notify to her the sitting of the Council of Trent, and to request she would send an ambassador to it, and permit the prelates of England to attend it. Some objected to the Pope, that this was showing too great a condescension towards persons who had formerly separated from the Church. 'Nothing,' said the worthy pontiff, is humiliating to gain souls to Christ.' Both the King of Spain and the Duke of Alva seconded * * * the Pope's request, but the Queen was inflexible; * * * she therefore refused to permit the abbe to enter any part of her dominions."

The reader will also find it in Bailey's "Jurisdiction and Mission of the Ang. Epis.," p. 65; in Hardwicke's "Reformation," and in scores of other reliable works. I have never seen the story controverted or even questioned.

CHAPTER XVIII.

ANGLICAN JURISDICTION AND CATHOLICITY.

"Men cannot set up a new Church, so we think, and we bless God that we have the old Church cleansed and purified."—*Bishop Lee, the Presiding Bishop of the Church in the U. S. (Second Letter to the Assistant Bishop of N. Y.)*

WHEN the bishops of the whole Anglican communion, English, Irish, Scotch, American, Colonial, and Missionary, from all parts of the world, assembled together at Lambeth, in the year of our Lord 1867, the Synod declared "that there was one true Catholic and Apostolic Church, founded by our Lord and Saviour Jesus Christ; that of this true Catholic and Apostolic Church, the Church of England and the Churches in communion with her are living members; and that the Church of England earnestly desires to maintain freely the *Catholic* faith as set forth by Œcumenical councils of the Universal Church."

A National Church might have valid orders, and yet by heresy or schism have cut itself off from Catholic Christendom and have lost its *jurisdiction*. If all jurisdiction flows from the Bishop of Rome (which is the modern Ultramontane fiction), then, in casting off his authority, our Church became schismatic. But it is enough to say that this Ultramontane theory is a recent innovation—*nuper inventum et ante haec tempora inauditum.*

Our Church in the British period owed nothing to the Bishop of Rome. According to the ancient canons of the universal Church, every provincial Church possessed *inherent jurisdiction*,[1] and notably the *autocephalous* Churches, as of Cyprus and *Britain*. When Augustine received the Archbishopric of Canterbury, it was not as a *lieutenant* of the Roman Pontiff, but " as an independent bishop of a See in a country which had never been included in the Patriarchate of Rome,[2] as the "*Papa alterius orbis.*"[3] Gregory, in fact, appointed Augustine to be Archbishop of *London* (though by the authority of the *King of Kent* he was actually placed in Canterbury instead of London,[4] and Augustine was consecrated by French bishops ; but Gregory ordered that " for the future the Archbishop should be consecrated by his own synod " (*i. e.*, in England), and that his jurisdiction should extend over the whole island.

---

1. See Bishop Forbes on Art. XXXVII., and Bailey on the "Jurisdiction and Mission of the Ang. Epis.," Sec. IV.

2. *Id.*, p. 44. Cf. also note, p. 96, of "The Eng. Ref.," by the Rt. Rev. J. Williams, D. D., LL.D., Bp. of Conn. "The Roman Patriarchate," says he, "included the ten provinces placed under the *Vicarius urbis*, namely: Italy, south of the Italic Diocese, and the three adjacent islands." The editor of the "Church Times" says: "We know from Ruffinus (and the matter has been thoroughly worked out by the great French Catholic scholar, Dupin, in his treatise *De Antiqua Disciplina*) that the Roman Patriarchate extended over no more than the ten "suburbicarian" provinces of Italy—those under the civil jurisdiction of the Roman prætor—and the islands of Sardinia, Corsica, and Elba. What decides Patriarchal authority is the right of consecrating Metropolitans. And the Popes did not get this power, even in North Italy, till the days of Gregory the Great. All the West, outside the limits named, was and is extra-Patriarchal."

3. Coit's Early Hist., etc., note, p. 140. "*Pope of another world.*"

4. The Christian Kings of England always had a share in appointing bishops. See [*e. g.*] the general synod of the English Ch., A. D. 1072, where it was decreed among other things: "If the Archbishop of York shall die, his successor, accepting *the gift of the archbishopric from the King*, shall come to Canterbury to receive canonical ordination."—Wm. of Malmsbury, Hist. of the King's Book, 3, p. 265.

The English Church was, therefore, *complete in itself*. And as to its Archbishops, the learned canonist, Thomassinus, says : " The confirmation of the *Roman See* was not to be waited for." The Archbishops both of Canterbury and York were generally appointed by the king, elected by the clergy or Cathedral Chapter, and consecrated in England. Until into the twelfth century only two Archbishops of Canterbury, and none of York, were consecrated by the Bishop of Rome ; nor is there even "any clear instance of the Pope's confirming the election of English Metropolitans till the time of Richard, Archbishop of Canterbury, in 1174." The English Church was never lawfully dependent on Rome, or Constantinople, or any other foreign See for her jurisdiction or ecclesiastical right to exercise her Catholic orders and spiritual power within definite territorial limits. " The English clergy derive their jurisdiction from their own bishops, and these from their bishops who went before them back to the beginning, as every Christian Church whatever derived theirs, without one thought of the Bishop of Rome, for some 1200 years, and as the whole Eastern Church derives hers until this very day."[5]

" The only difference in the ' English Catholic Church,' as it existed previous to the dynasty of the Tudors, and as it stood at the termination of the reign of William III., was that certain ecclesiastical abuses had arisen, which

---

5. Haddan Apost. Succ. in the Ch. of England, p. 262. It should be remembered that the Bishop of Rome wished the Council of Trent to declare that all jurisdiction comes from "the chair of St. Peter." This, however, the council expressly refused to do. See Forbes on the Arts, Art. XXXVII., p. 774.

were corrected by Parliament and the clerical synods in convocation; but the identity of the 'English Catholic Church' was never destroyed. That sect which is now commonly called 'Roman Catholics,' are nothing but a mere body of dissenters from the 'English Catholic Church,' and have never, constitutionally speaking, been arbitrarily deprived of a vested right."—(" Delolme on the English Constitution," quoted in Greave's "Vindication of the Right of the Anglican Chr.," etc., p. 152.)

The Anglican Reformers certainly had no idea of committing the sin of schism or of making a *Protestant* church. They simply designed—and in the Providence of God accomplished—the freeing and purifying of so much of the Catholic Church as came under their own jurisdiction. As Bishop Williams remarks : " There is not the smallest thought of separating from the unity of the Catholic Church of Christ, far less of founding a new Church. The law of historic continuity is all along asserted and acted on."[6] The continuous *identity* of the Anglican Church is distinctly asserted in the Preface to the English Prayer Book, in this passage : " The service *in this Church of England, these many years*, hath been read in Latin." It was, therefore, *this same Church of England* before as well as after the translation of its Prayer Book into a language understanded of the people.

But even had the English Church been guilty of schism (which she was not), it would have been justifiable (if ever a schism could be), for the corruption of Western Christendom had become intolerable. Even the Bishop of Rome himself, Adrian VI., who labored so hard for

---

6. Eng. Ref., pp. 122-3.

reform during his brief pontificate (but as Bishop Williams naively remarks, " Reforming popes seem to have had but short reigns"), freely admitted that " many abominations had existed for a long time, even in the Holy See. Yea, that all things had been grievously altered and perverted." Unlike the so-called "reformers" on the continent, who broke altogether with the past, and kept neither jurisdiction nor orders, our Church retained both, and indeed used as much care that *on her part* there should be no schism from the rest of the Catholic Church, as that there should be no loss of the Apostolic Succession or the Orthodox Faith. Canon xxx. of the Anglican code, in allusion to the Reformation, says :

" So far was it from the Church of England to forsake and reject the Churches of Italy, Rome, Spain, and Germany, or any other such like Churches, that it doth with reverence retain those ceremonies which do neither endanger the Church of God, nor offend the minds of sober men ; and only departed from them in those particular points wherein they were fallen from themselves in their ancient integrity, and from the Apostolic Churches, which were their first founders."

At the election and Consecration of Parker, there was no intimation of such a thing as his receiving and holding any different office in the Catholic Church from that of the sixty-seven previous occupants of the Throne of St. Augustine. The mandates for his election and Consecration did not say that the Catholic Church being now at an end in England, a Protestant Archbishop would be elected for a Protestant church : but, on the contrary, after alluding to the vacancy occasioned by the death of " the Lord

Reginald Pole, last and immediate Archbishop," they ordered the election, confirmation, and Consecration of his successor *in the same office, in the same Church.*[7] Indeed, one Bishop—Kitchen of Llandaff—held his sacred office under Henry, Edward, Mary, and Elizabeth, never for a moment imagining that he had been a bishop in more than one Church all the while. Out of 9,400 clergy, only 189, at the most, refused to accept the reforms which, however important, were merely an *episode* in the continuous life of the Anglo-Catholic Church. Queen Elizabeth always professed herself a Catholic. When Pius IV. invited her to the Council of Trent in the same terms as the *Protestant* Princes, she returned an indignant remonstrance, saying that "an invidious distinction is made between me and such *other Catholic* potentates as have been invited to this Council." She also wrote to the German Emperor and some other Roman Catholic Princes, declaring: "There is no *new* faith propagated in England; no religion set up but that which was commanded by our Saviour, preached by the primitive Church, and unanimously approved by the Fathers of the best antiquity." Archbishop Parker, in his last will and testament, declared: "I profess that I do certainly believe and hold whatsoever the Holy Catholic Church believeth and receiveth." The mere casting off of the *usurped* dominion of a foreign prelate, who had no more right to the obedience of England than the Bishop of Delaware has to the obedience of Canada, did not in the least mar the Catholicity of our Church. During the reigns of Henry and Edward, and to the eleventh year of Elizabeth—1531 to 1570—the English Church reasserted

---

7. See Letters Patent in Chapter XVII.

her independence of Rome,[8] and yet those English Churchmen who really believed in the supremacy of the Roman Bishop, none the less worshipped and received the Sacraments in the parish churches, just as before. As Lord Chief Justice Coke said, in 1607 : " Generally (of) all the Papists in this kingdom, not any of them did refuse to come to our Church and yield their obedience to the laws established. And they all continued, not any one refusing to come to our churches during the first ten years of her Majesty's government." The Queen also asserts the same in a message to the French Government, in 1570, saying : " They did ordinarily resort * * * in all open places, to the churches, and to Divine service in the church, without any contradiction or show of misliking." It was the same also in Ireland.

Thus the whole nation was peaceably settling down to the old Church, " Catholic, Reformed, and Free," when, in 1570,[9] the Bishop of Rome, Pius V., issued his famous bull, entitled, " The Damnation and Excommunication of

---

8. It must be remembered, too, that for some 200 years previous it had been unlawful for any English Churchman to receive any appointment from Rome, or make any appeal to Rome.

9. "On *April* 27, 1570, the shameful mandate went forth, bidding all who would obey Pius V. to break with their own English Church, to secede and form conventicles, to abandon and dethrone their sovereign, and to subject their country, if they could, to a foreign invader."—*Curteis*' " *Dissent in its Relation to the Church of England.*"

"The Church of Rome at the present day cannot be identified with the Church of England previous to the Reformation; the Roman Catholic bishops in England and Scotland are bishops of foreign sees, and neither they nor those who have been schismatically consecrated for the sees in Ireland, which at the time of the Reformation were canonically filled, can trace any descent from the bishops of the ancient churches in these kingdoms; the now bishops of the Church of England being the only representatives by episcopal succession of the ancient Celtic and Anglo-Saxon churches; and the strongest illustration of this position is that the votaries of the Roman Catholic religion are distinguished by

Elizabeth "[10]—deposing the Queen, forsooth, absolving all her subjects from their oath of allegiance, and commanding them to withdraw from the Church. A mere handful of Englishmen, in disloyalty to the Catholic Church, and in treason to the Government, seceded and formed the *Roman Schism* or Italian Mission in England.

We never excommunicated them; we never broke fellowship with them; we have never repelled them from our altars. As St. Cyprian said of the Novatian schismatics in the third century, "We did not depart from them, but they departed from us."[11]

The petty Schism thus started aimed at nothing less than the complete subjugation of the Catholic Church and the State of England, to a certain bishop residing in Italy. But despite Latin anathemas, Jesuit plots and Spanish Armadas, GOD saved both His Church and the State.

The Roman schism in England has been a failure. It is a mere parasite and exotic having no organic connection with the ancient tree, no lineal descent from the dear old Catholic Church of St. Alban and St. Chad, Augustine, Theodore and Langton. It was not until 1850 that the Bishop of Rome presumed to intrude diocesan bishops into English Sees, in direct violation of the thirty-sixth Apostolic canon re-enacted in substance again and again by

---

the adoption of a new creed, which the English Catholic Church at no one period of her existence ever recognized."—"*Delolme on the English Constitution.*"

"These are weighty words; they show that the Church of England reformed itself constitutionally, the bishops and clergy in their convocations, the Parliament and the King representing the laity, assenting alike to the changes. This is the Church of England, and no foreign bishop has any lawful authority in its borders."—*Rev. J. A. Greaves.*

10. See Coit's Early History, etc., Note, p. 70.
11. De Unit. Eccl., p. 256.

councils provincial and general.[12] Pius IX., moreover, in making *Westminster*, instead of Canterbury, the Metropolitan See of his English schism, seemed to forget that his *infallible* predecessor, Boniface, in the seventh century, decreed that *Canterbury* should forever be the Metropolitan See of all Britain, no matter what changes should take place, pronouncing dreadful curses on any one who should presume to alter his decree.[13]

I leave it to any candid reader to say which are the schismatics, the Anglo-Catholics, who have remained in the old Church cleared of corruptions but not shorn of any mark of Catholicity, or the few Recusants who at the beck of a foreign prelate left their Mother Church and reared altar against altar?

The English Church never claimed to be *Protestant*, never once officially wrote the word. As the fogs of the eighteenth century clear away, as people become more familiar with the history of the Church and the principles of the Reformation, it will be looked upon as one of the marvels of history that we Anglicans should ever for one moment have imagined ourselves anything but *Catholics;* that we should ever, even in careless and casual conversation, have yielded the name, the privilege, and the honor of Catholicity to the Latin intruders, or allowed ourselves to be called by a misnomer borrowed from German sectarians. It is like a wealthy miser who persists in calling himself *poor*, till he comes to believe that he is a *pauper*.

It should be remembered that William III., "the dull

---
12. Bailey's Juris. and Miss. of the Ang. Epis., p. 68.
13. Id., p. 47, quoted from William of Malmsbury.

usurper of Orange" (as Bishop Coxe calls him), being desirous to identify the Catholic Church of England with Dissenters and continental Protestants, sent a message to convocation in which he speaks of his "interest for the *Protestant* religion in general, and the Church of England in particular." Even this indirect association of our Catholic Church with *Protestantism* was not allowed to pass Convocation, and after a thorough discussion, "an address of thanks was presented to the King in which the word *Protestant* as applied to the English Church was omitted."[14] The unchurchly King was angry and mortified, and showed his unrighteous indignation by proroguing Convocation and not allowing it to sit again for ten years.

The English Church in her authorized prayers says: "We pray for the good estate of *the Catholic Church.*" [Query: Is this a prayer for Popery?] Again: "That it may please Thee to rule and govern Thy Holy Church Universal."— *Sanctam Ecclesiam tuam Catholicam.* Thirteen times a year every Englishman is expected to make that grand and stately confession which begins: "Whosoever will be saved it is before all things necessary that he hold the *Catholic* faith," and which abounds in such expressions as "The Catholic Faith is this," and "We are forbidden by the *Catholic* religion," and in the Coronation Service the Sovereign is invested with the ring as "the ensign of kingly dignity and of defence of the CATHOLIC FAITH."

---

14. Hore's Eighteen Centuries, p. 448. It is worthy of note, just here, that the official title of the Romish Communion is not the "Catholic Church," but "The Holy *Roman* Church," or "The Holy Catholic Apostolic *Roman* Church." (See Creed of Pius IV.) Land left by will to the "Catholic Church" in England, has been awarded not to the Roman Schism in England, but to the English Church. (See Ch. Ecl., Apr., 1885, p. 68.

Even we American Churchmen (though we took the civil title "Protestant Episcopal") still claim to be and are that part of the Catholic Church which has *lawful jurisdiction* in the United States, and we authoritatively pray that we may die "in the communion of the *Catholic* Church." 15

---

15. The greatest mistake the Church in the United States ever made was the gradual acceptance, as a *civil title*, of the name "Protestant Episcopal"—which means (according to our missionaries who have labored to translate it into Chinese) "The Contradictory Bishop's Church!"

In the first place our Church is *not* protestant in the original ecclesiastical sense of the term, which is equivalent to *Lutheran*, having been conferred on German separatists on account of their *protest* against the Diet of Spires.

In the second place, our Church is not protestant in the modern popular sense of the term, which means *not Catholic*. God forbid that we should ever cease to be Catholics.

In the third place, our Church is not protestant in the strict technical sense, of protesting or remonstrating against the abuses of a *superior authority*, which, in spite of abuses, is nevertheless a *lawful* authority. We do not (strictly speaking) *protest* against Rome, for such protest would imply that Rome has *authority* over us, against some exercise of which we protest. But Rome has *no* authority over us; consequently we do not *protest*. We merely fall back on our *ancient, inherent, co-ordinate Catholic independence*. This was admirably set forth by Dr. Thrall, in the General Convention of 1883.

We are protestant only in the general, loose, vague and vapid sense in which *every* organization is protestant against *every other organization* which in any way differs from it—the same sense in which we (and *all* Christians) are protestant against Judaism, Mohammedanism, and Unitarianism; the same sense in which the Church of Rome is *protestant* against us and against the Orthodox Catholics of the Orient; the same sense in which the word could be applied to any school of medicine or philosophy, any political party, any social club. Now in all seriousness and common sense, is it worth while to qualify the Catholic Church in the United States by such a title as that?—a title *at best*, meaningless; *at worst*, foully misleading; a title which our Mother Church in England refused to countenance; which even the Church of Ireland (the *least* Catholic of all the branches of the Catholic Church) repudiates with scorn and indignation; which only one or two (and they the most insignificant) of all the legion of protestant sects have incorporated into their legal designation. Who of us does not agree with Dr. Fulton, when he says: "I should be glad if the name 'Protestant' could be dropped from the title page of our Book of Common Prayer"! (Am. Ch. Rev., Jan., 1885, p. 315.)

As to the other adjective, EPISCOPAL, while it is *true*, it is simple *tautology*. "Episcopal!" Why, the word *Catholic*—nay, the very word *Church* connects and implies all that. One might as well say a *vertebrate man*, or a *stellar star*,

In the words of the late venerable Dr. Thomas W. Coit: "To prejudiced Protestants who ignorantly eschew the word *Catholic* as dangerous, it may be enough to say, it is ridiculous (not to use a more solemn word — blasphemous) to say in church, in God's presence, 'I believe in the Holy Catholic Church,' and to repudiate or dishonor the word in *man's* presence." (Early Hist. Note, p. 6.)

"The separation," says Dr. Samuel Seabury (late Professor in the General Theological Seminary, New York), "was from the Court of Rome in respect to its claim of jurisdiction in England, and not from the Church of Rome in respect to any points of faith or order that had been ruled by the Catholic Church. Leaving the Bishop of Rome to govern the Churches of Rome, and the Churches also of

---

as an "Episcopal Church." Moreover, the Church does not belong to the Bishops, but the Bishops to the Church. If we must call our Church "Episcopal" just because it has Bishops, why not call it *Presbyterial* because it has Presbyters ? Presbyters are just as distinctive a mark of the Catholic Church—of the Catholic Church exclusively—as Bishops are, for no body can have Presbyters without having Bishops to make them. The fact of our having *Presbyters* differentiates us as widely from all protestant bodies as the fact of our having *Bishops*, for a Presbyter is a man ordained to the Christian Priesthood by a Bishop.

Then, too, as one has said: "The term 'Protestant Episcopal' has never been *formally adopted* as a title for our Church. * * * The title stole in upon us like a thief in the night. * * * Who put it there [on the title-page] ? What printer, what private member of a committee, what unauthorized person ? In vain have I searched the records of those days to find that the Convention ever adopted the title-page to the Prayer Book. * * * It was never formally adopted as such by the Church here in her corporate capacity. The fact is, the question concerning a proper title for the Church never came up. The utmost that can be said is that the title has only had a mere *quasi* adoption."—("*Failure of Protestantism*," pp. 25 and 27.) The report of the committee of the House of Bishops, at the Gen. Conv. of 1883 (signed by the Bishops of W. N. Y., Georgia, and Michigan), declares that the "name Protestant Episcopal was *forced* upon us by external pressure of circumstances." And the Bishop of Chicago says, in his Convention address, 1884 (See Ch. Ecl., Aug., 1884, p. 429), that this title "was at no time deliberately selected and applied to herself by the Church in this country."

Finally, the name P. E. is never used by intelligent Churchmen except in

such other countries as deemed it for their benefit to continue subject to his jurisdiction, the Church of England, under the protection of the State, resumed the responsibility of governing herself and her members agreeably to the word of God and Catholic tradition. No change was made which offended the consciences of her members. The Church remained Apostolic and Catholic, and gave to her clergy and children this golden Rule of Faith :

" Preachers shall, in the first place, be careful never to teach anything from the pulpit, to be religiously held and believed by the people, but what is agreeable to the doctrine of the Old and New Testament, and collected out of that doctrine by the *Catholic Fathers* and ancient bishops.' (Decree of Convocation, 1571.)

---

official documents. "American Church" is the *usus loquendi;* THE CATHOLIC CHURCH IN THE UNITED STATES OF AMERICA would be more exact.

Our present civil title hurts us more than any other legacy of the eighteenth century. The old proverb says: "Give a dog a bad name, and hang him." The poor fellow may be as faithful as "Fido," but his name ruins him. It is true our nickname (P. E.) does not touch the essence of our Catholicity; but it requires constant explanation, and it hinders the work of the Church, the education of our people, and our intercommunion with other parts of the Catholic Church which are justly suspicious of a Church "which owns so bad a name." We might call ourselves *The Prayer-Bookers*, or *The Anti-Atheistic Ecclesiastical Church Militant here upon Earth*, as a civil designation. It would, of course, be disrespectful to our Holy Maker; but we would none the less continue to be the Catholic Church in the United States of America. Is it not best to call her what she is ? The General Convention of 1883, *from considerations of expediency*, failed to adopt our rightful name. But as the Rev. J. H. Greaves, of Virginia, says (see his "Vindication of the Right of the Anglican Churches to the Use of the Name Catholic," p. 54): "If the question had been as to the *right* to use the title [Catholic], we may be quite sure that the whole body would have voted for it." Such RIGHT will not long have to wait on a timid and (after all) mistaken *expediency*. The day is coming—God hasten it—when our legislators [a majority of the House of Bishops is said to be already in favor of it] will give our Church her rightful name, to which our present *nom de guerre* will give place as "Snowdown's Knight" to "Scotland's King," or as *Il Boudocaue* to "Harown Alraschid;" and "P. E." will in the future be looked upon merely as the *al as* of our youthful dallyings, the *nomen fictum* of our protestant escapades. Our rightful name will then bear fruit to the glory of God.

CHAPTER XIX.

THE ATTITUDE OF DISSENT TOWARDS EPISCOPACY.

"A self-formed Priesthood, and the Church cast forth
To the chill mountain air."
—*Lyra Apostolica*, p. 143.

"It is required now, just as much as in the days of Christ's ministry on earth, that no man shall take the honor of the Christian *Priesthood*, but he whom Christ, as Head of the Church, hath chosen and ordained to that office."—*Bishop McIlvaine*.

VERY different from the authoritative and Catholic reformation of the English Church were the revolutionary Protestant reformations on the Continent, which broke altogether with the past and lost the divinely commissioned ministry of the Church. Far be it from us, however, to condemn a movement which, though less successful, was perhaps as earnest and sincere, and, from the greater abuses of Rome on the continent, more imperatively *necessary* than our own reformation. The candid student of history, however, must admit that for the Lutherans and Calvinists to leave the corrupt and tyrannous papal Churches of Europe was one thing, but that for English Christians to behave in the same manner toward the already freed, purified, and comprehensive Catholic Church of England was another and a very different thing.

The changing attitude of those who left the Historic Church, toward the Apostolic Ministry is, to say the least, remarkable and instructive. (a.) First they revered the Episcopate, longed to retain it, and when they found they had lost the Apostolic Succession, sought earnestly to recover it. It is well known how Luther and Melancthon believed in Episcopacy. Their confession of faith,[1] speaking of bishops, says: "The Churches ought necessarily, and *jure divino* to obey them." Melancthon wrote : " I would to God it lay in me to restore the government of bishops. For I see what manner of Church we shall have, the ecclesiastical polity being dissolved." Beza protested : "If there be any (which you shall hardly persuade me to believe) who reject the whole order of Episcopacy, God forbid that any man of sound mind should assent to the madness of such men." Calvin, in his commentary on Titus (I., 5), admits that there was no such thing as "the parity of the ministry." Again he says : " If the bishops so hold their dignity, that they refuse not to submit to Christ, no anathema is too great for those who do not regard such a hierarchy with reverence and the most implicit obedience." Says Blondel, a learned Presbyterian : " By all we have said to assert the rights of Presbytery, we do not intend to invalidate the ancient and apostolical constitutions of Episcopal pre-eminence, but that wheresoever it has been put down or violated, it ought to be reverently restored." The tremendous testimony of Grotius was quoted above in Chapter XI. And there is something touching and pathetic in the reply of Dr. Bogerman, President of the "Synod of Dort," to the English visitors (sent over by King James I.) when they reminded him that the Reformed Christians of Holland

---

1. Augsburg (part I., Art. 22).

had not retained the Episcopate. "It is not permitted us," said he, "to be so *blessed*"—"*Nobis non licet esse tam beatis.*" It is also well known that Calvin, Bullinger, and other Protestant leaders wrote to King Edward VI., in 1549, with a view to securing the Episcopal succession from England. The letter fell into the hands of some Roman Catholics, who forged a haughty and contemptuous reply.[2]

Such testimony might be multiplied to any extent. Grotius, Blondel, Chamier, Du Moulin, Cassaubon, Beza, Bucer, Le Clerc, Baxter, Doddridge, and many more, yielded to the unanswerable argument for the universality of Episcopacy in the early days, and used to place its origin either with the Apostles, or at least as far back as A. D. 150. And it has been shown that if Episcopacy prevailed then it must have prevailed from the *beginning*, for no such stupendous a revolution could have taken place within fifty years of St. John's death.[3]

---

2. See Kip's Double Witness, p. 79.
3. This attitude of dissenters toward Episcopacy has been well described by Bowden, Mines, Kip and others in their well known books.

"There is yet another historical presumption, exceedingly strong, against those who now slight the apostolic ministry and orders. The unbroken and unquestioning usage of fifteen hundred years is in itself much. For how could it possibly happen, as Hooker well asks, that all that time, if the existing episcopacy were wrong, no one Church ever discovered the right order, or doubted the rightness of the order which did exist ? But the presumption is strengthened still further when it is added that those who now deny episcopacy did not begin by doing so, but were led by circumstances into the want of it, and then gradually, and by a manifest afterthought, came to make a merit of their own defects, and to defend as right what at first they only endured as unavoidable. * * * The controversy about episcopacy, or about orders, was not that which either originated the Reformation, or even occasioned it, or by which men's minds were stirred to urge that Reformation forwards. It was a controversy which grew out of circumstances, and was taken up after a time in order to maintain a position which *no reformed community had sought upon its own merits.*"—"*Haddan on Apostolical Succession,* pp. 131, 136, quoted by Rev. Wm. A. Rich.

(*b.*) Then came a period of blind self-vindication, when the Protestant organizations having (as a temporary expedient) set up a *non-Episcopal* ministry, seemed bound to give it a sort of *ex post facto* justification and validity by boldly asserting that it was, forsooth, the primitive order, and that Episcopacy or *prelacy* (as they preferred to call it) was a corrupt and tyrannous usurpation. This assumption had to be backed by the most arbitrary exegesis of Holy Scripture, and the most amazing handling of the Fathers imaginable—it was indeed *translating* them "by the hair of the head over to the side of Presbyterianism." This process reached its climax in the early part of this century, when Dr. Miller (for example) blindly and recklessly proclaimed that " for the first *two hundred* years after Christ " Episcopacy was unknown to the Church, but that " toward the close of the third century "—[Hear it, ye that have sat with me at the feet of St. Paul and St. John, Ignatius, Irenæus, Tertullian, Cyprian ! !]—" toward the close of the third century prelacy was gradually and insidiously introduced."(!)

Again he says : " We find no evidence whatever within the first FOUR (!) centuries that the Christian Church considered diocesan Episcopacy the Apostolic and primitive form. * * * It is not true that any one of the fathers within the first four centuries, does assert the Apostolic institution of prelacy." Dr. McLeod, of New York, even claimed that the sin of Episcopacy was so great that no bishop could be a minister of Christ, and that all ordinations by bishops were null and void.

Those were days of ignorant, bitter and unreasoning hostility to the Church, when our foes cried : " Down with it, down with it, even to the ground!" I thank God there is more kindliness and candor, as well as more truth and light, in the ecclesiastical controversies of to-day.

(c.) The extreme anti-historical, anti-catholic, anti-scriptural position of Dr. Miller and his school, has now given way to a sounder scholarship among Dissenters, and a better, though not yet perfect, appreciation of the overwhelming evidence on the side of primitive Episcopacy.

Dr. Schaff, a scholarly Presbyterian divine, and a profound student of Church History, in speaking of the Angels of the Seven Churches, frankly remarks: "The impartial reader must allow that this phraseology of the Apocalypse already looks towards the idea of Episcopacy in its primitive form; that is, to a monarchical concentration of governmental power in one person, bearing a patriarchal relation to the congregation, and responsible in an eminent sense for the spiritual condition of the whole.

"This view is confirmed by the fact that among the immediate disciples of John, we find at least one—Polycarp—who, according to the unanimous tradition of Irenæus (his own disciple, himself a bishop), of Tertullian, Eusebius, and Jerome, was, by Apostolical appointment, actually Bishop of Smyrna, one of the seven churches of the Apocalypse.

"Add to this the statement of Clement of Alexandria, that John, after his return from Patmos, appointed bishops; the epistles of Ignatius at the beginning of the second century, which already distinguished the bishop from the presbytery at the head of the congregation, and in which the three orders pyramidically culminated in a regular hierarchy; * * * and we assuredly have much in favor of the hypothesis, so ingeniously and learnedly set forth of late by Dr. Rothe, that the germs of Episcopacy are to be found as early as the close of the first century, and particularly in the sphere of the later labors of St. John. * * * In addition to this, however, the Episcopal system was simultaneously making its way also in other parts of the Church. * * *

"If now we consider the fact, that in the second century the Episcopal system existed as an historical fact in the whole Church, East and West, and was unresistingly acknowledged, nay, universally regarded, as at least indirectly of divine appointment, we can hardly escape the conclusion that this form of government grew out of the circumstances and wants of the Church at the end of the Apostolic period, and could not have been so quickly and so generally introduced without the sanction, or at least the acquiescence of the surviving Apostles, especially of John who labored on the very threshold of the second century, and left behind him a number of venerable disciples. At all events it needs a strong infusion of skepticism, or of traditional prejudice, to enable one in the face of these facts and witnesses to pronounce the Episcopal government of the ancient Church a sheer apostacy from the Apostolic form, and a radical revolution."[4]

Again Dr. Schaff says: "It is a matter of fact that the Episcopal form of government was *universally* established in the Eastern and Western Churches as early as the middle of the second century."

---

4. Schaff's Apostolic Church, pp. 539-541, quoted in that new and most convincing little book, "Plain Footprints, or Divers Orders Traced in the Scriptures," by Rev. H. R. Timlow, p. 10.

Dr. Fisher, of New Haven, also says: "All *candid* scholars must concede that the Episcopal arrangement in the form described may be traced back to the verge of the Apostolic age, if not beyond."

The concessions of Mosheim, Gieseler, Neander, and Hase, are scholarly and candid, and show that any fair view of antiquity compels the admission of the universality of Episcopacy. Their testimony is too long to quote here,[5] so I give but a single sentence from Mosheim, and one from Hase. The former says: "The order of bishops could not have originated at a period considerably more recent than that which gave birth to Christianity itself." And Hase says: "The Episcopate was the divinely appointed pillar which sustains the whole ecclesiastical fabric."

AN IMPORTANT CONSIDERATION.

If Christ appointed any ministry at all for His Church, it must be that ministry which, existing in the Early Church, has perpetuated itself through the ages.

The only ministry which, as an historical fact, has so perpetuated itself, is the *Episcopal ministry* — it, and it alone, has organic connection with those to whom Christ gave the divine commission.

Has that ministry no authority? Has it no claims upon Christian men? Let us reflect.

---

5. See these and many other like witnesses in "Plain Footprints," chap. 1.

CHAPTER XX.

THE ANGLICAN CHURCH AND CONFIRMATION.

> "*Veni Creator Spiritus,*
> *Mentes tuorum visita,*
> *Imple superna gratia*
> *Quae Tu creasti pectora.*"
> —Whitsun Hymn, by Gregory the Great.

> "*Sapientia, intellectus, consilium, fortitudo, scientia, pietas, timor, Domini.*"

> "Draw, Holy Ghost, Thy sevenfold veil
> Between us and the fire of youth."
> —*Keble's Christian Year.*

IN connection with the primitive order of bishops which the Anglican Church has retained in unbroken succession, comes the consideration of an important and Sacramental rite which it belongs to bishops alone to administer, viz. : Confirmation.

Confirmation is defined in the *Church Cyclopædia* as "The imposition of the bishop's hands, whereby the gift of the Holy Ghost is given to the person confirmed ; the strengthening of the soul by the grace of the Spirit." It is an Apostolic Blessing given to those who have been baptized, conveying to them grace and spiritual strength from God the Holy Ghost, to fit them for the worthy receiving of the Blessed Sacrament and the daily living of the Christian life. It is the completion of Holy Baptism, a sort of lay-ordination to that "royal priesthood"[1] which is the privilege of all believers. It was typified by the descent of the Holy Ghost upon our blessed Lord *after* His Baptism in the River Jordan.[2] It was implied in the words of St. Peter: "Be baptized every one of you, * * * and ye shall *receive the gift of the Holy Ghost.*"[3] It seems to be alluded to in the beautiful Hebrew parallelism of St. Paul: "But ye are washed [i. e., baptized], but ye are sanctified [i. e., confirmed], but ye are justified in the name of the Lord Jesus [i. e., in Baptism], and by the Spirit of our God [i. e., in Confirmation]."[4] The sevenfold gift of the Holy Ghost is "the inward part or thing signified;" the laying on of Apostolic hands is "the outward visible sign or form." It is variously called Confirmation, or the strengthening, from the idea conveyed in Eph., iii., 16; the Seal, from Eph., i., 13, and iv., 30; the Chrism, from I. St. John, ii., 27; and the Laying-on-of-hands, from Heb., vi., 2, where it is associated with repentance, faith and Baptism, as being one of "the principles of the doctrine of Christ," the "Foundation" of the Christian life.

That it was the custom of the Apostles themselves to confirm is clearly shown in the eighth chapter of the Acts. St. Philip the Deacon went down to Samaria, preached the Gospel, and baptized many converts. As a deacon he could preach and baptize, but could no more confirm than he could ordain. What was to be done? St. Luke tells us: "Now when the Apostles, which were at Jerusalem, heard that Samaria had received the word of God, they

---

1. I. St. Pet., ii., 9. 2. St. Matth., iii., 16. 3. Acts, ii., 38. 4. I. Cor., vi., 11.

sent unto them Peter and John; who, when they were come down, prayed for them that they might receive the Holy Ghost; (for as yet He was fallen upon none of them ; only they were baptized in the name of the Lord Jesus). Then laid they their hands on them, and they received the Holy Ghost." * * * "Through the laying on of the Apostles' hands the Holy Ghost was given."[5] Unless Confirmation had been an important rite, one of "the principles of the doctrine of Christ," the Apostles would hardly have taken the trouble to send two of their most prominent bishops, SS. Peter and John, to administer the rite to the baptized converts of St. Philip.

Nearly twenty years after this, St. Paul, passing through Ephesus, found there twelve men who had received the Baptism of St. John the Baptist, which was not Christian Baptism, not the "Washing of Regeneration," not the New Birth "of Water and the Spirit," but merely, as St. Paul showed them, a "Baptism of repentance." Then he preached Christ unto them, and they were Christened or received Christian Baptism. After that St. Paul "laid his hands upon them," and they received the Holy Ghost.[6] In other words, they were sealed and received the earnest of the Spirit in their hearts (II. Cor., i. 22).

These allusions to the Apostolic custom of Confirmation in the New Testament, are corroborated by the universal practice of the Church ever after. Baptism was held to be the initiation of a child (or an adult) into the Church; but Baptism was invariably followed, either at once or after an interval, by the laying on of the bishop's

---

5. Acts, viii., 14-18. 6. Acts, xix., 5-6.

hands. In cathedral towns and in small dioceses, where the bishop himself could be present at all Christenings, whether of infants or adults, the Laying-on-of-hands appears to have followed immediately after the Baptism, so that it came to be looked upon as almost a part of it. But where it was impossible for the bishop to be present at the Baptism, the Laying-on-of-hands was deferred until he could be present and perform the act in person "after the example of the Holy Apostles." Thus rose the system of regular Episcopal visitations in every parish, that all who were admitted into the fellowship of Christ's religion might be brought *en rapport* with the Chief Pastors of the Church, might receive the touch and the benediction of an Apostle. All this may be gathered from a few passages from the Fathers.

Tertullian (born A. D. 135), after speaking of Baptism, says : " Next to this the hand is laid upon us, calling upon and invoking the Holy Ghost through the Blessing."[7] St. Cyprian, the Bishop of Carthage (born about A. D. 200), says : "The custom has also descended to us that those who have been baptized be brought to the bishops of the Church, that by our prayer and by the Laying-on-of-hands, they may obtain the Holy Ghost, and be consummated with the *Seal of the Lord*."[8] St. Jerome (born A. D. 340) says : "It is the custom of our Churches that hands be laid on those who have been baptized and the Holy Ghost invoked over them." But lest any one should imagine that this Laying-on-of-hands was administered by the presbyters or deacons, he says explic-

---

7. Tert. *De Bap.*, vii., and viii.   8. Cyp. Epist., lxxiii., 8.

itly: "This is the usage of our Churches. The *bishop* goes forth and makes a tour in order to lay his hands and to invoke the Holy Ghost on those in the small towns who have been baptized by our priests and deacons."

But why multiply instances? Let it suffice to have seen that St. Paul declares this Laying-on-of-hands to be one of the "principles of the doctrine of Christ," that the allusions in the Acts show that it was the practice of the Apostles to lay their hands on the baptized. In addition to which the testimony above cited — of one who lived on the verge of the Apostolic age, of another in the next century, and of another in the century following — shows that it was the custom of the Catholic Church that this rite should be administered by the successors of the Apostles, with the imposition of hands, and with prayer for the gifts of the Holy Ghost.

Confirmation was therefore Apostolic and universal, a note of the Church, a mark of primitive Catholicity. Said a learned Presbyterian divine, while working his way back into the historic Church: "I could not find in antiquity any beginning to this 'Laying-on-of-hands,' but at the hands of the Apostles. I would trace it beyond the Apostles to the Jewish Synagogue, where I could find it even to this day intervening between Circumcision and the Passover."

Considering the primitive character, the Apostolic authority, the scriptural evidence, the testimony of the Fathers, and the universal practice of the Church, to say nothing of the intrinsic grace and practical utility of the solemn act which would give to every child of the Church the paternal benediction of an Apostle — which binds the font to the altar—it seems to me that no Church can claim to have continued in the fellowship of the Apostles, or to have retained *all* the marks of Catholicity, unless it has kept this "Venerable Blessing,"[9] this Apostolic rite.

The Holy Eastern Church with its eighty-five million members, has done so, albeit with a certain irregularity in the mode and form of administration. The Latin Church has done so, although the essence of the rite is somewhat obscured by various additional ceremonies. How is it with our own Church, the Catholic Church of the English-speaking race? I answer, on this point as on all the essentials of the Catholic religion — " the principles of the doctrine of Christ " — our Church has " continued steadfastly in the Fellowship of the Apostles."

The venerable Bede tells us how St. Cuthbert, Archbishop of Canterbury, early in the eighth century, used to go all over his diocese, bountifully distributing counsels of salvation, " and laying his hands on the baptized that they might receive the grace of the Holy Ghost." There is still extant a beautiful Confirmation office which was used in our Church's grand old diocese of York some twelve hundred years ago.

The prayer in our present Confirmation office, beginning: "Almighty and everlasting God Who hast vouchsafed to regenerate these Thy servants," has come down to us by the constant use of the Church from remote antiquity, probably from Apostolic times. It was used in England as far back as we have records of the services; it was

---

9. See a capital sermon with this title by the Rev. H. F. Hill, rector of Montpelier, Vt. It, with "Bishop Randall on Confirmation," and especially Bishop Lay's recent monograph on the subject may be used to great advantage in parish work.

used by St. Ambrose in the ancient cathedral of Milan, in the year 375, more than fifteen centuries ago, and still earlier; it is found also in the Confirmation offices of the Greek Church.

In the Anglican Church since the sixteenth century some of the unnecessary *accessories* of Confirmation, such as the use of holy oil, the signing of the cross, and the blow on the cheek, which had gradually been added to the simple sacrament of the Laying-on-of-hands, have been generally laid aside, and the rite is administered among us in its most primitive and Catholic form.

I know not what words the Apostles used at the precise moment of the imposition of hands; but they can hardly have used words much more appropriate than the sentence which our own Church puts in the mouth of the confirming bishop:

"Defend, O Lord, this Thy child with Thy heavenly grace; that he may continue Thine forever, and daily increase in Thy Holy Spirit more and more, until he come unto Thy everlasting kingdom. Amen." [10]

Indeed the mere witnessing of the sacred joyous service of Confirmation, in which the venerable Father in God, lays his hands on the children of the Church and blesses them in God's name, has been the means of bringing back many a wandering Christian to his own true home

While there is nothing in the nature of Confirmation to prevent its being properly administered to a little child,

---

10. The writer, however, begs to suggest to those who are interested in P. B. revision, whether the meaning of Confirmation would not be more clearly expressed if the first word, "Defend," were changed to *confirm*—Confirm, O Lord, this Thy child, etc. The meaning would really be the same for the defense alluded to comes only through being "strengthened [confirmed] with might by His Spirit in the inner man." Eph., iii., 16

immediately after Baptism (as is the usual custom in the Greek Church), the whole Western Church—both Anglican [11] and Roman [12]—has thought good to order that none shall be confirmed but such as understand the rudiments of Christian faith and duty, and are old enough to " renew the solemn promise and vow " that was made at their Baptism. No age is specified, but any ordinary child, properly brought up, ought to be desirous of Confirmation, and certainly sufficiently instructed, when from twelve to fifteen years of age, some much younger, others not so young. It is at least the design of the Church that children, made members thereof in infancy by Holy Baptism, shall be brought up as children, not as strangers ; and that as soon as they are come to years of discretion, they shall " be brought to the bishop to be confirmed by him," and then be admitted to the Table of the Lord. This is not " joining the Church ; " that was done fully and once for all in Holy Baptism, wherein the person is " regenerate and grafted into the body of Christ's Church." Dissenters, therefore who desire to conform to the Church, ought not to feel aggrieved when they are asked to be confirmed. The ordeal called "joining the church," to which they may have submitted when they became communicants of their respective denominations, is not Confirmation, *nor indeed even analogous thereto.* So that to thoughtful Christians who have been brought up in non-conformity to the historic Catholic Church, Confirmation, instead of being in any sense an obstacle,

---

11. See third rubric after Catechism in P. B., closing exhortation in Baptismal Office, and preface to Confirmation Office; also Canon 61 of the Eng. Ch.

12. For R. C. usage, see Catechism of the Council of Trent, III., 7. "The time there marked out for Confirmation is between seven and twelve years of age." In the Anglican Church the usual age is from twelve to sixteen.

ought to be looked upon as one of the chief inducements for returning to the Church, in order to obtain a grace and a blessing to which as baptized Christians they were justly entitled, but of which they have been deprived by the insufficiency of the bishopless systems of Protestant dissent.

So keenly is "the conscious want of a connecting link between Baptism and Communion" felt by those who have lost the Apostolic rite of Confirmation, that most Continental Protestants (notably the great body of Lutherans) have retained the outward form of Confirmation even though they have no ministry empowered to bestow it. "I sincerely wish," said Calvin, "that we retained this custom of the Laying-on-of-hands, which was practiced among the ancients." The Presbyterians and the Baptists in this country have officially declared their belief in it.[13] Had Confirmation, even as an empty form and without the Apostolic Ministry, been retained among our dissenting brethren, I am very sure that the heresy which denies Baptism to little children would never have made such havoc as it has in the religious life of this age. It is largely for want of Confirmation that Baptism has been transferred, with deplorable results, from infancy to adult age, in order to have some rite or ceremony of preparation for first Communion.

To all thoughtful Non-conformists, as well as to Churchmen, who have not fully grasped the meaning of Confirmation, I beg to speak a serious and loving word — call it preaching, if you will :

You believe in prayer ; you believe that God in answer to prayer gives special grace through His appointed ordi-

---

13. See Randall on Confirmation.

nances. Now go back in thought to the first age of the Church. Suppose you are one of those Samaritans whom St. Philip has converted. You have repented of your sins; you have professed your faith in the Lord Jesus Christ; you have been baptized into the Church. But St. Philip tells you that two of the chief pastors of the Church, the Apostles Peter and John, are coming down from Jerusalem to give you their official benediction, to lay their hands on your head and to invoke the Holy Spirit upon you. With what eagerness would you seize the precious opportunity! You would hasten to the place appointed; and as soon as you saw the benignant face of St. Peter or heard the loving voice of St. John, and realized that you were in the presence of one whom your Divine Master had commissioned as an Apostolic Bishop or Overseer of His Church, would you not rejoice to have him lay his hands on your head and bless you in God's name? Well, that is Confirmation. The bishops who visit our parishes every year come with the same office and authority as Peter and John, when they made the first Episcopal visitation of Samaria. If you believe in God; if you desire grace and help and strength,— come in faith, and as the good bishop after the example of his predecessors, the Holy Apostles, lays his hands on your head and blesses you in God's name, you will be blessed indeed.

In Confirmation, then, as in the sacrament of Regeneration, the Catholic Faith, and Holy Orders, the Anglican Church has continued steadfastly; and it is permitted us to see another golden strand in the cord which binds our Church to the Catholic Church of the Apostles, the Church which Christ founded on the Rock.

CHAPTER XXI.

THE ANGLICAN CHURCH AND THE BREAKING OF THE BREAD.

> "And then—as when the doors were shut,
> With Jesus left alone—
> The faithful sup with Christ, and He
> In breaking bread is known."
> —*Bishop Coxe, Christian Ballads.*

IN the history of eternity there has been but *one* true sacrifice—that of the Son of God Who made "by His one oblation of Himself once offered, a full, perfect, and sufficient sacrifice, oblation, and satisfaction for the sins of the whole world." This, the so-called sacrifices of the Patriarchal and Jewish dispensations foreshadowed; to it they pointed; from it they derived whatever of meaning, virtue, grace they possessed.

In like manner, our great High Priest, at the offering up of Himself, "did institute, and in His holy Gospel command us to continue a perpetual memory of that His precious death and sacrifice." The Eucharist, so far as its *sacrificial* character is concerned, differs from the sacrifices of the elder dispensation chiefly in point of *time*. They prefigured; it commemorates. They were a type; it is a memorial. They were the shadow on the dial before the hour of noon; it the shadow on the dial after the sun has past the meridian.

Christ bade His Church: "Do this for My memorial."[1] And the Church has done it, not as a renewing of Christ's sacrifice, but as a commemoration of it, a pleading of it before the Father, a "showing of the Lord's death till He come."[2] And so from St. Paul[3] and St. Ignatius,[4] nay, even from our Lord Himself,[5] to the American Prayer Book,[6] the Table of the Lord has been authoritatively (as it is almost always popularly) called THE ALTAR, because on it is celebrated the sacrificial memorial of the one great Sacrifice.

Scholarly readers will recall the eloquent passage in Origen's Second Homily, in which he speaks of seeing "Churches built, and ALTARS not sprinkled with the blood of flocks, but consecrated by the precious blood of Christ." Also the clear statement of Athanasius, in his Disputation against Arius, in the Council of Nicæa, in which he says that Christ "sent forth the Apostles, furnishing a Table, that is, the HOLY ALTAR, and on it heavenly and immortal Bread."

---

1. *Eis ten emen anamnesin.* St. Luke, xxii., 19. 2. I. Cor., xi., 26.
3. We have an altar, etc. Heb., xiii., 10; cf. also I. Cor., x., 18, 19, 20, 21.
4 "St. Ignatius, who lived in the Apostolic age itself, calls the Lord's Table the "*Altar.*" See Epist. to the Philadelphians, Chap. iv. Other early fathers frequently allude to the Christian altar." Blunt, An. P. B., p. 158.
5. St. Matth., v., 23 and 24. See Sadler's commentary on this passage: "If the Sermon on the Mount is to be for the guidance of the Church in all time, then there must be in God's Church, at all times, something which can properly be called an 'altar,'" etc.
6. See *Office of Institution,* Am. P. B., 4th rubric, *et passim.* Also the English Coronation Service and the English Canons. It is fair, however, to say that the English Coronation Service was never presented to Convocation, and has thus never received the sanction of the Church. It is a purely *State* service. It is important to remember this, as (while it uses the word Catholic) it also uses the word Protestant in the King's oath. William III. introduced the word as a slap on the face of the Church for refusing to sanction it. Of course, it is interpreted to mean simply *not Romish.*

This aspect of the Holy Eucharist has been by some distorted, and by others entirely ignored. Judged by the usage of the early Church, the Romanists have disproportionately exaggerated it, and the Protestant Dissenters have lost sight of it altogether—giving not even a *minimum* of recognition to the divine system of priest, altar, sacrifice.[7] Between these two extremes, the Anglo-Catholic Church has maintained a safe, primitive, and practical medium. Like the early Church, she gives due recognition to the sacrificial idea by requiring (as she has always done) that no one but a lawfully ordained Priest (*sacerdos*) shall present the "Pure Offering" upon the Holy Table, consecrate the Eucharist, and pray the Father to "accept this our Sacrifice of praise and thanksgiving." The ideal expression of the Anglican view (which, as has been said, is the primitive) is to be found in the Scottish and American Liturgies, especially in that meaningful passage: "We, Thy humble servants, do celebrate and make here before Thy Divine Majesty, with these Thy holy gifts which we now offer unto Thee, the Memorial Thy Son hath commanded us to make."

On the other hand, our Church leaves no room for the undue and disproportionate magnifying of this aspect of the Sacrament of the Altar. (See Article xxxi.)

The Eucharist, however, according to the teaching of Christ and St. Paul, and according to the usage of the Early Church, as apparent in the primitive Liturgies and the writings of the Fathers, was not only a memorial of Christ's sacrifice, but also a Holy Communion or sacramental means of communicating to us the highest of all

---

7. See Bp. Andrewes', vol. v., p. 66, on "Altar, Priest," etc.

God's gifts of grace, uniting us to Him and to one another in the blessed "Communion of Saints." As St. Paul says: "The Cup of Blessing which we bless, is it not the Communion of the Blood of Christ? The Bread which we break, is it not the Communion of the Body of Christ? For we being many are one bread and one body; for we are all partakers of that one Bread."[8] The gift conveyed is nothing less than the Body and Blood of Incarnate God, whereby we are made partakers of Him—as St. Peter says, "partakers of the divine nature."

Look at the Bible-history of the Holy Communion. Our blessed Lord in His memorable discourse at Capernaum (St. John, vi.), said: "I am the living Bread which came down from heaven; if any man eat of this Bread, he shall live forever; and the Bread which I shall give is MY FLESH which I will give for the life of the world."

No wonder that the Jews strove among themselves, saying, "How can this man give us His flesh to eat?" For a mere man to utter these words, would have been the height of madness, and the Jews would have been right. But it was INCARNATE GOD Who spake; He meant what He said, and therefore He repeated His assertion only more emphatically: "Verily, verily, I say unto you, except ye *eat the Flesh of the Son of Man, and drink His Blood,* ye have no life in you. Whoso eateth My Flesh, and drinketh My Blood, hath eternal life; and I will raise him up at the last day. For My Flesh is meat indeed, and My Blood is drink indeed. He that eateth My Flesh, and drinketh My Blood, dwelleth in Me, and I in Him. He that eateth Me, even he shall live by Me."

---

8. I. Cor., x, 16 and 17.

These words were so strange, so unlike the words of any one else, that many of our Lord's disciples said: "This is a hard saying, who can hear it?" And many of them from that time went back and walked no more with Him. Nevertheless He would not retract His words, those "words of eternal life."

Doubtless the faithful ones who still clung to Him were troubled, and cast in their minds what He might mean; but they had not long to wait. For on the night on which He was betrayed, "Jesus took bread, and blessed it, and brake it, and gave it to the disciples, and said : "'Take, eat ; THIS IS MY BODY.' And He took the cup and gave thanks, and gave it to them, saying, 'Drink ye all of it; for THIS IS MY BLOOD.'"[9]

He said we must eat His Flesh and drink His Blood, and then to show us what He meant, He instituted the Holy Communion, saying : "This is My Body," "This is My Blood." St. Paul also teaches that the unworthy receiver of the Bread and Wine, is "guilty of the *Body and Blood of the Lord*."[10] His sin consists in "not discerning the Lord's Body."

St. Ignatius speaks of certain heretics, who "confess not the Eucharist to be the Flesh of our Saviour Christ."[11]

Justin Martyr, who gives us the first graphic account of the administration of the Holy Eucharist, says : "We do not receive these elements as common bread and common drink, but we have been taught that the food which has been eucharistically blessed is the Flesh and Blood of that same Incarnate Jesus."[12] Similar testimony might

---

9. St. Matthew, xxvi., 26–28. 10. I. Cor., xi., 27. 11. Ad. Smyr., Ch. vii.
12. 1. Apol., LXVI.

be brought forward to any extent showing that in the Holy Communion the Body and Blood of Christ are (as our article says) "given, taken, and eaten."

On the other hand, our blessed Lord and St. Paul taught, and the Early Church believed, that the bread and wine, although after Consecration properly called the Body and Blood of Christ, nevertheless are still bread and wine, having no change of substance. Christ calls the consecrated wine His Blood, but He also calls it the "fruit of the Vine."[13] St. Paul calls the consecrated bread not only the Body of Christ, but still bread, "for," says he, "we are all partakers of that one bread."[14] And again "As often as ye do eat this bread;" and "Whosoever shall eat this bread;" and "So let him eat of this bread."[15] The Fathers also assert the same. Says St. Irenæus: "The bread from the earth, receiving the invocation of God, is no longer common bread, but the Eucharist, consisting of two things — an earthly, and a heavenly."[16] St. Chrysostom says that the bread "when once Divine Grace has, through the intervention of the priest, sanctified it, is worthy to be called the Lord's Body, although *the nature of bread remains.*"[17] Theodoret says that Christ "honored the symbols which are seen with the title of bread and wine, *not changing their nature, but adding grace to the nature.*"[18] And Gelasius, Bishop of Rome, A. D. 492, says: "The grace of the Body and Blood of Christ which we receive is a Divine thing, wherefore also we are by the same made par-

---

13. St. Mark, xiv., 25. 14. I. Cor., x., 17. 15. I. Cor., xi., 26–28. 16. Adv. Hær., IV., 18, 5. 17. Epis. ad Caes., Opp. T., III., p. 744, Ed. Ben. 18. T., IV., 25, Ed. Sch.

takers of the Divine nature; and yet *the substance and nature of bread and wine ceaseth not to be.*"[19]

Now, if we care anything for the teaching of Christ and of St. Paul, and anything for the belief of the Catholic Church in its purest days, we must admit two things: First, that the bread and wine are in some true sense the *Body and Blood of Christ;* and secondly, that they are still *bread and wine.*

It is altogether unnecessary to assume that there is any contradiction or inconsistency in this twofold truth. From Augustine, and even Irenæus, the Church has had a simple and comprehensive doctrine which saves both sides of the truth, viz., that so well expressed in our Catechism, that a Sacrament has two parts, the "outward visible sign, and the inward spiritual grace." The Bible itself demands this definition.

Such was the belief of the early Church; and our Liturgy, Catechism, Articles and Homilies show that such is the doctrine of the Anglican Church to-day. "What," says the English Church Catechism, "is the outward part or sign of the Lord's Supper? Bread and Wine, which the Lord hath commanded to be received. What is the inward part or thing signified? The Body and Blood of Christ, which are verily and in deed taken and eaten by the faithful in the Lord's Supper."

Diverging from this, the Catholic Doctrine of the Holy Eucharist are two errors—both of which overthrow the very nature of a Sacrament, viz., (a) The doctrine of the *real absence* of the Bread and Wine; and (b) The doctrine of the *real absence* of the Body and Blood of Christ—both

---

19. *De duab. Christi naturis.* The passage is quoted in Sadler's Ch. Doct. and Bib. Truth (p. 137), a book which every intelligent layman ought to read and study.

of which are equally opposed to the Church's Scriptural and Catholic Doctrine of the *Real Presence*, the substantial reality, of *both* parts of the Sacrament.

I. The first of these errors is called Transubstantiation It denies the outward visible sign by declaring that aftei Consecration there is no bread and no wine at all, but only the actual Body, Blood, Soul and Divinity of Christ. And yet that Jesus Christ, Incarnate God, thus present, deludes His worshippers by the Protean trick of *resembling* a piece of bread and a cup of wine—albeit no bread and wine are there, for the whole substance of the bread and wine has ceased to be, having been converted into the substance of the Body and Blood of Christ, into " Christ whole and entire,"[20] but the " accidents " of the bread and wine, having supplanted the proper accidents of Christ's human Body remain to mock us.

This doctrine of Transubstantiation was foreshadowed by Paschasius Radbertus, in 831, but ably opposed by Rabanus Maurus and Bertram of Corbie, while in the tenth century the "Paschal Homily" of our own Aelfric, Archbishop of York, shows that the error had not then gained a footing in the Church of England. Lanfranc, Archbishop of Canterbury, in 1070, was the first to teach Transubstantiation in our Church; and in 1215, this rationalistic hypothesis, which "is repugnant to the plain words of the Scripture, overthroweth the nature of a Sacrament,

---

20. See Council of Trent, Sess. XIII., Ch. 4. See also Catechism of Co. of Trent, Pt. II., C. IV., q. XXXI., which teaches in addition that in this Sacrament are contained "whatever appertains to the true nature of a body, such as bones and nerves." Canon III. of Sess. XIII., also teaches that "the whole Christ is contained under each species." From this premise it was easy to deduce the practical heresy of Communion under one species. See Sess. XXI., Canons I. and II.

and hath given occasion to many superstitions," was declared an article of the Faith (!) by the Fourth Lateran Council.

It must of course be acknowledged that Transubstantiation was for several centuries taught by the clergy of our own Church in England, though it is probable that all the while the general average of English Churchmen, guileless of Aristotelian metaphysics and scholastic subtilties, held substantially the same view of the nature of the Blessed Sacrament that they hold to-day. It is needless to say that one important part of the English Reformation was the restoring of the primitive, consistent, scriptural doctrine of the *two* parts of the Sacrament, and the *Real Presence of both*.

Out of the theory of Transubstantiation there gradually arose in western Christendom a most shocking and impious abuse, the withholding of the chalice from all but the Celebrant himself. This half-Communion or Communion under one kind is nothing less than the robbing of Christ's people of the Blood of Christ, and a sacrilegious mutilation of the Blessed Sacrament.

Christ had said, "Except ye drink the Blood of the Son of Man ye have no life in you;" and when He gave the consecrated wine (as if guarding against this very abuse) He said: "Drink *all* ye of it." The teaching of St. Paul is equally conclusive: "So let him eat of that bread, *and drink of that cup.*" The Catholic Church throughout the world administered under both kinds—the Liturgies and all the Fathers testify to this. Bishops of Rome (and our Roman Catholic brethren would have us believe them all infallible!), notably Leo the Great and Gelasius I., declared this half-Communion a heresy, and ordered those who refused the chalice to be excommunicated.[21] As late as 1095 the Council of Clermont, under the presidency of Urban II., Bishop of Rome, decreed that "no one shall communicate at the altar, without receiving the Body and the Blood separately and alike, unless by urgent necessity and for caution."[22] The mutilation of the Sacrament began about the twelfth century,[23] though in the thirteenth, St. Thomas Aquinas speaks of the primitive practice (Communion in both kinds) as lingering in some Churches.[24] It did not become general in our own Church till after the Council of Constance (1415), which decreed it; it was never willingly acquiesced in by our laity, and sometimes the clergy used to administer a chalice of *unconsecrated wine* (*!*) for the sake of appearances and to pacify the people. The sacrilege was of short duration in our Church, for the chalice was unanimously restored by Convocation, December 2, 1547; and with the exception of the four years of Romanist reaction under Queen Mary, the Sacrament of the Altar has ever since been administered to our people in its integrity, as Christ appointed.

II. The second great error which overthrows the nature of a Sacrament is commonly called Zwinglianism.

It is the doctrine of the real absence, not of the bread

---

21. See Leo Hom. XLI., and *Gelasius ap Gratiam de consecrat*, quoted in Littledale's Plain Reasons, xxxiii., p. 83. Also "England versus Rome," by H. B. Swete, M. A., p. 160.

22. See Brown on the Articles, p. 733.

23. *Cardinal Bona* admits this. See Bingham II., 808.

24. In S. Joann., VI. and VII. The Greek Church, of course, has never refused to the laity the Sacrament of the Blood of Christ.

and wine, but of the *Body and Blood of Christ*. It reads a negative into God's most solemn affirmation. It transubstantiates our Lord's declaration, "This IS My Body," into This is NOT My Body. As Transubstantiation ignores the outward visible sign, so Zwinglianism refuses to "discern" the inward part or thing signified, which, St. Paul teaches us, is the essence of the unworthy reception of the Sacrament. The Catholic doctrine accepts both. Just as touching the Incarnation, Unitarians deny that Christ is God, the Docetæ deny that He is Man. But He is both, and the Catholic Church adores Him, God and Man, the blessed *Theanthropos*.

According to Zwinglianism, the Holy Communion is a bare, empty sign, and as such may be administered without priest, or altar, or divine Liturgy ; and among American Dissenters is now, with fanatic presumption, usually administered without wine ;—vapid, outlandish, unauthorized compounds being substituted.

Zwinglianism has, of course, never received any ecclesiastical sanction in the Anglo-Catholic Church, either before or since the sixteenth century. Our doctrinal and liturgical standards are as careful, on the one hand, to guard against it, as, on the other hand, to guard against Transubstantiation; allowing, however, between these two extremes a large and charitable measure of Christian liberty.

Our Church, therefore, continues steadfastly in "The Breaking of the Bread." We Catholics prize and love the outward symbols which remind our dissenting brother of the broken Body and the out-poured Blood ; while, with our Roman brother, we reverence and "discern the Lord's Body," receiving that "spiritual food and sustenance to our great and endless comfort," holding each side of the truth without disparagement of the other.

> "Whene'er I seek the Holy Altar's rail,
> And kneel to take the grace there offered me,
> It is no time to task my reason frail,
> To try Christ's words, and search how they may be;
> Enough, I eat His Flesh and drink His Blood,
> More is not told—to ask it is not good.
>
> I will not say, with these, (25) that bread and wine
> Have vanished at the consecration prayer;
> *Far less*, with those, (26) deny that aught divine
> And of immortal seed is hidden there.
> Hence, disputants! The din, which ye admire,
> Keeps but ill measure with the Church's choir."

---

25. Romanists.   26. Zwinglians.

CHAPTER XXII.

"THE PRAYERS."

"They continued steadfastly in the prayers." (A mark of the Early Church.)
—Acts, ii., 42.
"Take with you words and turn to the Lord."—Hosea, xiv., 2.
"If all the liturgies of all ancient Churches throughout the world be compared amongst themselves, it may be easily perceived that they had all one original mould."—*The Judicious Hooker.*

TO some it may be a surprise to be told that liturgical worship is a mark of the early Church, and hence a note of Catholicity, but it is assuredly so. I would not say that a body of Christians having the Faith, the Ministry, and the Sacraments, would be necessarily un-Churched if they were to give up the Liturgy (as for a time the Catholic Church of Scotland did, with results melancholy and disastrous), but such a Church would be incomplete, not fully Catholic, and sure to deteriorate. Indeed, I believe a purely human organization with a Catholic Liturgy (like the Irvingites) is more likely to keep the Faith, than a Church without the Liturgy would be. It behooves us, therefore, (*a*) to understand and appreciate the fact that the Early Church had its " Divine Liturgy," as well as its Faith, Ministry, and Sacraments; and (*b*) to realize that our own Church, the Catholic Church of the English speaking race, has preserved, in its essential integrity,

Catholic worship, as well as those other marks of the primitive Church in which we have already seen her historic continuity.

Of all the kinds of authorized public worship, among Jews and among Christians, no such thing was ever known, until recent times, as a non-liturgical service. The usual custom of Anglo-American Dissenters in delegating their worship to the extemporaneous devotion of a single leader, would have appeared as absurd to a Jew, or to an ancient Catholic Churchman, as it does to-day to those of us who have learned what "Common Prayer" really is, who have been taught "not to bring unbeaten oil into the Sanctuary."

The Tabernacle and Temple service, which was ordained by God, was absolutely liturgical. The worship of the synagogue, if not of Divine ordering through Ezra, had, at least, Divine sanction, and was approved and devoutly participated in by the Son of God during His earthly life. It also was absolutely liturgical.

Fragments of the Mosaic ritual are given us in the Old Testament, and the whole in the writings of the Rabbis. Thus in Numbers, vi., 24–26, we have the divinely ordered form of priestly Benediction : "In this wise ye shall bless the children of Israel : The Lord bless thee and keep thee ; the Lord make His face to shine upon thee, and be gracious unto thee ; the Lord lift up His countenance upon thee, and give thee peace."[1] In Deuteronomy are given the liturgical forms to be used by the people in making the offering of first fruits,[2] and of the tithes of the

---
1. Our Church retains this ancient blessing in the Visitation Office
2. Deut., xxvi., 5-11, and 12-15.

third year, and the form used by the elders of a city in which murder had been committed.[3] The Psalms also were nothing less than a divinely inspired book of devotions, and were regularly chanted or intoned by the vested priests and white-robed choristers in the temple. When Hezekiah remodeled the Jewish worship, we read that he "and the princes commanded the Levites to sing praises unto the Lord with the words of David and of Asaph the seer; and they sang praises with gladness, and bowed their heads and worshipped."[4]

We learn from the Talmud the whole arrangement of the services in connection with the sacrifices, the sabbaths, and the holy days. Accurate translations may be found in Lightfoot's Temple Service. The Jewish ritual also furnished forms for all special occasions—circumcisions, marriages, burials and the like. And we have in minute detail the forms of worship used at the Passover, used therefore by our Lord at the "Last Supper," and constituting the norm of the Christian Liturgy or Order for the Administration of the Holy Communion.

In opposition to all this, Dissenters often reply: O, Christian worship is not based on the Temple Service but on that of the synagogue!—which, they assume, was very much of the nature of an extemporaneous "prayer-meeting." Let us see. One has but to enter a synagogue to-day in order to see that the service which the Jews have kept up for more than two thousand years is as distinctively liturgical as that of any part of the Catholic Church. Indeed a stranger happening into a synagogue might almost think that the service of Morning or Evening Prayer was that of

---

3. Id., xxi., 7.   4. II. Chron., xxix., 30.

a somewhat ritualistic congregation of Churchmen. The reading of Scripture lessons according to *The Calendar*, the chanting of Psalms, the intoning of beautiful prayers, especially the eighteen[5] collects which Ezra is said to have composed at the time of the return from the captivity, and which were certainly used in the time of Christ, bear as little resemblance to the modern " prayer-meetings," " experience-meetings," " gospel-temperance-meetings," *et id genus omne*, as does the high Celebration at St. Paul's cathedral to the " love-feast " of a " camp-meeting." A graphic description of the synagogue services is accessible to all in Geikie's Life of Christ, vol. I., chap. xiii.; in Prideaux' Connection, part I., book vi., p. 375, and in many other works.

Does it ever occur to the advocates of bald extemporaneous services how unnatural is the supposition that the Apostles, trained to liturgical worship in every detail of religious service, should have wrought a revolution in the very idea of worship, inconceivable to the oriental mind, and which would have appeared as irreverent and distasteful to them, as would the total abolition of the Prayer Book to devout Anglicans to-day ? Our Saviour certainly never uttered one word against the established forms of Jewish worship in which He Himself regularly and devoutly participated. St. John Baptist taught his disciples to pray ; [6] and Christ gave His Apostles the Lord's Prayer, which the Church has ever since universally employed in public and in private worship. It is worthy of note also that every

---

5. A 19th collect was added early in the Christian era, praying against Christians.
6. St. Luke, xi., 1.

petition in this prayer is to be found in the Jewish services.[7] In His agony in the garden, our Saviour used the same words in prayer three times; and when He, the Son of God, was dying upon the Cross, in His closing words to His Father (as one has said) "He used that golden form of prayer which David as His prototype, composed," "My God, my God, why hast Thou forsaken me?" (Ps. xxii.) and, "Into Thy hands I commend my spirit." (Ps. xxxi: 5).

The Church under the guidance of the Apostles soon shaped to itself, by adaptation and by composition, a liturgical service. In Acts iv., we have a picture of the Christian assembly in Jerusalem, as "they lifted up their voices to God with one accord," in a beautiful prayer which breathes the spirit of the early Church, a sort of Christian psalm, carefully composed according to the rules of Hebrew Parallelism, and evidently said or sung in concert. The Colossians were bidden to teach and admonish one another "in psalms and hymns, and spiritual songs"[8] which certainly could not have been extempore. The only early instance of unpremeditated and irregular worship (if worship it may be called,) is the abuse which existed for a time in the troublesome and self-willed congregation of Corinth, and to the rectification of which St. Paul so strenuously exerted himself.[9] His closing injunction in this connection may well be the Church's motto in all ages: "Let all things be done decently and in order."

The Liturgy, in the strict sense of the word, means the service used in celebrating the Holy Eucharist. It admits of no doubt that our Saviour, at the Last Supper, followed

---

7. See Lightfoot on St. Matt., vi., 9–13, and Horne's Incrod. to Scrip., V. iii., p. 296.
8. Col., iii., 16.   9. See I. Cor., xiv., especially vs. 26

the usual ritual of the Passover, inserting at the most appropriate places the Eucharistic blessing of the bread and wine, and the distribution of the consecrated Elements. It is, moreover, reasonable to suppose that He gave the Apostles directions as to the way in which they were to " do this." Be that as it may, they certainly could never have celebrated that Holy Communion without recalling and reproducing the outline of the Paschal service which the Master had used. His example was command enough, even if He did not explicitly order them to follow it; and as a matter of fact they did follow it. Wherever they went they carried with them the same outline of the Liturgy, and that, too, based on the Paschal Sacrifice. Although it was not generally (if at all) committed to writing till in the second century, yet it retained all its parts, and had only verbal differences in the most widely severed portions of the Church.

In the great centers like Jerusalem, Ephesus, Rome and Alexandria, the Liturgies used bore the impress of Apostolic individuality, while still keeping to the general form of Catholic unity. Thus arose four great types of the primitive Liturgy, called, respectively : (*a*) The Liturgy of St. James, used in Jerusalem (and, in a slightly modified form, in Antioch, known as the Antiochian, Clementine or Apostolic Liturgy); (*b*) the Liturgy of St. John, used in Ephesus, Gaul, Spain, and Britain ; (*c*) the Liturgy of St. Peter, used at Rome ; and (*d*) the Liturgy of St. Mark, used at Alexandria.[10]

---

10. These four Liturgies are the basis of all modern Liturgies. That of St. James is still used in the East, and is the basis of the Græco-Russian service; that of St. John is the basis of the Anglican, and also of the old Gallican and Mozarabic; that of St. Peter, of the modern Roman use; that of St. Mark, of the Coptic rite.

These all have twelve parts or divisions in common. The order in which these parts occur is not always the same ; the substance of each is the same, and even the verbal expression, though not identical, is so similar as to demonstrate a common origin. They differ less from each other than the four great races of men whom God " hath made of one blood for to dwell on all the face of the earth,"[11] and who may all justly claim a common origin from Noah, by whose sons " was the whole earth overspread."[12] After Scripture lessons and a sermon with which the service usually began, the twelve parts common to all ancient liturgies are as follows :

    I. The Kiss of Peace.
    II. Lift up your hearts.
    III. The Tersanctus.
    IV. Commemoration of the Institution.
    V. The Oblation.
    VI. The Invocation.

(The three last form the Prayer of Consecration, or Canon of the Mass.)

    VII. Prayer for the living.
    VIII. Prayer for the faithful departed.
    IX. The Lord's Prayer.
    X. Union of the consecrated Elements.
    XI. The Communion.
    XII. Thanksgiving.

This is the order of parts according to the Liturgy of St. James.[13]

---

11. Acts, xvii., 26. 12. Gen., ix., 19.
13. For the arrangement of the other Liturgies, see Blunt's Annot. P. B., p. 148; Cutt's Turning Points in Gen. Ch. Hist., p. 142, and Kip's Double Witness, p. 105. See also, for some specimens, Sadler's Ch. Doct. and Bible Truth, p. 204.

The four varieties of the early Liturgy are at least as much alike as the four Gospels, which have so much in common that we are sure they are each based on the one oral Gospel which the Apostles taught for twenty years before they wrote down the first word.

The Apostolic Liturgy is, in its substance, older than the written Gospels and Epistles. St. Paul himself several times quotes from liturgical forms used in the Early Church. This fact is clearly shown in Neale's Essays on Liturgiology (pp. 411–474), is often alluded to by Conybeare and Howson, and is admirably set forth by a layman of our own Church in a most instructive monograph on the Divine Liturgy.[14]

The worship of the early Church was liturgical, musical, reverent, symbolic, and, as soon as circumstances allowed, ornate. When the younger Pliny was Governor of Bithynia, A. D. 112, he wrote a letter to the Emperor Trajan, in which he gives us our first post-Apostolic glimpse of Christian worship. The Christians, says he, "are accustomed, on a stated day, to meet before daylight, and to say antiphonally a hymn to Christ [*dicere secum invicem carmen Christo*] as to God, and to bind themselves by a Sacrament [or oath, Latin *Sacramentum*] not to commit any wickedness."

The next description of Christian worship is given by Justin Martyr before A. D. 140:

"Upon the day called Sunday we have an assembly of all who live in the towns or in the country, who meet in

---

14. I refer, of course, to "The Divine Liturgy in the Book of Common Prayer," by Geo. W. Hunter, pub. by James McCauley, Philadelphia, 1881. See p. 104; also, for St. Clement's quotations, p. 90.

an appointed place; and the records of the Apostles, or the writings of the Prophets are read, according as time will permit. When the reader has ended, then the Bishop [or president] admonishes and exhorts us in a discourse that we should imitate such good examples. After that we all stand up and pray, and as we said before, when that prayer is ended, bread is offered and wine and water. Then the Bishop, also, according to the authority given him, sends up prayers and thanksgivings; and the people end the prayer with him, saying, Amen. After which distribution is made of the consecrated Elements, which are also sent by the hands of the deacons to those who are absent."[15] He also speaks of the Christians offering up "solemn rites and hymns."[16]

The prayer of consecration or "Canon of the Mass," is of course the vital and essential part of the Liturgy. It is impossible here to reproduce any ancient Liturgy in full; but while referring the reader to Neale's translations, to Hammond's great work, and the little book of Hunter mentioned above, I will give a brief description of the so-called Clementine Liturgy which agrees with that of St. James, being probably that form of it which was used in Antioch.[17] It is undoubtedly the earliest complete Liturgy which has come down to us, for it is contained in the eighth book of the Apostolic Constitutions, which though probably not compiled until the third or fourth century, is made up of material of much earlier date. The four great Liturgies may be traced back in substantial integrity

---

15. For the whole passage see Justin's Apol. I., Ch. 65-6-7.
16. Apol. I., 13.
17. See Probst, p. 231, quoted by Hunter.

to the fifth century, St. James' Liturgy to the fourth, and this form which I am about to quote, certainly to the third or earlier.[18] They can also be traced by fragments and actual quotations so far back that there can be no doubt that they were used substantially as we have them in the age next succeeding that of the Apostles, and were based on the oral Liturgy which the blessed Apostles used with the memory of the Last Supper fresh in their minds, and which Proclus (Patriarch of Constantinople in the fifth century) asserts they agreed upon before they parted for their several fields of work.

The first part of the Clementine Liturgy—the part which we call the Ante-Communion or Proanaphora—begins with readings from Holy Scripture (which at an early date, probably by St. Jerome in the fourth century, were arranged into the Gospels and Epistles for the day.[19]) Then the Bishop says the lesser Benediction (which St. Paul quotes in II. Cor., xiii., 14), "The grace of our Lord Jesus Christ, the Love of God the Father, and the fellowship of the Holy Ghost be with you all."

[*And let all answer*] "And with thy Spirit."

Then follows the sermon; and after that a deacon dismisses the catechumens, and utters a bidding prayer, which bears a most striking resemblance to the corresponding part of the Jewish Paschal Office immediately

---

18. Hunter says of it: "We have here sacred words used by apostles and martyrs day after day and week after week, older, possibly, than the Gospel of St. Matthew; older, probably, than the Epistles of St. Paul; older, most of them, certainly than the loveliest and dearest of all writings, the Gospel of St. John." P. 26.

19. The altar readings both of the ancient and modern Anglo-Catholic Church often differ from the modern Roman arrangement, in which case we generally follow the old order of St. Jerome, from which Rome has often departed. See Blunt, Annot, P. B., p. 70.

after the discourse, bidding the people pray for the Church and the world, for bishops, priests, deacons, etc., for "the babes of the Church" (an incidental proof, by the way, of infant baptism). The bishop,[20] who is here called the High Priest, says the prayer corresponding to our prayer for the Church Militant. Then comes the Offertory, when "the deacons bring the gifts to the bishop at the altar," and the wine is poured out. Just here occurs an important rubric:

"When the High Priest has prayed by himself with the priests, and has put on his shining garment,[21] standing by the altar, and having made with his hand the sign of the Cross upon his forehead, let him say:

"The grace of the Almighty God, etc., be with you all."

[*And let all with one voice say:*] "And with thy Spirit."

[*The High Priest.*] "Lift up your mind."

[*All.*] "We have unto the Lord."

[*The High Priest.*] "Let us give thanks unto the Lord."

[*All.*] "It is meet and right."

[*And let the High Priest say:*]

[THE PREFACE.] "It is verily meet and right, before all things, to hymn to Thee, the only true God," etc. Here follows a very long ascription of praise (which we have cut down to the Short Preface and proper Prefaces of our Communion Office) obviously based on the "Hallel" of the Passover ritual. It closes, of course, with the

---

20. In this copy of Liturgy the Celebrant is supposed to be a Bishop: It is directed to be used by a Bishop at his first Eucharist after his Consecration.

21. The clergy of the early Church, like the Jewish ministry, wore proper vestments as soon as it was practicable to do so.

Ceraphic Hymn, though in a somewhat fuller form than our own, "Therefore with angels and archangels," etc., the whole congregation uniting in the "Holy, Holy, Holy, Lord God of Hosts," etc. The bishop then says a prayer which embodies a pharaphrase of the Creed, and also corresponds slightly to our "Prayer of Humble Access," followed by the solemn Canon of the Mass, which I give in full that all may see how remarkably our Prayer of Consecration agrees with it:

"Remembering, therefore, what things He endured for us, we give Thee thanks, O, God Almighty, not as we ought, but as we are able, and fulfill His command.

[THE INSTITUTION.] For in the night in which He was betrayed He took bread in His holy and spotless hands, and when He had looked up to Thee His God and Father, He brake, and gave to His disciples, saying, This is the mystery of the New Covenant, take of it, eat. This is My body, which is broken for many, for the forgiveness of sins. Likewise, when He had mingled the cup with wine and water, and hallowed it, He gave it to them, saying: Drink ye all of this, for this is My blood, which is shed for many for the remission of sins. Do this in remembrance of Me. For as often as ye eat this bread, and drink this cup, ye do show forth My death till I come.

[THE OBLATION.] Remembering, therefore, His passion and death, and resurrection from the dead, and return into the heavens, and His future second appearing, in which He shall come with glory and power to judge the quick and the dead, and to give to each one according to his deeds, we offer to Thee, King and God, according to

His command, this bread and this cup, giving thanks to Thee through Him, in that Thou hast thought us fit to stand before Thee, and to sacrifice to Thee.

[THE INVOCATION.] And we beseech Thee that Thou wilt favorably look upon these gifts which now lie before Thee, O Thou God, who needest naught, and be well pleased with them in honor of Thy Christ, and send down upon this Sacrifice Thy Holy Ghost, the Witness of the sufferings of the Lord Jesus, that He may make this bread the Body of Thy Christ, and this cup the Blood of Thy Christ, that they who partake thereof may be strengthened in piety, may obtain remission of sins, may be delivered from the devil and his deceit, may be filled with the Holy Ghost, may be made worthy of Thy Christ, may obtain eternal life, since Thou art reconciled to them, O Lord Almighty."

I give here the corresponding prayer in our Prayer Book to show how primitive our Liturgy is:

THE INSTITUTION. "All glory be to Thee, Almighty God, our Heavenly Father, for that Thou, of Thy tender mercy, didst give Thine only Son Jesus Christ to suffer death upon the cross for our redemption; Who made there (by His one oblation of Himself once offered) a full, perfect, and sufficient sacrifice, oblation, and satisfaction for the sins of the whole world; and did institute, and in His holy Gospel command us to continue a perpetual memory of that His precious death and sacrifice, until His coming again: For in the night in which He was betrayed, He took bread; and when He had given thanks, He brake it, and gave it to His disciples, saying: Take, eat, this is My Body, which is given for you ; do this in remembrance of Me. Likewise, after supper, He took the cup ; and when He had given thanks, He gave it to them, saying, Drink ye all of this ; for this is My Blood of the New Testament, which is shed for you, and for many, for the remission of sins ; do this, as oft as ye shall drink it in remembrance of Me.

THE OBLATION. Wherefore, O Lord and heavenly Father, according to the institution of Thy dearly beloved Son our Saviour Jesus Christ, we, Thy humble servants, do celebrate and make here before Thy divine Majesty, with these Thy holy gifts, which we now offer unto Thee, the Memorial Thy Son hath commanded us to make; having in remembrance His blessed passion and precious death, His mighty resurrection and glorious ascension; rendering unto Thee most hearty thanks for the innumerable benefits procured unto us by the same.

THE INVOCATION. And we most humbly beseech Thee, O most merciful Father, to hear us; and, of Thy Almighty goodness, vouchsafe to bless and sanctify, with Thy Word and Holy Spirit these Thy gifts and creatures of bread and wine ; that we, receiving them according to Thy Son our Saviour Jesus Christ's holy institution, in remembrance of his death and passion, may be partakers of His most blessed Body and Blood." * * *

After the prayer of consecration follow some special intercessions for the living and for the faithful departed, which we have in the concluding part of the Canon and also in the prayer for the Church Militant. Next comes the *Gloria in Excelsis*, though in a shorter and more ancient form than that of other Liturgies, including our own. The Communion follows, the bishop, priests and deacons first receiving, and then the people in order, " with reverence and godly fear."

"[*And let the bishop give the offering, saying:*] The Body of Christ. [*And let him that receiveth, say:*] Amen.

[*And let the deacon take the cup, and giving it, say:*] The Blood of Christ, the Cup of Life. [*And let him that drinketh, say:*] Amen.

The 34th Psalm follows, corresponding to our Communion Hymn. And the concluding prayers correspond with our post-Communion prayer.

This is a fair specimen of the early Liturgy, tne chief and central service of the primitive Catholic Church. And as we compare our own with it, we may well thank God that our Church has " continued steadfastly in the prayers."

CHAPTER XXIII.

THE ANGLICAN CHURCH AND "THE PRAYERS."

"In beauty built and might
For Apostolic service
And high liturgic rite."
—*Bishop Coxe, Christian Ballads.*

"Here rises with the rising morn
Their incense unto Thee,
Their bold confession Catholic
And high Doxology.
Soul-melting Litany is here,
And here, each holy feast,
Up to the Altar duly spread
Ascends the stoled Priest."
—*Same.*

THE striking resemblances which we have noted between the Liturgy of our Prayer Book and the Liturgies used in the Early Church are not the result of chance nor of imitation, but of hereditary possession and unbroken usage. Our Church *inherited* Catholic worship just as she inherited Catholic Faith, Order and Sacraments.

The "Liturgy of St. John,"[1] used in Ephesus, until the fourth century, was very early carried to Gaul, Spain and Britain, receiving, of course, certain modifications as the

---

1. The Liturgy of Ephesus, though commonly called the "Liturgy of St. John," is thought by many to be more properly the Liturgy of St. Paul, as it was really he who organized the Church in Ephesus, and ordained Timothy as the first bishop of that city.

needs of the Church required. It was used in Gaul until the time of Charlemagne, who introduced the Roman Use, about A. D. 800 ; and in Spain until the eleventh century, when there also it was superseded by the Roman — although since the sixteenth century it has been, and is still, used in Toledo, in a college and chapel endowed for that purpose by Cardinal Ximenes.

The British Church was no more indebted to Rome for her Liturgy than for her other marks of Catholicity. She used a form of the Liturgy of St. John, substantially identical with that used in Gaul. When Augustine found that the British Christians used a somewhat different form of worship from that to which he had been accustomed in Rome, he was very much perplexed, and wrote to Gregory, the Roman bishop, to know what to do. Gregory's answer was most wise and charitable ; and to it we are indebted for the preservation of our own beautiful and independent Liturgy, which, based on that of St. John, is still our glory and the precious vehicle of our devotions. Instead of forcing the Roman form on the Anglo-British Church, Gregory wrote to Augustine :

"You, my brother, are acquainted with the customs of the Roman Church in which you have been brought up. But, it is my pleasure, that, if you have found anything either in the Roman or the Gallican or any other Church, which may be more acceptable to Almighty God, you carefully make choice of the same ; and sedulously teach the Church of the English, which is at present new in the Faith, whatsoever you can gather from the several Churches. * * * Select, therefore, from each Church those things which are pious, religious and correct ; and when you have made these up into one body, instil this into the minds of the English for their use."²

Augustine, of course, made not a few modifications in the direction of the Roman Use, which was, perhaps, at that time the more elaborate and complete service. But as a great majority of the Saxons were converted by the missions of the old Celtic Church, the English race clung tenaciously to its independent ritual. As a matter of fact the Roman Missal and Breviary were never used in England's Church, except in some of the monasteries. Attempts to enforce the Roman Use (as at Cloveshoo, A. D. 747), encountered a stern resistance, a resistance in some respects more successful than certain other Italian encroachments met with. In 1085, St. Osmund, Bishop of Salisbury, revised the offices of the Church, and his revision (known as the Sarum Use) became quite general throughout our Church. Certain dioceses, however (as York, Bangor, Hereford, and London till 1414), retained to some extent local Uses, all of which, however, were clearly independent of the Roman Use.

Very extensively during the Saxon period, and almost wholly after the Norman Conquest, the offices of our Church were said in Latin for obvious reasons.³ Moreover, many corrupt additions had crept into our formularies of worship, such as prayers, hymns and litanies which paid

---

2. Greg. opera, II., 1151, Ben. Ed. and Bede's Eccl. Hist., I., 2. 7.
3. Latin was a sort of universal lauguage in the West, for devotional purposes far superior to the *vernacular* which was undergoing constant change, especially after the Conquest. Our Church has no objection to the use of Latin where it is understood by the congregation; accordingly an authorized Latin version of the P. B. was put forth for use in the universities and classical schools in England, and the opening service and sermon at convocation and at some of the diocesan synods in England, are still in Latin. Even in the parish churches,

to saints and angels and especially to the Mother of our Blessed Lord, an almost idolatrous veneration, clearly forbidden in Holy Scripture and unheard of in the primitive Church. Then, too, the calender was so cumbered up with superfluous Saint's Days, and the services were so complicated, and the daily offices in the monasteries left so little time or inclination for daily prayers in the parish churches that a reform in our devotional system was as clearly called for as the other reforms, in the sixteenth century, of which we have already treated. And in the Providence of God this, like the others, was effected gradually and without any break of continuity.

The invention of printing now enabled the Church to put Prayer Books as well as Bibles in the hands of the people, and became a powerful instrument for reform. Something in the way of devotional reform was accomplished in 1516, probably through the influence of Cardinal Wolsey, and more in 1531. The " Prymers " and " The Mirroure of our Ladye " followed, giving in English, the Epistles, Gospels, Litany, and other parts of the services, with explanations. In 1541 the Lessons were ordered to be read in English. Three years later the Litany was admirably revised and authorized to be sung in English. In 1547 Convocation adopted an " Order of the Communion " in English to be appended to the usual Latin Liturgy, and providing for the restoration of the chalice to the laity.

---

where the English clergy are obliged to say Matins and Evensong every day, *if no congregation be present*, the service may be said in Latin. Had the government allowed the Irish Church to retain Latin after the Reformation, instead of forcing English upon it, the probability is that a large majority of the native Irish would have remained in the Old Church, instead of being driven into the Roman schism. The Irish were used to Latin, but hated English.

And finally on Whitsun Day, 1549, the whole service of the Church—viz.: "Matins" and "Evensong," "The Holy Communion commonly called the Mass," and many special offices—was universally adopted in superb idiomatic English, by authority of Convocation and Parliament. This great work, commonly called the "First Prayer Book of Edward VI.," is, in the judgment of competent liturgiologists, the most perfect form of Catholic worship ever used in the Church of God.[4]

Although this Prayer Book was in some respects new— the old services being purified and simplified as well as translated, and the "Seven Hours" being condensed into the two offices of Matins and Evensong—yet it was essentially identical with the old, and Archbishop Cranmer offered to prove that "the order of the Church of England, set out by authority of Edward VI., was the same that had been used in the Church for fifteen hundred years."[5]

There have been several subsequent revisions of the Prayer Book, but the English, Scottish, Irish, and American Books, to-day, differ but little from the Prayer Book of 1549, the Scottish being the most perfect of the four, and the American next. Still the differences are so slight that the different members of the Anglo-Catholic family are hardly aware of any diversity in their grand, pure, ancestral system of divine worship—which, as a service of *Common Prayer* is far superior to the Roman system in which participation in the worship is almost exclusively limited to the clergy and the choir, besides being *far* less

---

4. A capital reprint of this book, with a preface by Dr. Dix, may be had of the "Ch. Kalender Press," New York.
5. Bp. Jeremy Taylor's Works, vii., 292.

primitive and pure, and "in a tongue not understanded of the people." As to all kinds of non-liturgical worship, no comparison is possible; they are not to be mentioned in the same breath.

As one looks at the whole question of public worsnip, and remembers how precious the Prayer Book is to many a Christian heart outside the Anglican Church,[6] it becomes a matter of wonderment that any body of English speaking Christians, even after they had cast off their allegiance to the Historic Church, should ever have given up the liturgical worship of the sanctuary. Luther and Calvin, and Knox and Wesley,[7] and almost every leader of sccessions from the Church believed in the liturgical system, and put forth elaborate forms of public prayer, which are still largely retained by continental Protestants. But for more than two centuries almost all English and American Dissenters have had the strange notion (not taught by their founders nor dreamed of before in all Jewry and Christendom) that liturgical worship was unscriptural, insincere, unedifying !—a sentiment characteristically expressed by "Sam Lawson," when he said: "Now readin' prayers out of a book, that ere' don' strike me as just the right kind o' thing. For my part I like

---

6. Dr. Adam Clarke, a distinguished Methodist, said: "The liturgy is almost universally esteemed by the devout and pious of every denomination, and, next to the translation of the Scriptures into the English language, is the greatest effort of the Reformation. As a form of devotion it has no equal in any part of the Universal Church of God. Next to the Bible, it is the Book of my understanding and my heart." Similar testimony, especially in this country during the last twenty years, might be multiplied to any extent.

7. In classing Wesley among the leaders of secession, it must be remembered that he was such only indirectly and unintentionally. He lived and died a loyal Catholic priest, and his dying injunctions to his followers were never to leave the Church of England.

prayers that come right out of the heart."⁸ As though, forsooth, a prayer born in the intellectual throes of extemporaneous utterance on the part of the leader, and followed by the audience on the *qui vive* of uncertain expectancy and mental adoption, could somehow be more devotional, more directly from the heart, than the chaste, hallowed, familiar devotions of the Prayer Book, when, the mental effort of recollection and invention—the cerebral struggle with syntax and vocabulary—being in abeyance, the whole energy of the soul is centered in the heart, and the heart itself lifted to God in the ecstacy of pure and ennobling worship.

This truth, with others, is strongly, but with no real lack of charity, expressed by a leading Presbyterian minister on the eve of his return to the Historic Church :

"To be losing my time and patience, and to be injuring my devotional taste and temper with the 'gifts' of the brethren in a stupid prayer-meeting, when I might be wafted toward heaven in the sublime strains of a holy liturgy ; to be frequenting a more public service, where prayer was curtailed, and Holy Scripture almost excluded, and a few short verses of rhyme sung only as an interlude or rest, and all this, done systematically, to make room for a labored sermon," etc., etc., " when by a single step I might enter the larger liberty of a Church which breathes, and believes, and prays, and praises as she did when Irenæus, Ignatius and Polycarp beheld her glory, and the noble army of martyrs died for her as the pure spouse of Christ —all this had now become a burden too great for me to bear."⁹

---

8. Mrs. H. B. Stowe's "Oldtown Folks," p. 326.
9. Mines' Pres. Clerg., p. 140.

How did such a system of public service ever arise and gain adherents, not to say devotees, among Christian men? It will be a surprise to many to be told that it was largely the work of Jesuits in England,[10] who, in the disguise of zealous Protestants, made some weaker members of the Church and the larger portion of Nonconformists ill affected toward the Church's worship, in order to create divisions, anarchy, and confusion, that on the ruins of England's Faith, they might erect, as on heathen soil, a foreign and corrupt Church. They were successful in ruining the public worship of Dissent, but the Church of England, "the Bulwark of the Reformation," kept the Catholic worship, which, in turn, has kept her from manifold ill. And we may now thank God that English-speaking Christians of every name are more and more coming back to the principles of Prayer Book Worship. The remarkable Presbyterian Book of Common Prayer, compiled by the devout and scholarly Dr. Shields, of Princeton, the earnest efforts of Drs. Hopkins and Hitchcock, also among the Presbyterians, and of other like-minded men in different denominations, and the superb liturgy compiled by the little sect of Irvingites, are a few among many indications that the prejudice against liturgical worship is being done away. There has been, too, a sudden waking up to the fact that hymns, which are for

---

10. "They (i. e., extemporaneous services) were contrived by popish emissaries disguised in the garb of Protestantism, and pretending the utmost abhorrence of what they stigmatized as the corruptions of popery still existing in the English Church. The object was to produce division and dissension, as the surest mode of bringing the reformed religion into disrepute, and regaining the ascendency once enjoyed by the Roman pontiff. For this purpose, among other things, they were loud in their invectives against the liturgy," etc.—*Sermons on the Church*, by the Rev. G. T. Chapman, D. D., p. 188.

the most part nothing but rhythmical prayers, are as distinctly liturgical as the Litany or the Psalter ; and if it is right to sing liturgical prayers in verse, it can hardly be wrong to say or to sing them in prose.

It cannot be claimed that our Prayer Book is absolutely perfect, but it is at least marvelously good.[11] Cast in the words of Holy Scripture (for more than nine-tenths of it is taken directly from the Bible), framed on the general plan of primitive Apostolic worship, of which it is the lineal descendant, cleansed from all mediæval corruptions, expressed in the purest style of the best of modern languages, consecrated by the devout use of generations of saints who now rest in Paradise, and withal adapted to the devotional needs of the rich and of the poor, of the high and of the lowly, in this and every age, we may well thank God for the Book of Common Prayer, rejoicing that our beloved Church has "continued steadfastly in THE PRAYERS."

---

11. See a notable article by Dr. Shields in the Century (Nov., 1885). Speaking of the liturgical movements among the sects, the learned Presbyterian declares: "It must have its logical conclusion in the English Prayer Book as the only Christian Liturgy worthy the name. * * * The English Liturgy, next to the English Bible, is the most wonderful product of the Reformation." He adds, that if the reunion of American Christianity ever comes, "it must come through the spirit of Protestant Catholicism, of which the English Liturgy, properly amended and enriched, would be the best conceivable embodiment." —p. 84.

CHAPTER XXIV

THE CLOSE OF THE ARGUMENT FOR THE CHURCH'S AUTHORITY BASED ON HISTORIC CONTINUITY.

> "One only Way to Life;
> One Faith, delivered once for all;
> One holy Band, endowed with Heaven's high call;
> One earnest, endless strife;—
> This is the Church the Eternal framed of old.
>
> "Smooth, open ways, good store;
> A Creed for every clime and age,
> By Mammon's touch new moulded o'er and o'er;
> No cross, no war to wage;—
> This is the Church our earth-dimmed eyes behold.
>
> "But ways must have an end,
> Creeds undergo the trial flame,
> Nor with the impure the Saints forever blend,
> Heaven's glory with our shame:
> Think on that hour, and choose 'twixt soft and bold."
>
> —*Keble on Dissent.*

IN connection with the prayers in which our Church has continued steadfastly, it is worthy of note that even in the manner and the accessories of public worship, our Church has followed the general course marked out by the primitive Church.

Dissenters usually *sit down* to pray and often to sing praises, and almost all of them, at their Communion services, receive the elements in the same undevotional posture. It is the custom of Churchmen, enforced by rubic and canon law, to make *bodily* reverence an accompaniment, or rather a part, of divine worship, the general principle being for the congregation to kneel in prayer, to stand in praise, and to remain seated during other parts of the service, such as the lessons and the sermon. That this change of position is a rest in itself, and relieves the monotony of a long service is a practical argument in its favor ; but the real ground of it is the authority of primitive example and unbroken Church usage, which is after all the natural expression of the devotional instinct.

Perhaps some one will say: What has the position of the muscles and bones of my body to do with the prayers of my soul? What difference does it make whether the angle of articulation between the *femur* and the *tibia* be an angle of 90 or of 180 degrees? — that is to say, whether the knee be bent or no. Well, as a matter of physical anatomy it makes no difference ; as an act of bodily exercise it profiteth little. But as a matter of religious service, of sincere devotion, it marks the difference between the reverent worshipper and the irreverent. What difference does it make whether a man enter a drawing-room with proper decorum, or with hat on and hands in pockets? Why, just the difference between a gentleman and a clown. We strive to be polite, urbane, considerate of others ; and well we may. Domestic decorum, social civility, and grace of manner, born of the instinctive courtesy which renders honor to whom honor is due, not only prove the kindly heart within, but by a well known law of reciprocal action, minister to and increase the same. He who would be courteous must *act* courteously; and he who would be reverent in heart must be reverent in his outward demeanor. There is then such a thing as divine courtesy, the humble, reverent, etiquette of God's House, the grand and worshipful decorum of the palace and court of the Great King. What! shall we be polite to our fellow-men, and rude to our Heavenly Father? Shall we regard even the artificial conventionalisms of society, and forget the ritual of God's Church? Shall we observe the proprieties of the parlor, and not respect the sanctities of Jehovah's temple? Shall we present a petition to an earthly prince, on bended knee, and (like English courtiers) bow even before the *empty* throne of majesty; and yet, when we offer our prayers to the King of Kings, shall we sit bolt upright, or stand without so much as a feeling of awe before God's Altar Throne? Surely to ask such questions is to answer them.

And as to Scriptural warrant and primitive example, what a cloud of witnesses surrounds us! See Abraham "bowed toward the ground" in the plains of Mamre,[1] and his servant Eliezer, when by the well of the city of Nahor, "he bowed down his head and worshipped the Lord."[2] Witness Moses and Aaron on their faces before the Ark of God,[3] and David throughout his life of prayer. Witness Solomon at the dedication of the Temple, "before the altar of the Lord, kneeling on his knees, with his hands spread up to heaven."[4] Call to mind that memorable occasion when "Jehosaphat bowed his head with his face to the ground, and all the inhabitants of Jerusalem fell before the Lord, worshipping the Lord."[5] Witness Daniel when, with his windows open toward Jerusalem, "he kneeled upon his knees three times a day, and prayed and gave

---

1. Gen., xviii., 2. 2. Gen., xxiv., 48. 3. Num., xx., 6; xvi., 22, etc. 4. I. Kings, viii., 54. 5. II. Chron., xx., 18.

thanks before his God."[6] Behold our Divine Master — in His agony in the garden He "fell on his face and prayed."[7] See the Martyr Stephen,[8] and St. Peter,[9] and St. Paul,[10] on their knees in prayer. St. John also gives us a glimpse of angelic ritual in heaven. He looks, and lo! "the four and twenty elders fall down before Him that sat on the throne, and worship Him that liveth forever and ever, and cast their crowns before the throne. * * * And all the angels fell before the throne on their faces, and worshipped God."[11] The same principle of reverence was carried into the early Church. St. Paul says: "I bow my knees unto the Father,"[12] and "at the name of Jesus every knee should bow,"[13] while St. James, the first Bishop of Jerusalem, used to spend so much of his time in the true attitude of devotion, that his knees became like the knees of camels.

There are, of course, among the different races of men, certain differences in the manner of expressing reverence. Western races uncover the head as an act of reverence; Orientals remove the shoes, which is as natural to them as lifting the hat is to us. Races differ also as to their posture in prayer. Some stand, some kneel, some prostrate themselves. Customs, even among the same people, may differ from age to age. The ritual of the early Church required the congregations to kneel at public prayer on week days, fast days, and even on all Sundays in Lent and Advent; but on other Sundays, and on all high festivals, the people stood in prayer, in order to show that the Lord's Day

---

6. Dan., vi., 10. 7. St. Matt., xxvi., 39. 8. Acts, vii., 60. 9. Acts, ix., 40.
10. Acts, xx., 36, and xxi., 5. 11. Rev., iv., 10, and vii., 11. 12. Eph., iii., 14.
13. Phil., ii., 10.

was not a penitential day, not the "Sabbath" (as modern
Dissenters call it), but a holy and joyous festival. The
distinction, however, did not long remain in the West.
The general sense of Christians seemed to be that kneeling is the proper attitude for prayer — the chief exception
being that the minister, when he performs what our Prayer
Book calls a distinctively "sacerdotal function," should
stand. The distinction, however, while it lasted, was only
between kneeling and standing in prayer. Such a thing
as the modern, lazy, don't-care kind of ritualism which
sits down to worship, was never dreamed of in the Church,
save as being allowable for cripples, invalids, and those
who through some unusual illness or fatigue are unable to
kneel. There is, moreover, a devout custom which has
been universal in the Church for some sixteen centuries,
and probably quite general from the beginning, viz., bowing at the mention of the sacred name of JESUS, wherever
it occurs, but especially in the Creed and *Gloria in Excelsis*.
When American patriots at a political meeting hear the
name of Washington, they applaud ; when the followers
of Incarnate God, assembled for worship, hear that Holy
Name in which He wrought out their redemption, they
bow, in grateful, loving, reverent adoration. Angels worship Jesus Christ. The Father Himself has commanded
it, for we read : " When He bringeth in the First-begotten
into the world, He saith, 'and let all the angels of God
worship Him.'"[14] And if angels adore Him, shall not we
who are redeemed by Him? As soon, therefore, as "heresies of perdition" led men to "deny the Lord who bought
them," and to refuse to worship Christ, the very sound of

---

14. Heb., i., 6. See also Rev., v., 6–14.

Jesus' Name became to orthodox Christians an invitation, nay a challenge, to adore Him, to proclaim "Worthy is the Lamb that was slain," to feel like Thomas when he cried: "My Lord and My God!"[15] It is true that most of us bow only in the Creed and the *Gloria in Excelsis*, but in theory our Church keeps up the old custom, for she bids her children adore whenever in Divine service the name of Jesus is heard. See the fifty-second of Queen Elizabeth's injunctions (A. D. 1559) and the eighteenth canon of the English Church (passed in 1603, and still in force), which says:

"And likewise, when, in time of divine service, the Lord Jesus shall be mentioned, due and lowly reverence shall be done by all persons present, as it hath been accustomed."[16]

It is then a part of our continuity in Scriptural and Apostolic worship to ask our clergy and people to be reverent in their demeanor, to "glorify God with their bodies and their spirits which are His." Many of our dissenting brethren see the propriety of this; and in times of special religious fervor Presbyterians, Congregationalists, and still more frequently Methodists, kneel in public prayer; while in private prayer, or about the "family altar"—freed from the unnatural restraints of the "meeting-house" and the pitiable self-consciousness which is born of uncatholic individualism, these same people are always wont to kneel

---

15. St. John, xx., 28.
16. See a learned layman's treatment of this subject, "By What Laws the Am. Ch. is Governed," by S. Corning Judd, Am. Ch. Rev., Jan., 1882, pp. 214–216. Also speech of Sir Edw. Dering, in House of Commons, quoted in Mine's Presb. Clerg., pp. 236–237.

in reverent and devout worship, in which I have rejoiced and do rejoice to unite with them.

The same principle of Anglo-Catholic continuity applies to the Church Year. The Bible and all Jewish History set before us the idea of sacred seasons, the round of festival and fast. The early Christians largely observed the Mosaic year. St. Paul "hasted to be at Jerusalem the Day of Pentecost."[17]

Soon three great Christian Festivals, Christmas, Easter, and Whitsun Day, took the place of the three great Jewish Feasts, while Good Friday succeeded to the solemn Day of Atonement, the ante-type to its type. Indeed, from the very day of the Lord's Resurrection, a weekly Easter, THE LORD'S DAY, took the place of the Sabbath.

If Americans who lightly esteem the Church's Year—but go wild over the "May Anniversaries" of tract societies, boards of commissioners, and the like, who enter with zeal into Luther and Wiclif celebrations, and keep political, biographical, scientific, literary and domestic anniversaries and centennials—would reverently place themselves back in Apostolic times, they would see that the rise of the Christian Year was authoritative and inevitable. For example, it is inconceivable that the blessed Apostles could ever have found themselves in the Paschal Season without recalling the events of Holy Week. Suppose it is A. D. 53. The Jews are occupied with the Passover. What memories, O what memories must crowd upon an Apostle's mind ! Twenty years ago to-day they nailed Him to the Cross for our sins. *Let us fast and pray.* Or: —This is the anniversary of that glorious morn when our

---

17. Acts, xx., 16.

Master rose from the dead. *Therefore, let us keep the Feast.* And so the Christian year began. Taking Easter as a specimen, I quote the words of Dr. Blunt:[18] "They who went about 'preaching Jesus and the Resurrection,' and who observed the first day of the week as a continual memorial of that Resurrection, must have remembered with vivid and joyous devotion the anniversary of their Lord's restoration to them. It was kept as the principal festival of the year, therefore, in the very first age of the Church, and Easter had become long familiar to all parts of the Christian world so early as the days of Polycarp and Anicetus, who had a consultation at Rome in A. D. 158, as to whether it should be observed according to the reckoning of the Jewish or Gentile Christians. [Irenæus in Euseb. v., 24.] Eusebius also records the fact that Melitus, Bishop of Sardis, about the same time, wrote two books on the Paschal Festival [Euseb. iv., 26], and Tertullian speaks of it as annually celebrated, and the most solemn day for Baptism. [De Jejun. 14, De Bapt., 19.] Cyprian, in one of his epistles, mentions the celebration of Easter solemnities [lvii.]; and in writers of later date the festival is constantly referred to as the 'most holy Feast,' 'the great Day' [Conc., Ancyra, vi.], 'the Feast of Feasts,' 'the Great Lord's Day,' and 'the Queen of Festivals. [Greg., Naz., Orat., in Pasch.]"

Our own Church, through all its deformations and reformations, has always had the same Christian Year. No break was made in the sixteenth century, no change save to weed the Calender of some superfluous days of recent origin and questionable propriety. As one has said:

---

18. Annot. P. B., pp. 103 and 104.

"The Christian Year is a lively and systematic exposition of the Christian Creed."

So it is with other points, such as the respective functions of bishops, priests and deacons, the form and manner of ordaining, the power and use of Absolution, the architecture and arrangement of churches, the vestments of the clergy, etc.

A single word as to the last. The Jewish ministry was ceremonially vested by divine command. It is not likely that the Christian ministry would forego a custom so natural, reverent and appropriate. As soon, therefore, as the Church was able to have regular and well-ordered services, the clergy appear to have worn a distinctive dress in their public ministrations. Many think that the "cloak" which St. Paul "left at Troas," was an Episcopal vestment. St. James in Jerusalem and St. John in Ephesus used to wear the mitre of the High Priest.[19]

During the ages of persecution, when the Church worshipped "in dens and caves of the earth," there is no clear evidence that the clergy in general wore vestments, but as soon as it was safe and practicable the custom became universal;[20] and has, of course, been perpetuated in the Anglican Church.

For all the distinctive features of our Church we have primitive precedent and historic usage almost absolutely uninterrupted from the beginning; and for most of them we have Catholic, Apostolic, Scriptural, Divine authority, while *none* of them are contrary to the Word of God.

---

19. See Polycrates, *ap.* Euseb., iii., 31, for St. John. Epiphanius asserts the same, and appeals to St. Clement as authority for the statement, *Haer*, xxix., 4. Hegesippus affirms it of St. James, *ap.* Euseb., ii., 23.

20. See Van Antwerp's Ch. Hist., vol. 1, p. 64.

There are a few matters of ceremonial and a few methods of work, certainly harmless and probably useful, for which ancient and quite general authority can be alleged, but which have fallen into disuse among us. Our Church has never condemned them, they can be fully restored at any time, and are decidedly non-essential, anyway. If there be one sign above another of our Church's justification, one key-note of the Anglo-Catholic position, it is the word CONTINUITY,—continuity in all the essentials of the Catholic religion of the kingdom of God.

It has now been shown that Christ founded an enduring Universal Church, with a perpetual ministry. The marks of that Church are apparent in Holy Scripture and in ancient history. Of the three great divisions of English-speaking Christians to-day, Anglo-Catholics, Roman Catholics, and Protestant Dissenters, to which ought we to belong?

The Dissenters have no historic continuity with the Early Church, and for the most part do not pretend to have; have lost the Church's ministry, the Christian Year, Common Prayer, and, to an appalling degree, the Faith, the Sacraments, the services, and the usages of Catholic antiquity; and have wholly lost the idea of authority and of unity in the kingdom of God.

The Roman Church has added to the Faith a few untrue, and many unnecessary dogmas; has over-ridden the Bible and the General Councils; has added creature worship to "The Prayers"; has mutilated the Chief Sacrament; has committed schism in four out of the five Patriarchates[21] and in the autocephalous Churches; has

---

21. It is the charge made by the whole Eastern Church that the Pope of Rome, as but *one* of five Patriarchs, has schismatically broken away from the other four.

thrust a fallible man into the throne of God on earth and has presumed to elevate a woman (albeit the holiest of the daughters of Eve) to the throne of the Adorable Trinity in Heaven. And whatever may be said for the authority of the Roman Church in Italy, as the national Church thereof, certainly within Anglo-Saxon Christendom it is nothing but a foreign, intruding, schismatic Church, having no mission and jurisdiction, and no historic continuity, no organic connection with the old Church of England.

The Anglo-Catholic Church, on the other hand, has retained, in unbroken continuity, all the essential elements of true Catholicity, while free from corrupt and unnecessary additions. She is Catholic; she is reformed; she is Scriptural; she is authoritative; she is that part of the kingdom of God which has jurisdiction over the Anglo-American race; she has continued steadfastly in the Faith, the ministry, the Sacraments, and the worship of the Apostolic Church. In a word, we may say to her:

> "*Antiquom obtines,*" [22]
> "How well in thee appears,
> The constant custom of the antique world." [23]

And as to those who have "gone out from us," but who love the Lord Jesus Christ, they are still our brothers, and the Merciful Father is the Judge of all, and will do right. Be ours the prayer of Hezekiah: "The good Lord pardon everyone that prepareth his heart to seek God, the Lord God of his fathers, though he be not cleansed according to the purification of the sanctuary." [24]

---

22. Ter. Andria, Act IV., Sc. iv., 817. 23. "As You Like It," II., 3, 56. 24. II. Chron., xxx., 18-19.

CHAPTER XXV.

THE ARGUMENT FROM EXPEDIENCY.

"Rise, Sion, rise, and looking forth,
Behold thy children round thee !
From East and West, and South and North
Thy scattered sons have found thee !
And in thy bosom, Christ adore
For ever and for evermore."

—From the *Haute de Klete* of St. John Damascene (Neale's "Hymns of the Eastern Church").

THE fact that Christ founded an authoritative kingdom on the earth, of which the Anglican Church is a pure and complete branch, ought to make a Churchman of every English-speaking Christian, irrespective of tastes, personal preferences, and considerations of temporary expediency.

The question is not : Which of the three systems (the Anglo-Catholic, the Papal, or the Protestant) do I like best ? but which is right, authoritative, divine ? We have found the Anglican so to be. Any other system, therefore, so far as English-speaking Christians are concerned, may logically be met with Tertullian's *praescriptio in limine* (like a case in court which is "quashed" or dismissed without a trial), for "what is new is none."

Nevertheless there are some people who care nothing for

authority, but consult only their own preferences. To such while freely admitting the good there is in all systems of Christianity, even the most defective, we need not fear to hold up the superior advantages of the Church in its organization and in its practical methods of worship, teaching and work.

Of the three systems of Christianity among us, the Anglican is the only one which both holds to the past and adapts itself to the present. The Roman, despite its many innovations, does hold to the past, but it is as far as possible from adapting itself to the present, being totally at variance with the genius—even the better genius—of modern times:[1] while as for Dissent, it breaks wholly with the past and in adapting itself to the present, too often sacrifices essentials of Christian doctrine and devotion to the itching ears and the restless, creedless spirit of modern society.[2] But the Church is at once stable and elastic, conservative and progressive.

All the elements of Catholicity are not only of divine authority (as we have seen), but are, in the long run, so practically beneficial that they may well challenge the admiration of the mere utilitarian. Indeed the bare imitation of some of them—*e. g.*, the Methodist imitation of the Episcopate, and occasional imitations of Catholic worship and Sacraments in various denominations—have been found so advantageous that there is a strong tendency on the part of many practical and farsighted Dissenters to adopt, as a matter of expediency in order to keep their children from flocking to the Church, many customs of the Church

---

1. See the Syllabus of Pius IX.   2. See II. Tim., iv., 3.

which they once condemned. The reading of the Bible in public worship, religious services at weddings and funerals,[3] the use of instrumental music, the singing of hymns and even chants and anthems, a lessening of the grim requirements for "joining the church," a milder and more Churchly treatment of Christ's little ones, a partial escape from the pestilent superstition touching the necessity of "instantaneous conversion,"—a cruel bug-bear which has frightened many a pure, gentle, sensitive soul away from all religion—the use of the Holy Cross—which used, with shocking profanity, to be called the "mark of the beast," a growing belief in Paradise or the immediate state, the imitation of Church architecture, a partial adoption of the Church's year, of the Church's nomenclature, of the Church's idea of worship (as distinguished from mere preaching and exhortation),[4] and even of liturgics, ministerial vestments, banners, processions, lights, ecclesiastical colors, and ritual in general, albeit sometimes strangely symbolic; more frequent Celebrations, and notably less

---

3. See "Puritanism; or a Churchman's Defence against its Aspersions," by the late Dr. Thomas W. Coit, D.D., of Berkeley.

4. "Of course it would be idle to expect those outside the pale to appreciate our system, because if they did they would be outside no longer. Nevertheless, there are from time to time remarkable and most touching indications of an instinctive yearning after Catholic faith and practice amongst those who as yet know them not. Here is an example: The congregation of Govan, a suburb of Glasgow, recently presented a testimonial to their minister, Dr. John Macleod, who in returning thanks referred to that happy time ' when the Church, *i. e.*, the Presbyterian bodies, would repent of the blunder she had so long committed in substituting the purely human invention of perpetual preaching and hearing of sermons, for that which undoubtedly was the distinctive ordinance of the weekly worship, the perpetual pleading by the holy priesthood of the power of the sacrifice for all men before the Throne of the Eternal, and the feeding upon the Heavenly food of the Body and Blood of our Lord.' We can only pray that this good man may soon discover where he may at once obtain what he wants."— *Church Times.*

disagreeable mannerisms,[5] unreasonable asceticism, and pseudo-Judaic Sabbatarianism; and, above all, more sweetness and beauty, and joy in the Christian life, with more charity for the Church,—all these things show a tendency, on the part of those whose ancestors left the Church, to return to the Church's bosom. They are a vindication of the Church's system, showing that its general features are not only harmless, but desirable and good. As Dr. Hopkins, the Presbyterian champion of liturgical worship, says "the tracks are all *one way.*" The tendency of devout and thoughtful Dissenters is unquestionably toward the Church. They wonder now at the fierce passions and petty whims which led their ancestors to break with the Historic Church. It is said that descendants of Luther are to be found in the Roman priesthood, and descendants of Cromwell in the priesthood of the English Church; while descendants of Cotton Mather, and indeed of almost every Puritan prominent in the early history of New England, are to be found among the clergy or the laity of the American Church.

The practical advantages of the Episcopal form of government are as obvious as the fact of its Apostolic authority is incontrovertible. But perhaps the argument which weighs most with outsiders who have not heard, or do not

---

5. In the reasonable, cultivated, urbane, and to all outward appearances *Churchly* Congregationalist one meets in Boston society to-day, it is hard to recognize a descendant of the so-called "Pilgrim Fathers," or the English Puritans of the seventeenth century, whose idiosyncrasies were a part of their religion. The reader will recall Macauley's vivid description of them: "The ostentatious simplicity of their dress, their sour aspect, their nasal twang, their stiff posture, their long graces, their Hebrew names, the Scriptural phrases which they introduced on every occasion, their contempt of human learning, their detestation of polite amusements, etc." Essay on Milton.

grasp, the argument from authority, lies in the usefulness and beauty of our dear old Book of Common Prayer. Said a Congregationalist minister who, like many of his brethren, is an appreciative observer of the Church :

"The proper name, because truly descriptive, for this Church, would be Church of the Prayer Book. As is the way with all other churches, so here the Church champions and leaders have many wise things to say about the Church and her perogative. But the pious multitude that frequent her courts, are drawn thither mostly by love of the prayers and praises, the litanies and lessons of the Prayer Book.

"And, brethren of every name, I certify you that you rarely hear in any church a prayer spoken in English, that is not indebted to the Prayer Book for some of its choicest periods.

"And further, I doubt whether life has in store for any of you an uplift so high, or downfall so deep, but that you can find company for your soul, and fitting words for your lips among the treasures of this Book of Common Prayer.

"*In all time of our tribulation; in all time of our prosperity; in the hour of death and in the day of Judgment; Good Lord deliver us.*

"As a consequence of the Prayer Book and its use, I note :

"The Episcopal Church preserves a very high grade of dignity, decency, propriety and permanence in all her public offices.

"In nearly every newspaper you may read some funny story based upon the ignorance or eccentricity or blasphemous familiarity of some extemporizing prayer maker. All of you here present have been at some time shocked or bored, by public devotional performances. Nothing of this sort ever occurs in the Episcopal Church. All things are done and spoken decently and in order.

"And so, too, of permanence and its accumulating worth of holy association, no transient observer can adequately value this treasure of a birthright Churchman.

"To be using to-day the self-same words that have through the centuries declared the faith or made known the prayer of that mighty multitude who, being now delivered from the burden of the flesh, are in joy and felicity.

"To be baptized in early infancy, and never to know a time when we were not recognized and welcomed among the millions who have entered by the same door.

"To be confirmed, in due time, in a faith that has sustained a noble army of confessors, approving its worth through persecutions and prosperities, a strength to the tried and a chastening to the worldly-minded.

"To be married by an authority before which kings and peasants bow alike, asking benediction upon the covenant that, without respect of persons, binds by the same words of duty, the highest and the lowest.

"To bring our new-born children, as we were brought, to begin where we began, and to grow up to fill our places.

"To die in the faith, and almost hear the gospel words soon to be spoken over one's own grave as over the thousand times ten thousand of them who have slept in Jesus.

"In short, to be a devout and consistent Churchman, brings a man through aisles fragrant with holy association, and companied by a long procession of the good, chanting as they march a unison of piety and hope, until they come to the holy place where shining saints sing the new song of the redeemed; and they sing with them."[6]

In the same strain, Dr. Phelps, of Andover, writes in a memorable epistle:

"A friendly study of the Episcopal Church discloses certain dominant *ideas*, which we who cherish Puritan traditions may with profit add to our stock of wisdom. One of these ideas is that of *the dignity of worship*. Of Christian worship no other branch of the Church universal has so lofty an idea as the Church of England and its offshoot in this country. In all the liturgic literature of our language, nothing equals the Anglican Liturgy. Its variety of thought, its spiritual pathos, its choice selection of the most vital themes of public prayer, its reverent importunity, its theological orthodoxy, and its exquisite propriety of style, will commend it to the hearts of devout worshippers of many generations to come, as they have done to generations past. For an equipoise of balanced virtues it is unrivaled.

" The liturgic forms of other denominations would be saved from some excrescenses and inanities if the venerable Book of Common Prayer were more generally revered as a model. * * *

" The spirit of worship is deepened by the use of liturgic forms, in which holy men and women of other generations have expressed their faith. The Lord's prayer has been the most potent educator of childhood and youth that the world has ever known."

---

6. Lecture on the Episcopal Church, by the Rev. Thomas K. Beecher.

He also observes:

"Another of the ideas dominant in the Church of England, which we do well to accept in such degree as our puritanic faith will admit, is that of the *unity and moral authority of the Church.* We have drifted to a perilous extreme in our advocacy of the principles of individuality in religious life. It often degenerates into individualism.

"The Church of England does good service for us all in conserving this Churchly idea without crowding it to the tyranny of the Romish hierarchy. Divine life is concentrated in one true and living Church. That article of the Apostles' Creed, 'I believe in the Holy Catholic Church,' has more than Apostolic authority. It is the Word of God. It represents the power which is to convert this world to Christ.

"When this idea of Churchly authority is presented in its biblical simplicity, the common sense of men approves it. Under right conditions the world reveres it."

He proceeds:

"The Church of England, furthermore, does good service in the conservation of the idea of the *historic continuity of the Church.* * * *

"This reverence for historic continuity as a factor in religious culture is found developed in no other Protestant sect so profoundly as in the Church of England. By her fidelity to it she does good service to the Church of the future."

Or in the words of the lecturer above quoted:

"The Episcopal Church furnishes (to all who need such comfort) the assurance of an organic and unbroken unity and succession, from Jesus Christ through the Apostles, by a line of authentic bishops, down to Bishop —————— of this diocese. * * *

"Citizens and Christians, all!—Because this Episcopal Church is a reformed Church and not revolutionary; because her book of prayer is rich and venerable above all in the English tongue; because her ritual promotes decency, dignity, prosperity and permanence; because her historic union through the Apostles with Christ comforts and satisfies so many souls; because she adopts her infant children and provides for them education and drill; therefore, from her own psalter let us take the words wherewith to bless her: 'They shall prosper that love thee. Peace be within thy walls, and plenteousness within thy palaces. For thy brethren and companions' sakes I will wish thee prosperity. Yea, because of the house of the Lord our God I will seek to do thee good.'"

Similar sentiments are often advanced by devout, unprejudiced Protestants, who see the beauty of the Church, and love her; but, having never grasped the Sacramental system, and the idea of the Church's unity and divine authority, are content to admire her from without. To such and to all our non-conforming brethren who study the Church at all, I beg to say a single word:

Love the Church for Christ's sake. And if we Churchmen, who at best are but unworthy sons of our Holy Mother, sometimes *appear* to be bigoted or uncharitable when we defend our Mother's honor, remember we do not *feel* so, and it is not for ourselves that we contend, but for *her*. A true Churchman's love for the Church is an enthusiasm, a celestial passion, such as no one has ever felt or can feel for a *human* organization.

> "I love the Church, the Holy Church,
> The Saviour's spotless Bride;
> And Oh, I love her palaces,
> Through all the land so wide;
> The cross-topped spire amid the trees,
> The holy bell of prayer,
> The music of our Mother's voice,
> Our Mother's home is here." [7]

Protestants often feel the spell which sometimes takes devout, impressionable, sentimental natures to the Church of Rome, where they become devotees. And it is a glory and a great advantage to any Church to be able to inspire an ardent and enthusiastic love in this cold age. But I affirm there is no charm on the cheek of her that sitteth upon the Seven Hills, which can for one moment hold comparison with the holy beauty of the Saviour's Bride, when she "looketh forth as the morning, fair as the moon, clear as the sun, and terrible as an army with banners." [8] Roman Catholics belong to the Church, and love the Church, and the *Roman* Church is, of course, a *part* of Christ's Catholic Church; but the *Papacy itself* is no part of the Church, but a blot upon it. The Papacy is indeed "terrible as an army with banners;" but it is the *non-papalized*, the *Catholic Church* alone, that is "beautiful as Tirzah, comely as Jerusalem." [9]

But on the fair and heavenly graces of our Mother, who of us is worthy to speak? As Macauley says of Athenian literature, "It is a subject on which I love to forget the accuracy of a judge, in the veneration of a worshipper, and the gratitude of a child." [10]

---

7. Bishop Coxe, Christian Ballads. 8. Solomon's Song, vi., 10. 9. *id.,* vi., 4.
10. Conclusion of Essay on Milford's History of Greece.

When one has grasped the Catholic idea, when one realizes for the first time that he is in that same old Church which God loved and purchased with His own Blood, the Church in which the blessed Apostles lived and died and are living still, the Church of the Fathers, the Saints, the Martyrs of yore, the Church clad in the white robes of early tribulation, and crowned with the garlands of Nicæa and Constantinople, the Church that lifted Britain from barbarism and made the Anglo-Saxon race "a chosen people," the leaders of the world—when, I say, the truth dawns upon one that he is in the Church of the Living God, and in that part of it which has continued most steadfastly in the Apostles' Doctrine and Fellowship, Sacraments and Prayers, there is given him an uplift of soul, a divine enthusiasm undreamed of before and not elsewhere to be obtained; doubt seems impossible, righteousness grows easier, love becomes immortal, and salvation is made as sure as the possibilities of human nature allow. The Catholic Churchman, and the Catholic Churchman alone, understands this:

"Ye are come unto Mount Sion, and unto the City of the Living God, the Heavenly Jerusalem, and to an innumerable Company of Angels, to the General Assembly and Church of the first born, which are written in Heaven, and to God the Judge of all, and to the spirits of just men made perfect, and to Jesus the Mediator of the New Covenant, and to the blood of sprinkling, that speaketh better things than that of Abel." And after such a description of the Church as that, well does the Apostle conclude: "See that ye refuse not Him that speaketh."[6]

---

6. Heb. xii., 22, 23, 24.

CHAPTER XXVI.

THE ARGUMENT FROM FUTURITY.

> "Wanderers! come home! When erring most
> Christ's Church aye kept the Faith, nor lost
> One grain of Holy Truth:
> She ne'er has erred as those ye trust,
> And now shall lift her from the dust,
> And REIGN as in her youth!"
> —*Lyra Apostolica*, p. 137.

To complete the reasons for being a Churchman according to the plan proposed, it remains to consider briefly the argument from futurity : Which of the three systems of Christianity in vogue amongst us has the brightest outlook? is surest to keep the Faith? offers the best basis for the reunion of Christendom?

I. A century ago the prospects of Anglo-Catholicism were far from encouraging. The Church was bound hand and foot by an Erastian government. Faith and piety, the Church idea and missionary activity were at a low ebb. But things have changed. The revival of Church life—begun in part by the Wesleys, and by the so-called Evangelical movement early this century, and carried out on Catholic lines by the Oxford movement since 1833—is one of the grandest revivals in the religious history of the world.

Since then the growth of the English Church at home

—where it still holds three-fourths of the population—among the colonies, and in heathen lands, is, for present character and promise of permanency, such as no other religious body can show.

The Church in the United States was almost annihilated by the Revolution; it took fifty years for it to recover even a foothold in this land. Since then its progress has been very satisfactory, and, on the whole, rather more rapid and substantial than that of any of the denominations. Its position is honorable and unique in the religious life of the Western world. It is looked up to and respected by all classes. Its future is bright, and growing brighter all the while.

The Anglo-Saxon race is now the dominant race of mankind. The English language, the most universal, as it is the most perfect of modern tongues, is now spoken by at least a hundred million people. At the present rate of increase it will not be long before there will be five hundred million men speaking the English language and moulded by Anglo-Saxon influences—among which influences the oldest, most characteristic, most permanent, and most potent for good, is the Historic Church, everywhere identified with the English-speaking race. In hundreds of European cities, and in the military and commercial centers of Asia, Africa, South America, and the islands of the sea, wherever a community of Englishmen is to be found, there is almost sure to be an Anglican chapel in the midst of them. Besides which the Book of Common Prayer has been translated into nearly a hundred different languages.

Heretofore when comparisons have been made between the English Church and the Roman, there has always been an element of numerical unfairness, the English Church being but *one* national Catholic Church, and the Roman Church being a vast conglomeration of a number of national Catholic Churches, which had lost their ancient independence. The only fair comparison would have been as between the Church of England and some *one* national Church of about the same size, say the Church of France, or the Church of Spain, or the Church of Italy. But the time is coming when the national Catholic Churches of England, Scotland, Ireland, the United States, Canada, Australia, India, South Africa, and other colonies—to say nothing of the "Old Catholics," or reformed part of the historic Church in Europe, now in full communion with the Anglo-Catholic, and not to mention the "Orthodox Catholic Eastern Church" with its eighty-five million members —will surpass the Tridentine Consolidation in numbers, as they do already in social, intellectual, moral, and spiritual influence, and that, too, without any tyrannous and un-Catholic centralization. Indeed, so far as the ethnic, political, commercial, linguistic, and ethical prospects of the Anglo-Saxon race are an indication, the outlook of the Anglo-Catholic communion is brighter by far than the outlook of the Roman, whose constituency is almost wholly confined to the less moral, less intelligent, less dominant, less progressive, less rapidly increasing, less promising races of Southern Europe and South America, among whom infidelity (especially in France and Italy), is sapping the very life of religion, of society, and of the state.

Romanism is at its best where it has intruded into the jurisdiction of the Anglo-Catholic Church. It is, if I may so say, forced to be on its good behavior. But aside from its being here an unjustifiable *schism*,[1] which has, in the long run, no right to expect the blessing of God, the outlook of the schism amongst us is not good. Despite most strenuous efforts put forth in England, and in spite of a large Hibernian immigration, the Anglo-Roman schism has been relatively losing ground, having now barely three and a half *per cent.* of the population where a few decades ago it had from four to five *per cent.* And of that small percentage *not one-sixth are English.* As Mr. Gladstone computed in 1878, "probably not less than five-sixths are of Irish birth," and the remaining sixth contains many *aliens* from the continent. The idea that an *Italian schism* will ever dominate the English race, while the Catholic Church of England stands, is simply frenzy.

In America the growth of the Italian mission has been rapid and substantial, not, however, from its inherent fertility nor from its earnest and faithful proselytism, but as the result of a most enormous and unprecedented influx of foreign co-religionists from Ireland, Germany, and elsewhere. The Romano-American papers often proclaim a net increase, say of 100,000 souls, during a given year. It sounds well. But during the *same* year, *more* than 100,000 Romanists have been added by *immigration* without which the "net increase" would have been a *minus quantity.* A candid Roman Catholic prelate recently remarked that if his Church had kept all Roman Catholic immigrants and their children, it would have some 20,000,000 adherents in this country, instead of which it has but little over 6,000,-

---

1. "The guilt of schism rests on the Church of Rome, and the Roman Church since A. D., 1570, has occupied in England the position of a permanently schismatical body."—The Rev. Wm. A. Rich.

000. It is, moreover, out of harmony with the spirit and genius of American institutions and popular liberty; and can only bring itself into harmony therewith by an act of *felo de se*, the Syllabus of the late "Infallible" *Pio Nono*, being witness.

The United States is the Paradise of Protestantism. Owing to the character of the early settlers, and the almost total destruction of the English Church during the Revolution, sectarianism here far outnumbers both the Church and the Roman schism. Its prospects are brighter here than anywhere else. Nevertheless, in the judgment of thoughtful men, both within and without the Church, its total lack of authority, its uncertainty in matters of faith, its conflicting, multitudinous divisions and sub-divisions, its tendency to further disintegration, and its dependence on "spasmodic religion," are against its permanency and ultimate success as the religion of the English-speaking race.

Protestantism is, moreover, about to pass through a fearful ordeal. It has always blindly proclaimed itself *The Religion of the Bible:*—"The Bible and the Bible only the religion of Protestants." But Protestantism is now beginning to be uncertain whether the Bible is inspired ; what constitutes the Bible ; whether there is any Bible at all. Protestantism rejected the Church, and put in its place that Book which is a child of the Church. The New Testament was written by Churchmen, and was not completed till the Church was more than sixty years old. The canon of Scripture rests on the authority of the Church, which is "The Witness and Keeper of Holy Writ." Destroy the Church, and you have logically lost the Bible. Logic is inexorable, and will at last make itself felt. Protestantism is going to wake up to this fact. Then those who want the Bible will come back to the Church, while those who refuse to conform will be left *Scriptureless* as well as *Churchless*.

There is such a thing as whole communities laboring for generations under a logical delusion (as St. Paul says, "Blindness in part is happened to Israel").[2] The delusion of Dissent—which I venture to call *Protestant paralogism*—is that the testimony of early Fathers and councils must be accepted on the subject of the canon of Holy Scripture, but not on the subject of the Church—its Creed its threefold ministry, its Sacraments, etc. The Presbyterian, Doctor Miller, who could appeal to St. Ignatius as authority against Unitarianism, but in the next breath reject him *in toto* because of his testimony in favor of Episcopacy, is a fair specimen of the demoralized reasoning faculty of Dissent. There is, forsooth, an *Ecclesia Docens*, conciliar authority, patristic testimony, and Catholic tradition, when private judgment wants such things; there is no *Ecclesia Docens*, no conciliar authority, no patristic testimony, no Catholic tradition, when private judgment wants none. *Alpha est* and *alpha non est* have been sleeping together in the brain of Protestantism. By and by the landlord will find that he really cannot accommodate them both; that he cannot consistently hold that there is a Church, and that there is no Church. If he decide that there *is* a Church, then he must conform to it; if he decide that there is *no* Church, then he must give up his Bible, for without the Church he cannot know what

---

2. Rom., xi., 25.

the Bible is, and the same authorities which tell him of the Bible, tell him also of the Church. What will be left of Protestant Dissent when it gets through this ordeal, God only knows. From such an ordeal, however, the *Churchman* has nothing to fear. Take away his Bible if you can; he still has the Gospel chrystallized in the Creed and the Liturgy, in the Sacraments and in Catholic tradition. In a word, he has the CHURCH OF THE LIVING GOD, THE PILLAR AND GROUND OF THE TRUTH; and having the Church, he has all, and can get back his precious Bible, for the Church tells him what it is.

II. The Anglican Church offers the strongest guarantee for the keeping of the Faith—" When the Son of Man cometh, shall He find the Faith on the earth?"[3] Were it not for the Anglican and Greek Churches, the answer would be doubtful indeed.

In the various Churches which are conglomerated into the "Holy Roman Church," the Catholic Faith is overlaid (not to say smothered) with the creed of Pius IV., a part of which is uncatholic and false, and with the false dogmas of the Immaculate Conception and the infallibility of the Bishop of Rome. The old Faith in which the saints and martyrs were saved is not enough now. A man must also believe unsupported assertions, historical contradictions, at least one blasphemous conceit, and a host of *adiaphora*, or be damned. And one of the saddest spectacles the sun sees, is the apostacy from all faith which Rome is causing among her children to-day by enforcing falsehoods. Rome, *as a Church*, still holds the whole Cath-

---

3. St. Luke, xviii., 8.

olic Faith, but multitudes prefer to risk damnation by believing nothing, rather than to lower themselves to the level of superstition, credulity, and "gullibility" necessary to make one believe what nature and common sense, history and the Bible, the undivided Church and God Himself proclaim to be foolish and untrue. I refer, of course, to the impious nonsense of "papal infallibility" and the dogma of the Immaculate Conception of the Blessed Virgin—which latter, by the way, is a fine illustration of the truth (!) of the former, as *fourteen* "infallible" pontiffs declared it a *heresy*, and *one* "infallible" pontiff (Pius IX., in 1854) declared it a dogma of the Faith and necessary to salvation!! (See Littledale's "Plain Reasons," p. 167.) It is said that a little girl in a Roman Catholic convent school naively defined faith as, "The gift of God, whereby we believe what we know to be false." It is a kind of faith needed in Rome to-day.

And granted a man knows the Roman faith to-day, what will it be to-morrow? Is *infallibility* the last article of the Creed? "Infallibility" may promulgate a new creed to-morrow, in which vagaries as false and absurd as itself may be declared *de fide* and necessary to salvation, *e. g.*, the ubiquity of St. Joseph, the *apotheosis* of St. Mary, the real presence of the *lac Virginalis* in the Eucharist (for Roman theologians already teach that *St. Mary* is present in the Eucharist, and especially that the *lac Virginalis* is received along with the Sacrament of the Blood of Christ, (see Pusey's Irenicon, p. 160, *Et Seq.*), or the sanctity and salvation of "Pope Alexander VI." Rome is uncertain in matters of faith.

Protestant Dissent comprises so many different faiths

and even different religions, that it is hard, in this connection to speak of it as a whole. But even of the very essence of the Faith, the Incarnation of the Eternal Consubstantial of Son of God, Sectarianism has been and is making shipwreck. Almost everyone of the Presbyterian congregations existing in England in the seventeenth century has long since become Unitarian. The apostacies from Christianity to Socinianism, of the French, Dutch, Swiss, and German Protestants, are simply appalling. In the early part of this century a large proportion of the Trinitarian Congregationalists of New England denied the Lord that bought them. But in Connecticut where the Church was strong, Unitarianism never gained a foothold. No parish of the Anglican Church ever went over to Unitarianism.[4] The conservative spirit of Anglicanism, fortified by the Creeds, the liturgy, and the Church Year, [5] makes it less likely that the Anglican Church will either add to or detract from the Faith than that either Rome or Dissent will do so, or more properly will continue to do so. We Anglo-Catholics recognize that "the Faith which was once delivered to the saints," is a final revelation. The Creed is settled. Our aim is to hold it. Rome's idea is to develop it; while the Protestant idea is for each man to pick out his own creed from the Bible, or rather from such parts of it as meet with his approval, and from his own inner consciousness.

Given three such systems of keeping the Faith, it

---

4. King's Chapel, Boston, is no exception, for the Church had been seized by Congregationalists before the Apostacy occurred. They, and not Churchmen, were responsible.

5. "Our festival year is a bulwark of Orthodoxy as real as our confession of faith."—*Archer Butler.*

stands to reason that the Anglo-Catholic is surest to succeed. Nevertheless, we must admit that we hold these treasures in earthen vessels; and it behooves us, as the Church directs, three times a week to pray: "From false doctrine, heresy and schism, good Lord deliver us," and from our heart of hearts to offer the petition of Trinity Sunday (which used to be said *daily* in our Mother Church): "We beseech Thee that Thou wouldst keep us steadfast in THIS FAITH."

III. Finally, which system offers the best basis for the reunion of Christendom?

That the Papal system which in one year, this century, lost fully 2,000,000 of subjects (including bishops and priests) to the Orthodox Catholic Church of Russia, [6] which cannot even hold its own in France and Spain and Italy, can ever succeed in bringing the Catholic Churches of the Orientals and Anglo-Saxons, and the four hundred Protestant sects, under the Roman yoke, is manifestly absurd. Rome makes no concessions. She has burned the ships behind her. The dogma of Papal Infallibility must be retracted before Catholics or Protestants will be able to have communion with the Latin Church. It is a doctrine so absurd, so blasphemous, so obviously false, that the Papacy itself is cracking under the strain of it.

If Rome would bring about the reunion of Christendom, let her take away the *Papacy* and mitigate the doctrinal and devotional excesses touching the Mother of our Lord. There would remain then but little to hinder a Godly union and concord between the three great

---

6. See Dr. Neale's "The Bible and the Bible only, the Religion of Protestants," p. 7, and Alloc. of Greg. XVI., Nov. 16, 1839.

branches of the one Catholic Church. But this is simply to return to the fundamental principles of the Anglo-Catholic Church, as the old Catholics on the Continent have been doing ever since the Vatican Council. Thoughtful Roman Catholics of the Gallican School, have often acknowledged that, if the union of Christendom ever comes, it must be through the medium of the Anglican Church. [7]

No plan for the reunion of Christendom, however, must pass over the four hundred Protestant sects, some of which lack little of Catholicity save the Apostolic Ministry. Between Historic Christendom and Protestant Christendom there is just one connecting link, and that is the Anglican Church. That she is Catholic we have seen. That she is thoroughly and scripturally reformed, even radical Protestants admit, for they insist on calling her "Protestant," and our Church is allowed on all hands to be the bulwark of the Reformation. No reasonable and devout Dissenter objects to joining in the worship of the Anglican Church, and Anglican religious writings are current among all Protestants. For orthodox Dissenters to conform to the old Church is no sacrifice of principle. A man, for instance, may not be fully convinced as to Apostolic Succession, but that need not hinder his coming into the Church, which demands of her children only the sim-

---

7. See Pusey's Irenicon, p. 197, *et passim*. Even Ultramontane De Maistre could say: "Si jamais les Chretiens se rapprochent, comme tout les y invite, l semble que la motion doit partir de l' Eglise de l'Angleterre." (Considerations sur la France, c. II., quoted in the Irenicon, p. 216) If Christians ever come together again, as they all desire, it is evident that the movement must originate with the *English Church*.

Joseph Le Marche, the celebrated ultramontane, said that the Anglican Church, touching, as she did, upon what was great and noble in Protestantism and upon the fundamental truths of Catholicism, was the chemical solvent to bring about a possible united Christendom.

ple faith of the Apostles, the Creed. Surely he cannot think a clergyman who is episcopally ordained, is any less a priest or minister than one congregationally ordained ; that is, not ordained at all.

Nothing in all the world so retards the progress of Christianity as the divisions among Christians. In seeking re-union, therefore, we ought all of us to be willing to give up non-essential innovations and to restore vital or desirable things which have been dropped. If Rome would leave off insisting on such innovations as the infallibility and supremacy of the Bishop of Rome, and the other leading novelties which in the nature of things cannot be essential, the result would be a return to unadulterated Catholicism, to the principles which underlay the ancient Church, and which are to-day the basis of the Holy Eastern, the Anglican, and the Old Catholic Churches.

On the other hand, let Protestants simply restore what they have cast off, at least the Apostolic ministry which Christ ordained, the primitive universal Creed and Sacraments, accepting enough of the Divine Liturgy to insure the regular administration of the latter, and Protestants would find themselves Catholics of the Anglican, Oriental, primitive type.

All Protestants combined cannot reasonably expect Catholic Christendom (viz.: The Anglican, the Greek, and the Roman Churches, to say nothing of the old Catholics, Nestorians and Copts) to give up the Nicene Creed and the Apostolic Succession. Almost nine-tenths of Christians are Episcopalians, believing in the Episcopal form of Church order, and in the necessity of Episcopal ordination ; and they have always believed so from the beginning. They believe that to give up their Apostolic Succession would be to un-Church themselves forever. But no Protestant believes that (from his own standpoint) it would unchurch him to have the ministry of his church ordained by a bishop instead of a layman.

In short, Christians have erred in two ways. The Romanists have added many things. The Protestants have cast off many things. Between these two extremes lies the only ground of union, and that ground happens, in the providence of God, to be occupied by the Anglo-Catholic Church. She has all the good things which Rome has—the Creeds, the Bible, the Ministry, the Sacraments, the worship and the traditions of the Catholic Church—without the objectionable additions. At the same time she certainly has all the good things which Protestants have, without their defects.

In effecting the re-union of the scattered sheep of Christ, the Anglican plan would not necessitate the submission of all Christians to the English Church, but merely a return to Catholic Faith, order, Sacraments and worship among us all, so that there might be inter-communion. All the Anglo-Catholic Church would ask for herself, is that she be recognized as the Catholic Church of so much of the world as fairly comes under her jurisdiction, viz.: the British Empire and the American Republic. The other Churches would only need to return to their ancient integrity, and there would at once be full inter-communion.

I do not say that Christendom will ever be united on Anglo-Catholic principles; but I do affirm that the only reunion which can take in both extremes must be on the general principles of the reformed Catholic religion, which are the peculiar heritage of the English-speaking race. "Thus saith the Lord: Stand ye in the ways, and see and ask for the old paths, where is the good way, and walk therein."[8] To-day Dissenters are looking more and more favorably on the old Mother Church; and wherever reform is being attempted in the down-trodden national Churches of the Roman obedience, it is the Anglican Church that is looked to for help and for guidance; it is the Anglo-Catholic Reformation, rather than the revolutions of Luther and Calvin, that is taken for a pattern. Dissenters, Jansenists, old Catholics, Nestorians, Copts, look to us for help and inter-communion. We have partial and growing inter-communion with the Greek Church, and have many bonds of sympathy even with our cruel sister, the Church of Rome. If any other part of Christendom can offer a better starting-point for re-union, what is it?

To sum up, then, because on the whole the Anglo-Catholic Church has the brightest outlook, as the dominant religion of the dominant race of men: because it is the surest to keep the Faith till the Master comes; and because it offers the only possible basis for the re-union of Christendom, there is stronger reason, based on the argument from futurity, for being a Churchman rather than for being a Recusant or a Dissenter. But be the outlook what it may; be the present condition of our Church as gloomy as when there were but seven thousand worshippers of God in all Israel, the fact remains that, of the three divisions of English-speaking Christians, the Anglo-Catholic Church is the one which, in accordance

---

8. Jer., vi., 16.

with the Bible and with history, has continued most steadfastly in all the essentials of Apostolic Faith and Fellowship, Sacraments and Worship, and which alone has Divine authority and lawful jurisdiction over the children of God in the British Empire and the American Republic.

"*O Holy Jesu, King of the Saints and Prince of the Catholic Church, preserve Thy spouse, whom Thou hast purchased with Thy right hand, and redeemed and cleansed; the whole Catholic Church from one end of the earth to the other; she is founded upon a rock, but planted in the sea, O preserve her safe from schism, heresy, and sacrilege. Unite all her members with the bands of faith, hope, and charity, and an external communion, when it shall seem good in Thine eyes. Let the daily sacrifice of prayer and sacramental thanksgiving never cease, but be forever presented to Thee, and forever united to the intercession of her dearest Lord, and forever prevail for the obtaining for every of its members, grace and blessing, pardon and salvation. AMEN.*"

FINIS.

www.ingramcontent.com/pod-product-compliance
Lightning Source LLC
Chambersburg PA
CBHW032117230426
43672CB00009B/1771